CITIES  SOVEREIGNTY

CITIES & SOVEREIGNTY

IDENTITY POLITICS IN URBAN SPACES

Edited by

Diane E. Davis and

Nora Libertun de Duren

Indiana University Press

Bloomington and Indianapolis

This book is a publication of

Indiana University Press
601 North Morton Street
Bloomington, Indiana 47404-3797 USA

www.iupress.indiana.edu

Telephone orders   800-842-6796
Fax orders   812-855-7931
Orders by e-mail   iuporder@indiana.edu

⊚ The paper used in this publication meets the minimum requirements of the American National Standard for Information Sciences—Permanence of Paper for Printed Library Materials, ANSI Z39.48-1992.

Manufactured in the United States of America

Library of Congress Cataloging-in-Publication Data

Cities and sovereignty : identity politics in urban spaces / edited by Diane E. Davis and Nora Libertun de Duren.
    p. cm.
    Includes bibliographical references and index.
    ISBN 978-0-253-35577-5 (cloth : alk. paper) — ISBN 978-0-253-22274-9 (pbk. : alk. paper) 1. Urban policy. 2. Sovereignty. 3. Identity politics. 4. Ethnic relations. 5. City-states. 6. Metropolitan government. I. Davis, Diane E., [date] II. Libertun de Duren, Nora, [date]
    HT151.C5683 2011
    307.76—dc22

                                                                                        2010026757

1 2 3 4 5   16 15 14 13 12 11

Contents

Part 3 · Sovereignty, Representation, and the Urban Built Environment

Preface and Acknowledgments

The idea for this volume originated in the context of a larger initiative at MIT devoted to imagining the conditions under which Jerusalem might become a city of peace by the year 2050. Many of the chapters in this volume are revised versions of papers presented at a spring 2004 seminar series titled *Cities against Nationalism: Urbanism as Utopian Politics,* convened as a precursor to the Jerusalem 2050 project. The larger 2050 project, the seminar series that produced this book, and the Just Jerusalem Competition that these projects have spawned were all jointly sponsored by the Department of Urban Studies and Planning (DUSP) and the Center for International Studies (CIS) at MIT. Funding for these activities was kindly provided by CIS and the School of Architecture and Planning as well as DUSP. The editors especially want to thank CIS Director Richard Samuels, CIS Executive Director John Tirman, and former DUSP Department Head Lawrence Vale for their intellectual engagement and moral and institutional support of this project and all its related activities.

A Note on Dates

Unless otherwise indicated, all dates referred to in this volume take place in the Common Era (CE).

CITIES & SOVEREIGNTY

Introduction

Identity Conflicts in the Urban Realm

Diane E. Davis and Nora Libertun de Duren

Globalization and recent transformations in the international political system have catapulted the politics of identity into the contemporary lexicon and limelight. In contrast to much of the twentieth century, when the modern nation-state served as a source of national unity and party or class politics mediated between citizens and the state, in the current epoch political allegiances increasingly lie elsewhere. Individuals are more likely to acknowledge an unequivocal if not natural connection between their political aspirations and their individual identities—defined by ethnicity, religion, language, region of birth, or other socially ascribed statuses—than to unite behind larger nationalist projects that span these fault lines of individual difference.

With the existent system of nation-states coming under challenge in the face of accelerating economic globalization and post–Cold War political realignments, these identity politics fuel a re-emergence of subnational and transnational tensions that further call into question the political order and institutions of the modern nation-state. And with globalization ensuring that cities are becoming increasingly engaged in transnational flows that operate at scales and through activities outside the reach of national institutions, the promise of national unity further diminishes. Cities are more likely to become the locus of identity conflicts than to transcend such conflicts, calling into question the inherent cosmopolitanism of cities in today's world. In light of these changes, it seems inevitable that as multiple identities converge in cities and national institutions face limited capacities to control local populations, partisan violence would emerge.

To be sure, there is an illustrious tradition of scholarship identifying cities as sites where difference can be negotiated and transcended, owing either to a pragmatic tolerance engendered by the need to coordinate different groups (Durkheim 1933), or to the development of values of tolerance and acceptance as residents experience the benefits of diversity (Weber 1958). But it is all too clear that in many cities of the world today, pragmatism or civic values—assuming they do emerge—are not enough to assure peace, and the consequences for citizens have been less than desirable. On a world scale, among the various identities that are producing some of the most violent conflicts in today's cities, those revolving around ethnicity and religion stand out. After being held at bay for much of the second half of the twentieth century, often through more universal political ideologies advanced in service of particular nation-states, ethnic and religious conflicts have re-emerged with a vengeance in the post–Cold War world. They have been especially visible in postcolonial countries still struggling with non-democratic forms of government wrought by the encounter with empire, as in the Middle East and parts of East Asia.

These conflicts appear on a variety of scales and in a range of forms, many of them quite violent. Most also appear to be highly targeted in scope. From guerrilla warfare and terrorist attacks aimed at key installations, to coercive state occupation of strategic spatial locations—be they opposition-based urban and regional strongholds or important border regions—the terrain of everyday political struggle over *who* has the legitimacy to govern a people and on the basis of *what* identity categories seems to be scaling down from the nation-state. Struggles over the Enlightenment ideals of universal citizenship and equality have given way to more territorially circumscribed subnational levels where race, ethnicity, or religion are often the principal basis for making representational claims. In the context of these transformations, cities are ever more likely to stand at the front lines of battle and conflict. Around the globe, metropolitan populations are increasingly thrust into the violence, while in these embattled cities the commitment to civil rights and democratic deliberation are frequently cast aside in the quest for security.

Cities and Identity Conflict

The central place afforded cities in the new world "disorder" owes partly to the fact that cities, historically, have played host to diversity and difference, and thus they are more likely to hold within their borders a concentration of heterogeneous populations prone to be pulled into struggle when mutually exclusive ethnic or religious identities become the basis of national politics. Yet it also owes to the fact that globalization has brought increased heterogeneity to a larger number of cities around the world, as accelerating transnational migration flows and the rise of the information economy hike both the supply and demand for low wage immigrants in so-called global cities (Sassen 1991; 1998). Such flows of people create an environment ripe for ethnic and religious violence, often fueled by the struggle for cultural recognition, especially in regions of the world like Europe, where many immigrants differ from the majority populations of their host countries in ethnicity, race, or religious tradition. Complicating matters is the growing tendency for spatial polarization based on income and ethnicity in contemporary cities. In the words of Marcuse and Van Kempen, both globalization and the growing ideological belief that states and cities are helpless to counter the market forces that separate rich and poor have helped produce "partitioned cities" (2003, 3) in which new forms of division (as compared to the past, at least) lead to the exclusion of a large minority from participation in the mainstream of the economy (Marcuse 2002, 29) in ways that add to the cultural tensions and the increased violence of cities today.

Just as important, however, is the fact that cities all over the world are increasingly becoming the sites for "spectacular military and paramilitary violence," to use the words of Derek Gregory, owing to post–Cold War struggles to create new empires of global influence.[1] When in the course of these struggles new technologies of warfare confront old forms of resistance or power, or vice versa, the nature of contemporary battle space changes, and the city frequently stands at the center of these contestations. Grenade attacks in theatres and other public buildings by Chechen separatists in Moscow are one example, as were the 9/11 attacks on New York City's World Trade Center, the subway bombings in Madrid and London, and the skillfully organized militia attacks on the hotels and public buildings of Mumbai in December 2008. In those parts of the world where nation-states or their leaders are either weakened or continually challenged by violently opposing forces, social and political control of the city frequently becomes the stepping-stone to securing power at the level of the region or nation (Davis 1994; Myers and Dietz 2002). In such conditions, perhaps best exemplified by the case of Baghdad, cities themselves become ever more militarized, turning into the central locations for continued violence over state formation.

It is still too early to know whether global geopolitics is imploding into the urban world, to paraphrase Leonie Sandercock;[2] but it is not too premature to identify ethnic, religious, racial, and nationalist conflict in (or against) cities as facts of twenty-first-century life. The cosmopolitanism of cities may have served as a magnet for those committed to tolerance and enlightenment ideals in earlier centuries, thereby buttressing the emergence of both state and societal commitments to tolerance, social integration, and a stable political order, much along the lines theorized by Emile Durkheim and Max Weber long ago (Tajbakhsh 1991).

But in the brave new world of multiculturalism and identity politics, it may be precisely the difference and diversity of cities that drives contestation and conflict, or that makes cities symbolic of modernity and change sufficiently to generate fundamentalist attacks (Buruma and Margalit 2004). When the nation-state or other competing identity-based groups or institutions vying for sovereignty among diverse populations insert themselves into those cities, conflict can become intractable and deadly.

To underscore these patterns and their implications for violence or social disorder is not to suggest, as Stanley Milgram (1970) did, that violence is a natural consequence of difference and that society is corrupted by heterogeneity and anonymity. Rather, it is to bring back a focus on the territorial bases of identity politics and sovereignty struggles, and to consider their impact on cities and on the emergence of urban conflict and violence. In this formulation, neither diversity nor identity is understood to be the sole source of conflict. Rather, it is the built environmental or even sovereignty context in which identities take root that is much more likely to be the source of tension. What is needed is a new way of understanding the apparent correlation between urban conflict and identity politics. In this volume, we consider the proposition that the resurgence of ethnic and religious conflicts in cities around the world owes more to the competing, overlapping, or mismatched territorialities of the institutions that seek to govern urban life than to any essential irreconcilability of the identities themselves.

In trying to understand the complex of identities and networks of sovereignties that are more or less likely to lead to conflict in and against cities, we also must think more carefully about the concept of nationalism, distinguishing between so-called nationalist conflicts that are based on allegiance to the modern nation-state and other more essential identities that might have different territorial reference points. Building on Benedict Anderson's (1991) efforts to link the concept of nation to an "imagined community," and Arjun Appadurai's (2003) efforts to understand the territorial bases of identity politics, we must be prepared to ask whether those involved in urban violence or conflict are organizing themselves at the level of the individual, the community, the city, or the nation, and whether it is the mismatch or hierarchical ordering of these levels or competing sovereignties that creates tension or dissatisfaction. Will those committed to identity politics direct their struggles toward the creation of new institutional configurations that better suit their newly circumscribed "national" or identity boundaries, or will they be struggling for new ways of being included within existing institutional contexts? A central aim of this volume is to understand conflicts in terms of the scales, political institutions, and identities—whether ethnic, religious, or otherwise—around which those struggles are cast.

Analytical Aims

The essays included here examine the relationship between identity-based conflicts, cities, and sovereignty using a variety of comparative and historical cases and diverse disciplinary points of entry. What turns the benign differences and cultural diversity that generally exist in cities into intractable conflicts; and under which conditions will these conflicts undermine the sovereignty or power of nation-state, and why? Is there a historical dynamic at work that connects the rise of identity politics and shifts in the scale or nature of sovereignty—be it based on the city, the nation-state, or a larger global level (in the form of empire or other politico-institutional arrangements that locate decision making at scales greater than the nation-state)—to the likelihood of urban conflict? Stated differently, are certain cities more conflictive under certain forms of sovereignty, defined here as the territorial scale of governance, representation, and citizenship? What sovereignty hierarchies or forms of "nestedness" among cities, nations, or empires will produce cooperation as opposed to conflict on the urban scale, and why? Might other institutions, spatial practices, or identities also need to be in place in order to sustain urban harmony or solidarity as opposed to conflict; and if so, what are they and on what scale do they operate?

In many ways, these questions can be seen as variations on a set of themes well examined by classical sociologists, urbanists, historians, and political scientists who sought to understand the emergence of modern nation-states or capitalism and the role that cities played in these developments. Social scientists have long focused on the city as the incubator for larger transformations in society and governance. From understanding the rise of new forms of solidarity and integration in cities and their impact on social and economic modernization (Durkheim 1933; Smelser 1959), to the study of how and why cities have been central to the rise and maintenance of democratic structures and practices (Weber 1958; Katznelson 1981; Castells 1983), to appreciation of the role played by cities as sources of capital in the rise of coercive capacities, war-making, and state formation (Tilly 1992), questions about urban dynamics have long been central to the study of political and social transformations. But in recent years, studies of the relations between cities and sovereignty have fallen out of favor, perhaps because the increasing specialization of academia has undermined the interdisciplinary forms of inquiry that linked these domains to each other. But as we enter a new millennium and as the relationship between cities, nations, global structures, and political processes is changing in dramatic ways, it is time to follow the lead of Saskia Sassen (2008) and Matthew Sparke (2005), among others, and reconsider some of these age-old questions by applying them to the current world in which we live.

The importance of this endeavor is more than just theoretical, or formulated purely in the service of academic knowledge. As we see virulent forms of violence and political conflict in cities around the world ranging from Baghdad to Darfur to Kosovo to Rotterdam to Jerusalem, we must acknowledge the practical urgency of our aims. After all, we must be prepared to understand the origins and larger dynamics of these urban conflicts if we want to offer suggestions about how to avoid such destructive patterns in the immediate or long-term future.[3] To the extent that we can show that the intractability of these conflicts might owe as much to the nature of the sovereignty arrangements in which these cities and their citizens are embedded as to the growing resurgence of identity politics, or that the latter might in fact fuel the former as well as vice versa, leading to vicious cycle of spiraling violence, we will be in a stronger position to offer normative propositions that could hasten a return to the diversity, tolerance, and cosmopolitanism long associated with the urban sphere. If this can also serve as a stepping-stone to generating peace and political stability on the national or even global scale, then the gains would accrue far beyond the city even while keeping this analytic domain a central focus.

In the service of answering these theoretical questions and achieving these normative aims, this volume presents nine essays and a concluding chapter that examine various aspects of the identity-city-nation nexus. The essays embody the interdisciplinary perspective of scholars trained in the fields of sociology, urban planning, architecture, political science, and history. The papers span a variety of scales, regions, and time periods, focusing on questions about identity politics and urban conflict from the vantage point of the city, the nation, the subnational region, or the transnational context in both the past and the present. They also focus attention on different units of analysis, so to speak: the individuals involved in urban or national identity conflicts, the built environment or architectural forms that display or transcend these tensions and conflicts, and the political or governing institutions that mediate or produce these conflicts. Combined, they offer a sense of the multiplicity of ways that ethnic, religious, or other identity conflicts emerge from or are reflected in the everyday politics, spatial form, and operation of a city, and the impact that larger sovereignty contexts have on these dynamics.

Structure of the Volume

Each part of the volume develops a different subtheme related to the larger framing questions, drawing primarily on evidence from case studies of cities that have been affected by nationalist movements, sovereignty conflicts, and/or identity conflicts. The conclusion theorizes the extent to which sovereignty arrangements or urban form can trigger violent identity conflicts in the city. It builds on the conceptual and empirical findings presented in the chapters, examining the relationships between cities and sovereignty in more theoretical terms while also situating the larger aims of the volume in a tradition of urban scholarship that privileges the city as the site of tolerance and diversity. As it seeks to explain how and why urban differences may be tolerated in some cases but produce violence in others, the conclusion highlights the role of democratic institutions and practices essential to realizing the promise of the city.

Part 1 focuses on *Modes of Sovereignty, Urban Governance, and the City.* In this section three chapters explore the impact of different modes of sovereignty (empire, colonialism, and the nation-state) on the city, paying special attention to how various sovereignty conditions affect governance and social conflict—or cooperation—in the urban realm. The cases under study include Jerusalem—first under the Ottoman Empire and later in the transition from imperial to colonial rule—and India and Vietnam under colonial rule. While the paper on India and Vietnam sustains a network model of urban conflict in which violence is more or less likely to emerge dependent on how institutions or groups sustaining nationalist agendas are interrelated, the chapters on Jerusalem develop a more political approach focused on governance. That is, the essays on Jerusalem focus more on politics and urban planning, asking questions about how different sovereignty arrangements brought different forms of urban decision making about the city and its built environment. All three chapters respond to three well-defined questions about national sovereignty and the city-state nexus: 1) Which ethnic/national/racial groups compete for sovereignty at the level of the nation-state and which do it at the level of the city or other smaller or larger political territorialities? 2) Through which urban institutions and practices are the various territorial realms of identity politics linked? and 3) Does the form of this linkage affect the emergence of violent conflicts in the city?

The authors in part 1 find different answers to the question of whether conflict or cooperation will prevail, based on the history of each city under study, as well as the ways in which identity conflicts are exacerbated or diminished through urban governance or social policy measures. Nora Libertun de Duren presents the long sweep of history of the city of Jerusalem and examines the ways that different forms of sovereignty have affected urban governance and conflict. Focusing attention on the last days of Ottoman rule in Jerusalem, this chapter portrays the fragile balance of political forces seeking, yet incapable of establishing, control over their everyday lives and local politics. In this context, Libertun de Duren argues, religious identity takes on a dual meaning: first, it is the lived reality for most residents of Jerusalem; and second, it is the justification for European nations' intervention in urban matters, as these powers designate themselves protectors of the various religions in the Holy City. This paradoxical and fragile arrangement, which could not endure once the logic of the western-born nation-state prevailed, suggests that some of the most intractable violence in Jerusalem did not emerge from fanatical religious identity, or even from the concentration of multiple religions within the same city, but from the absence of a legitimized and pluralistically acceptable accord for how to live in difference within the same city.

The proposition that the institutional arrangements of ruling powers shape the character and likelihood of nationalist conflicts in urban populations is also the subject of Anne Raffin's essay, which traces the dynamics of identity politics in Indian Pondicherry under British colonial rule and in the Vietnamese city of Hanoi under French colonial power. In particular, she discloses how the implementation of policies designed to advance France's national political alliances (i.e., the post–World War I "Franco-Annamite collaboration") fostered or mitigated inter-ethnic conflicts within these colonial settings. Thus, she argues that the apparent homogeneity of colonial rule applied to the colonized does not negate pre-existing ethnic differences within colonial cities and nations. Rather, if not carefully considered, it is more likely to foster further ethnic violence.

The first section ends with an essay by Salim Tamari. With a focus on Jerusalem, the chapter examines how the British mandate superimposed its vision of a modern society to move the city away from its previous spatial occupation, in which religious and national identities mixed, to an urban vision implemented through changing urban forms and municipal regulations that led to more distinct group separation, in social and identity terms even if not spatially. He shows that British urban planners were stymied by the complexity of social and spatial forms, which could not easily be reduced to a single master plan, leading to interventions that created even more direct alignment between Jerusalem's spaces and religious identities.

Part 2, *Scales of Sovereignty and the Remaking of Urban and National Space*, looks as much at the overlapping forms of sovereignty and identity conflicts in cities as it does at the ways these tensions affect urban form and the city–nation nexus. The first essay in this section raises questions about competing or multiple sovereignties and the city–nation nexus. The Basque Country is a region in which nationalism is understood to be as much an urban and subnational or regional form of identity as one attached to the nation-state. Gerardo del Cerro Santamaría explores the ways that these alternative forms of nationalism build on transnational networks to challenge the national scale of sovereignty. He examines varying scales of sovereignty, tensions between urban and national development, and how they produce and are affected by identity conflict, along two different dimensions. One dimension is formed by the global connections that the city of Bilbao has established within the tradition and long history of Basque nationalism in order to move beyond the national context, even before the consolidation of transnational economic flows and the spread of a global culture of consumption were realities. Another is seen in the multiplicity of geographical relations produced within the Basque country in the contemporary era of globalization. These include the typical hierarchy of spatial institutions that extend from the global level, to the nation, to the region, to the city, and even down to architecture and the built environment.

In his examination of these two dimensions, del Cerro Santamaría shows that the construction of the Guggenheim Museum put Bilbao on the global map, thereby solidifying its international connections. He argues that the internationalization of Bilbao through iconic global architectural forms (to use the language of Leslie Sklair presented in the subsequent section) helped strengthen the nationalist aim of the Basque country, enabling the Basque people to challenge the sovereignty of the Spanish nation-state in the urban domain of Bilbao in ways that had eluded the Basque in earlier periods, ultimately allowing the Basque region to come closer to many of its historical goals of independence.

In the second chapter in this section, Agnès Deboulet and Mona Fawaz examine the interaction between religious groups, urban expansion, and national development, both political and spatial. Through a focus on the city inhabitants and their attitudes toward a new highway project linking the center of Beirut to its metropolitan periphery, in a direction straddling Hezbollah-controlled regions on the northern border of Israel, the authors show how plans and struggles over the urban development of Beirut became embedded in at least two tiers of contestation. One is the intranational conflict between different Lebanese religious groups over the political process and outcome implications of this particular highway expansion. This tier of contestation is itself embedded in a much larger regional contestation over sovereignty in Lebanon and in the larger orbit of the Middle East. The second principal axis of conflict involves identities more related to class and economic power: namely between those in the formal sector, who support a major national highway because of its economic developmental gains, who run up against the bottom-up resistance of informal settlements located along Beirut. Hence, the chapter portrays the tensions and overlaps between the ways in which national institutions and subnational ethnic groups struggle for sovereignty claims in and over the urban territory.

The final essay in this section, by Neil Brenner, takes a more macroscopic view of the urban challenges emerging from sovereignty contradictions, as well as the ways that the different institutional hierarchies of governance—or scales of sovereignty from local to national to transregional (as in the European Union) in which cities are embedded—will affect the potential for conflict and competition within and between different European cities. Rather than focusing primarily on the city–nation nexus, Brenner examines the historical and economic logics that alter traditional city-nation hierarchies by linking cities to transnational and mega-regional networks, and vice versa. In this regard, like del Cerro Santamaría, Brenner deconstructs the institutional logics of urban and national organization, while also doubting the legitimacy of traditional nation-state actors to regulate urban activities in today's globalizing world.

Brenner's chapter explores the mismatch between the bounded territoriality of urban institutions and the actual extension of power of the urban realm, as well as the disconnection between formal and substantive institutions for urban governance and its impact on the potential crisis of legitimacy of urban and national governments in a transnational context. Rather than posing dissolution of the state-city nexus in response to economic restructuring, as is often the scholarly response to globalization, Brenner presents its globalization-induced reconfiguration as a double-edged sword, where Western European cities are simultaneously empowered by reducing their dependency on the national state even as they are further pressured to become connecting nodes that link the global forces to sovereign nations. By doing so, he reverses the conventional order of questioning and asks how changes in urban conditions, owing to cities' embeddedness in a larger global hierarchy, can alter the role of cities and urban conflict in a given nationalist project. In essence, this approach focuses on the study of the macroeconomic conditions that render ineffective—or put under suspicion—governing institutions, even as it illuminates how and why this might breed conflict in or between cities.

Part 3, *Sovereignty, Representation, and the Urban Built Environment,* takes the volume beyond the sources of conflict, identity politics, or governance, and turns to their representation and urban semiotics. While the previous sections considered the nature and changing historical dynamics of the city-nation link and how they impact urban governance and urban social conditions, this final section shows how sovereignty concerns physically materialize or represent themselves in the urban realm. The authors in this section not only explore how the urban built environment is used to illustrate national identities at a variety of scales. They also show how control of urban form becomes the object of nationalist struggle in itself. Among the explanations given for these outcomes are the fact that national or global actors seek to control urban form either because they believe it can give proof of their sovereign powers, or conversely, because by controlling the urban form they can model society in ways that will evoke or create a nation through a shared repertoire of values that the built environment symbolizes.

The impossible dream of capturing or presenting city form within a purely nationalist discourse comes to light in the study of more contemporary forms of architectural practice, which serves as the subject of Leslie Sklair's chapter. As explored by Sklair, "iconic global architecture" may share many of the difficulties of manipulating the meaning of urban form that nation-states struggled with in earlier epochs, but the challenge of the contemporary period is different. In the current global context, the image of the city is constructed as the mirror, not of the sovereign nation, but of a global class of capitalists and consumers tied to no particular nation-state. Although it is not clear if this new "global semantic" is the outcome of a political project or the consequence of a shared sensibility, what is clear is that in contemporary cities of national and international significance, urban forms are designed for a preferred audience, which is not always its own urban citizenry. While this iconic global architecture might allow a given city to dispense with the conflicted exercise of symbolizing the nation, and in ways that could mitigate against nationalist conflicts in the urban realm, it also could mortgage the city's symbolic and spatial future to those who aim to package urban spaces into globally legible realms of consumption, leisure, and management, thereby bringing polarization and the possibility of new forms of urban conflict.

Both ways of conceptualizing urban space as a didactic/political tool are present in Lawrence Vale's discussion of capital cities. By examining the design of capital cities for the young nations of the twentieth century, Vale explores the many layers of visual representation that link national identity to the urban imaginary. Given its centrality within the nation-state, the capital city emerges as the designated carrier of this nationalist discourse. Its contents, however, are constantly under challenge, not just in terms of the definition of the identity of the nation, or with respect to the audience toward which this national discourse is directed (e.g., the education of the local citizen or the international image of the nation), but also with respect to the impossible task of finding an unequivocal link between the nation and the urban form. Yet it is precisely the irreducible complexity of the city that constantly exposes the artifice of an exclusionary national discourse.

This section ends with an essay by Eric Orozco, who examines Zionist architecture and a particular architectural design competition in Jerusalem for the Hurvah Synagogue. Orozco researches the circumstances that gave birth to and impeded the development of Louis Kahn's majestic project for this temple in Jerusalem. The nuances of the story reflect how architecture and urbanism were contested on the grounds of their symbolic appeal to different models of identity, a topic first introduced in this volume by Libertun de Duren and further addressed by Vale. Orozco argues that by selectively choosing which fragment of history to celebrate (Antiquity vs. Middle Ages vs. Modern Zionism) in the construction of the Temple Hurvah, both Kahn and the builders of Jerusalem were able to establish a new reference point for contemporary identity that drew inspiration from prior forms of political sovereignty without embracing all three equally or showing direct allegiance to any single one.

The volume closes with an essay by Diane E. Davis that reflects on the larger themes that unite the essays and re-examines how the case studies illuminate the nexus between cities, sovereignty arrangements, and conflict. Conflict in the city must be examined through attention to the specifics of its physical and social qualities. Further, even as there is not an unequivocal correspondence between urban form and urban social practices, spatial configurations set boundaries to social interaction in ways that may make violence more or less likely. This point has implications that entail not only the physical form of the city, but also the scales of sovereignty. We can hope that as globalization brings into question the effectiveness of national boundaries, it will also help us reconfigure sovereignty scales in ways that are most conducive to realizing the promise of the city.

Notes

1. The Gregory quote comes from a web-based review of *Cities, War, and Terrorism: Towards an Urban Geopolitics,* ed. Stephen Graham (Malden, U.K.: Blackwell Publishing, 2004). http://www.wiley.com/WileyCDA/WileyTitle/productCd-1405115742,descCd -reviews.html (accessed 12 April 2010).

2. The Sandercock quotes come from a web-based review of *Cities, War, and Terrorism: Towards an Urban Geopolitics,* ed. Stephen Graham (Malden, U.K.: Blackwell Publishing, 2004). http://www.wiley.com/WileyCDA/WileyTitle/productCd-1405115742,descCd -reviews.html (accessed 12 April 2010).

3. Clearly, there are many ways to understand the destructive, debilitating, and/or violence-related urban conditions that characterize so many of the world's cities. And

while our vantage point is the issue of sovereignty and how it affects ethnic, religious, and nationalist politics at the level of the city, there are several recent studies that make great headway in seeing these problems from the vantage point of urban political economy, and that take the city and/or capitalism as the unit of analysis. Among the best are Jane Schneider and Ida Susser (2003) and Mike Davis (1992).

References

Anderson, B. 1991. *Imagined Communities.* London: Verso Books.

Appadurai, A. 2003. "Sovereignty without Territoriality: Notes for a Post-national Geography." In *The Anthropology of Space and Place—Locating Culture,* ed. Setha Low and Denise Lawrence-Zuñiga, 337–349. New York: Wiley-Blackwell.

Buruma, I., and A. Margalit. 2004. *Occidentalism: The West in the Eyes of Its Enemies.* New York: Penguin Press.

Castells, M. 1983. *The City and the Grassroots.* Berkeley: University of California Press.

Davis, D. E. 1994. *Urban Leviathan: Mexico City in the Twentieth Century.* Philadelphia, Pa.: Temple University Press.

Davis, M. 1992. *Dead Cities and Other Tales.* New York: New Press.

Durkheim, E. 1933. *On the Division of Labor in Society.* New York: Macmillan.

Katznelson, I. 1981. *City Trenches: Urban Politics and the Patterning of Class in the United States.* New York: Pantheon Books.

Marcuse, P. 2002. "The Partitioned City in History." In *Of States and Cities: The Partitioning of Urban Space,* ed. P. Marcuse and R. van Kempen, 11–34. Oxford: Oxford University Press.

Marcuse, P., and R. van Kempen. 2002. "States, Cities, and the Partitioning of Urban Space." In *Of States and Cities: The Partitioning of Urban Space,* ed. P. Marcuse and R. van Kempen, 3–10. Oxford: Oxford University Press.

Milgram, Stanley. 1970. "The Experience of Living in Cities." *Science* 167: 1461–1468.

Myers, D. J., and H. A. Dietz, eds. 2002. *Capital City Politics in Latin America: Democratization and Empowerment.* Boulder, Colo.: Lynne Rienner.

Sassen, S. 1991. *The Global City: New York, London and Tokyo.* Princeton, N.J.: Princeton University Press.

———. 1998. *Globalization and Its Discontents.* New York: The New Press.

———. 2008. *Territory, Authority, Rights: From Medieval to Global Assemblages.* Princeton, N.J.: Princeton University Press.

Schneider, J., and I. Susser, eds. 2003. *Wounded Cities: Destruction and Reconstruction in a Globalizing World.* New York: Berg Press.

Smelser, N. J. 1959. *Social Change in the Industrial Revolution.* Reprint, Oxon: Routledge, 2006.

Sparke, M. 2005. *In the Space of Theory: Post-Foundational Geographies of the Nation-State.* Minneapolis: University of Minnesota Press.

Tajbakhsh, K. 2001. *The Promise of the City: Space, Identity, and Politics in Contemporary Social Thought.* Berkeley: University of California Press.
Tilly, C. 1992. *Capital, Coercion, and European States: AD 990–1992.* Cambridge, Mass.: Blackwell.
Weber, M. 1958. *The City.* Glencoe, Ill.: Free Press.

PART 1
MODES OF SOVEREIGNTY, URBAN GOVERNANCE, AND THE CITY

1

Jerusalem at the Beginning of the Twentieth Century

SPATIAL CONTINUITY AND SOCIAL FRAGMENTATION

Nora Libertun de Duren

> *We must establish our presence in the East not politically but through
> the church. . . . While our influence was still strong we could afford to
> conceal our activities and thus avoid envy, but now our influence in the
> East has weakened we, on the contrary, must try to display ourselves so
> that we do not sink in the estimation of the Orthodox population. . . .
> Jerusalem is the center of the world and our mission must be there.*
>
> —*1858 Russian Foreign Ministry memorandum*
> *(Wasserstein 2001, 60)*

In Jerusalem, modernity started in the ninth day of December 1917, when the
British forces commanded by (future Sir) Allenby entered the city, ending more
than four hundred years of Ottoman rule. Until then, the univocal mapping of
national institutions with territorial boundaries was foreign to the Holy City. At
the end of the nineteenth century, Jerusalem had been—not for the first time—
a site where civic and religious, eastern and western powers met. The city, whose
holiness was beyond temporal claims, was both the end of the contest and a means
to symbolize the legitimacy of the conqueror.

The period that preceded the full imposition of nation-state logic upon the
city was marked by a different arrangement of people, institutions and territory.
It is through the study of the interaction of these three that I try to capture the
complexity of the notion of citizenship in nineteenth century Jerusalem. This
chapter has three aims: first, to understand the city's configuration under the
Ottoman Empire; then, to describe how this citizenship model interacted with
European states; and finally, to trace these relationships in the spatial configuration of the city.

I have chosen this particular moment in Jerusalem's history because it was the last occasion when its institutions and residents did not operate in reference to a binary system of identity. The deep and antagonist separation of Jewish-Israelis and Muslim-Palestinians that we see today is localized spatially on the legacy of the British mandate. At that time, a congruency between religious identity and political jurisdiction was established as a criterion for dividing Jerusalem. Since that period, both Jews and Muslims have increasingly bound their lives to specific and exclusive locations. This is why I want to examine the very beginning of the twentieth century, before the modern nationalistic narratives were imposed on the organization of the city in ways that replaced the blurry geographies of national and religious territories characteristic of the Ottoman Empire. This vantage point helps me to explore how textures of identities work and sustains the search for alternative possibilities that can alter the current exclusionary logic of national spaces and their implementation in the occupation of urban spaces.

The Capitulations

National sovereignty, the notion of a univocal correspondence among people, land, and legal institutions, is a defining characteristic of the modern Western state. However, this connection was not present in early times. Rather, the indivisible bond between nationality and religion—as it was conceived before the European governments separated God from Government and Church from State—was attained by letting nationality flow beyond territorial boundaries.

Extraterritoriality, the legal form by which nationals of one country could be judged by their own law when residing in foreign land, was not uncommon in the Byzantine days. In order to encourage and organize commerce among people obeying different laws (and gods), the principle of extraterritoriality was often applied among European governments (Thayer 1923). Varangian merchants in the Byzantine Empire (according to a treaty of CE 904) and English merchants in the Russian Empire circa 1555, for example, were judged accordingly to the law of their own country, regardless of the physical location of their acts. "If a Russian should seek to steal from anyone in our Empire, the punishment for this act shall be severe; and if the theft has already been committed, twice the value of the stolen object shall be paid by him. Likewise, the rule is applicable to the Greeks in their relation with Russia and, furthermore, the guilty person shall be punished in accordance with the laws of his own country."[1]

The Ottoman Empire's adoption of this principle of "law-attached-to-subject" was reasonable in the fifteenth century context. "Capitulations"—the name ascribed to this specific model of extraterritorial privileges—were the ideal way to deal with the religious requirement of limiting access to Ottoman nationality only to true believers in Islam. By using this non-territorial system, commercial exchange with Westerners was made feasible. Otherwise, foreign merchants would not have been willing to reside within the empire; since according to Ottoman law, an infidel had no right to property and was not worthy of legal protection. Thanks to the Capitulations arrangement, the Ottoman Empire found a way to conduct international relations without breaking its own laws. As long as European nations kept a similar blurriness between legal and religious institutions and nationality, the Capitulations proved reasonably successful. However, after the Peace of Westphalia (1648), when modern European nations abandoned the principle of extraterritoriality in favor of the enforcement of local laws in correspondence to country boundaries, Ottoman power was weakened. Under these treaties, foreign nationals were given special benefits when in the empire's jurisdictions; but since legal systems were substantially unequal in Europe, no reciprocity was established.[2] Eventually, this ended up hurting the Ottoman government's ability to dominate its own territory. It was only in 1914, when Turkey entered World War I as an ally of German and Austro-Hungarian powers, that the Capitulations were officially rejected. The Turkish Ambassador submitted a note to the United States Secretary of State on September 1914. It reads "Sir: I have the honor to inform you that by Imperial Irade [decree] the Ottoman government has abrogated as from the first of October next the conventions known as the Capitulations restricting the sovereignty of Turkey in its relations with certain Powers. All privileges and immunities accessory to these conventions or issuing therefore are equally repealed. Having thus freed itself from what was an intolerable obstacle to all progress in the Empire, the Imperial government has adopted as the basis of its relations with the other Powers the principles of International Law" (Thayer 1914).

Jerusalem under the Ottoman Powers

The particularities of the population residing in Jerusalem did not escape the attention of the Ottoman Government. As a response to the demands that a large number of foreigners—residents, missioners and diplomats—imposed on the local administration, Jerusalem was given a special legal status. In 1874, while the rest of the Palestinian districts were still administered from Beirut, it was decided that the Holy City was to be governed by an exclusive "mutasarraf," or governor. Foreign residents were an extra challenge for Ottoman control, not because of their power, but because of their weakness. Being mostly part of non-Muslim religious communities or charity institutions, they required foreign nations' tutelage.

But this protection was not to be awarded for free, and as long as the Capitulation treaties were in effect, European countries took advantage of the unique legal arrangement to force their influence on Jerusalem's territories.

One of the most controversial issues in the administration of Jerusalem was the increased flow of Jewish migrants from Western nations, who had been formally barred since the early 1880s. However, since these migrants were foreign nationals, this prohibition was highly ineffective; in practice they were allowed to enter Palestine and stay under the protection of foreign consuls. From the perspective of the Ottoman power, not only religious, but also political reasons justified this prohibition. Within the Capitulations regime, the increased number of Jewish residents was likely to be used by European states to increase their own influence in Jerusalem. The same countries that disliked the presence of Jews in their own territories were happy to rise as their protectors when in Palestine. The situation was perceived to be so harmful to local government that one of the governors of Jerusalem—Tevfik Bey (1897–1901)—sent a letter to Istanbul proposing to force Jewish people to accept Ottoman nationality. The idea was to prevent European nations from taking advantage of being their protectors, because as Resid (the Governor who followed Tevfik Bey) said, "If total prohibition proved impossible, one should at least try to find the means to reduce the damage and harness Jewish power for Ottoman interest" (Kushner 1999, 83).

This "role of protector" was central to British policy in Palestine. In the middle of the nineteenth century, as a reaction to France being the protector of the Catholics (Latins) and Russia looking after the Christian Orthodox Church, England sought to fortify her own position in the Holy Land by being the guardian of the Jewish people.[3] However, since many of the Jews residing in Jerusalem were Russians émigrés, both Ottoman and Russian authorities objected to British policy. No European state wanted to lose the strategic advantage of having nationals within Jerusalem's boundaries who could justify its presence there.

After a series of diplomatic conflicts, by 1890 England was forced to limit its "protection activities" to only those Jewish residents who were also British nationals. The extent to which these extraterritorial powers in Jerusalem were used as political leverage is reflected in a 1914 irony. Almost twenty-five years before the Second World War, Germany—allied to Turkey in the First World War and with no territorial claims over Palestine—became the official protector of Jewish people in the Holy Land.

European designs on Jerusalem were not just opportunistic responses to Ottoman weakness but also a vestige of the unresolved internal contradictions of secular western nations. Even after the legal separation of church and state was fully incorporated into national laws, states found a justification for their actions in protection of religious values. The name of "Christendom" was the sword of territorial powers. The 1858 editorial note in the *New York Times* reads:

> To this immense territory [of the Ottoman Empire], and with this hetero-geneous people, the commercial States of the world are obliged to resort and deal; are obliged to maintain intimate intercourse, and send thither agents and traders. The religious sentiment of Christendom cannot refrain from attempt-ing the re-evangelization of the countries sanctified by the life and death of the great founder. A vast mass of the population are Christians, and they have strong affinities and sympathies with the churches of surrounding States. Thus every interest, sacred and secular, is involved in the preservation of order in the Ottoman Empire.

Governing the City

It is my interest to look at how the Ottoman Empire managed to govern under such conditions, with more than one third of its residents being "legally pro-tected" by foreign nations. In 1910, out of 69,900 residents in Jerusalem, there were 12,000 Jews and 12,900 Christians (Wasserstein 2001). Many of these resi-dents were economically inactive, surviving thanks to external donations—people whose reason for existence was just to be physically present in Jerusalem: in their own eyes to preach in the holiest place on earth; in the eyes of some European states, to help them embody their territorial claims.

The duality of actual residents and "residents' protectors" as actors in Jeru-salem meant that competition for city space happened at two different—yet inter-connected—levels: diplomacy and daily life. Foreign institutions advanced their interests through consulates who relied on diplomatic conventions; by using their legal rights they sought access to the territory. The approach of city residents was inverse: through the actual appropriation of the territory they looked for ways to institutionalize their rights.

Given that transactions and taxation related to property involving non-Ottoman residents were done through consular offices, secular life was difficult to manage. However, the main concern of Jerusalem authorities was "sacred-life" in the city, since any conflict could easily be converted into an international affair. Much of the daily task of the government of Jerusalem was to mediate in the residents' struggles for occupation of the sacred sites of the city. In most of the cases, what the parties contested was not the sanctity of a site, but the right of the other to be there. But although all groups claimed exclusive legitimacy, their incapacity to either renounce or to impose themselves forced them to the path of negotiations.

This was also related to the way residents defined their own religious affiliation. The people of Jerusalem at the beginning of the twentieth century did not identify themselves simply as Christians, Muslims, or Jewish; they constructed their religious identity with a zealousness and specificity that entailed drawing very circumscribed sub-boundaries within larger ecclesiastical groupings. There were "more than 45,000 Jews in Jerusalem divided into six sections—the Sepharadim of Spanish origins; the Ashkenazim chiefly of German, Polish and Russian extraction; the Jews of Yemen, Arabia; the Jews of Aleppo, Damascus and Bagdad, the Gurgeee, Persian and Bokhari Jews from the Caucasus, Persia and Turkestan, and the Karaim, Karaites from the Crimea. Every section had its separate organization and no representation in the local government because they were not united" (Wasserstein 2001). In addition, the identities of people of other religions were also broken down into a myriad of varieties: Latins, Franciscans, Greek Orthodox, Russian Orthodox, Armenians, Syrians, Jacobites, Copts, Abyssinians, Anglicans, Presbyterians, Arabs, Muslims, Sunis, Turks, and Bedouins, among others. All these groups acted out their distinct claims in their daily demands for Jerusalem spaces (Williams 1921). Moreover, their religious identities were crisscrossed by different nationalities. Holy City residents responded to different earthly laws. Mainly the codes of Turkey, France, Britain, Germany, Greece, Russia, Italy or United States were used to judge their actions.

Jerusalem's governors were under double pressure when administering the city. On the one hand they had to respond to Istanbul and to the Muslim world. On the other, they had to manage the pressure of European consuls, who were quick to object to any partiality that did not favor their constituencies, national or religious. In terms of the holy sites, most of the conflicts derived from questioning who deserved to be in which sanctuary. Given these constraints, the governors' approach did not rely on open coercion but on shrewd management. Three distinct strategies characterized their conflict over sacred spaces: use of a third neutral, double-deals, and attenuation.

The use of a "third neutral" served to deal with the contestation over spaces when parties shared more similarities amongst themselves than with the third—neutral—party. An example of this approach is recorded in an Ottoman mandate regarding the Easter ceremony. The various Christian groups would not agree to cede the religious privilege of guarding the keys of the Holy Sepulchre to each other, and in order to avoid conflicts among them, a Muslim family was made guard instead. In the same fashion, the windows of the Church of the Nativity were not cleaned by a devoted Christian but by an Ottoman employee; and when Copts and Abyssinians quarreled, a Catholic was the mediator. In other cases, such as in the cleaning of the Holy Sepulchre steps, it was fear of this same practice—a non-Christian performing a Holy Christian task—that compelled different parties to negotiate a solution among themselves.

The second strategy, the "double-deal," consisted in convincing each side that the government was favoring their cause. One way to do this was to let one party have its rights publicly legitimized, while allowing the other to actually enjoy them. For example, this was the procedure followed in the dispute between Latins and Greeks over the use of the Church of the Nativity passageway. The former had the legitimacy of their claim recognized, but the actual use permit was afforded to the latter. Another slight variation on this approach was when the right to a certain passage was given to the Copts, and then Abyssinians received exclusivity over a new path to the same area (Kushner 1999).

It seems that when either of these approaches was applied, the Jerusalem government did not feel threatened by the dispute. The situation was different when a European consulate backed up claims. In those cases, the contestation over city spaces was not perceived as a challenge to city order but rather as a way to undermine Ottoman authority over Jerusalem. "Attenuation" was a way to avoid having an urban conflict transformed into a diplomatic one. For example, Copts and Abyssinians were in constant conflict, but when Copts decided to become closer to British influence, the Governor of Jerusalem, Selma Ekrem, suggested giving them all Ottoman honors—so as to intervene in their gravitation toward English protection. This rationale closely resembles the suggestion made by another Governor, Resid, to give Jewish residents Ottoman nationality if their illegal immigration could not be prevented.

Britain was not alone in seeking ways to enlarge its influence in Jerusalem; other nations were also looking for means to legitimize their presence in the city. Eventually, the Ottoman government was unable to resist European powers and pulled out of Jerusalem. However, it is possible that it lasted longer than its own weakness would have led one to guess, precisely because of this contestation among Westerners. European nations were jealously guarding each other, never allowing any one of them to be too empowered in the city. When Russia wanted to become the protector of the Orthodox, the Greeks protested, and although France managed to be the protector of the Latins, the Italians, the Vatican, and the Franciscans were continuously challenging that right. It is not a coincidence that Jerusalem was taken by the "West" only after the Great Powers' alliance during World War I.

The Holy Places

Thinking through the dynamics of this period, when Jerusalem was a single jurisdiction with a multiplicity of nationalities and ethnicities—each one responding to a different legal constellation—one wonders how these interactions were reflected in the city's space. How did the European states—highly aware of national spatial boundaries—manage to operate under the logic of extraterritoriality, while still struggling for spaces of exclusive territoriality? For the Ottoman Empire, national and religious identities were one; for France, Britain, Russia, Italy and Germany at the beginning of the twentieth century, this belief was a powerful confounder through which they introduced their nationalistic interests in the midst of the city.

In Jerusalem, all claims are old, but none is older than the city itself. The contestation is over the legitimacy of the actors, not the holiness of the stage. Hence, the space is fixed and the demography is manipulated. The identity games that diplomacy played filtered into the architecture of the city. The Old City, composed by four quarters and circumvented by a rocky wall, could neither be divided nor completely unified.

The footprint of the Old City at the beginning of the twentieth century dated from the "Aelia Capitolina" time (CE 135–324), when Hadrian first destroyed the city and then rebuilt it after the Roman camp model. The courses of the wall—reconstructed during the Ottoman period—are located almost in the same place as the Roman ones. Inside of them, Hadrian traced a north–south road (Cardo) and an east–west road (Decumanus). During the Crusader Kingdom, these roads were used to mark four quarters: Syrian, German, Armenian, and Patriarch. Later, these same spaces were to be named the Muslim, Jewish, Armenian, and Christian quarters.

This practice of destruction and reconstruction and of reoccupation and renaming of city structures was not limited to these neighborhoods. With each new regime, the city received new temples and new names for the old ones. When Romans conquered the city, they built a Temple for Jupiter in the middle of the Jewish Temple, at the east side of the Wailing Wall. And when Moslems conquered Jerusalem in the seventh century, they renamed the area Haramesh-Sharif (Noble Sanctuary) and built a series of minarets within it. In the eleventh century, Crusaders called it Templum Domini and added the Baptisterium, the Temple Convent, and the Templus Salomonis. It was in the thirteenth century, with the Mamluk administration, that the religious compound received its current name: the Dome of the Rock.

When the Ottoman Empire conquered Jerusalem in 1517, they restored the Dome of the Rock to its full splendor and replaced its windows and decorations with those of the Suleiman aesthetic. They had considerable power over the city, and managed to transform many of the churches and temples into mosques. However, when the Empire's own powers started to decline, Western nations began to set a firmer foot in Holy Land. They did not limit themselves to protecting existing non-Muslim religious institutions, they also built new structures for their own creeds.

The increasing pressure European nations exerted to occupy further space in Jerusalem (as well as the increasing weakness of the local government) can be seen in how they encroached over the green belt that ran between the city walls and the old buildings, creating an even denser, yet more finely subdivided net of sacred territories in the city. By the middle of the nineteenth century, what had been a continuous strip of open space began to be filled by new houses in the Jewish quarter, and in the Christian quarter by the Convent and the Church of Saint Saviour and the Latin Patriarchae. Only the open space at the site of the Dome of the Rock was preserved. Even outside the Old City, the pressure to occupy the space was growing. Russians built the Saint Mary Magdalena Church and a huge religious compound on the Mount of Olives, and Germans founded a Lutheran Church next to the Holy Sepulchre. Jewish immigrants established themselves just outside of the city walls, in what later would be the Nachlat-Shiva and the ultra-orthodox Me' She' arim Jewish quarter. Noticeably, when British forces occupied the city in 1917, even before the fight was finished, they called the expert help of the Alexandria City Engineer—and later, in 1922, of Sir Patrick Geddes—to propose a plan for Jerusalem. The recommendation was to preserve Jerusalem's medieval character; and surround its wall by a belt of open space.

The Closure

This world of mischievous diplomacy was far too fragile to resist the pressures of the war. When the different sides felt that they had more to gain through military action than through compromise, negotiation was replaced by open confrontation. The Ottoman Empire allied with Germany, while the rest of European nations were drawing maps of their Holy Land share. In the words of one British War Office representative of the time, they were like "hunters who divided up the skin of the bear before they killed it" (Wasserstein 2001, 74). After the defeat of the Ottoman Empire, the issue of who would govern Jerusalem was still unclear. France and England were in the list of likely candidates, but the German Kaiser also suggested the Pope for the task. In 1917, England began their mandate and made public the Balfour Declaration "to facilitate the establishment of a Jewish National Home in Palestine." One year later, the Vatican proposed a Belgian for the government, since "politically Belgium is unable to overshadow anybody."[4]

This extreme contestation and instability deeply affected life in the city. In the last years of the Ottoman Empire, the living conditions in Jerusalem seriously deteriorated. Water and hygiene were scarce: malaria, cholera, dysentery and scarlet fever affected more than one fourth of the population. The infant mortality rate was tremendously high and trachoma was common among locals. As travelers to Palestine described, it was not rare to see blind people wandering around, with no particular direction, constantly murmuring prayers in the heart of the Holy City.

What can we conclude from this particular pattern of identity, power and place? Did this multifragmented space and discontinuity between law and territory prevent the city from experiencing ethnic conflicts, or just delay them and lead to an even worse outcome? Was the city's misery connected to its inability to move beyond its inherited sacredness, or was it precisely that fixity in the past that preserved Jerusalem over the centuries?

It is hard to provide an answer to these questions, or to establish a line of causality. However, there are at least four observations about this case that could be useful for tracing alternative configurations for Jerusalem's future. The first one is that we must distinguish between conflict among city residents, and the use of residents to dispute conflicts about the city (or about concerns beyond it). The second is that dependency on institutions independent from the city comes at a very high price: residents of Jerusalem were deprived of their resources when World War I began and excluded from participating in the decision-making processes when the moment to choose a new government came. Third, national powers rely on negotiation only when they cannot fully impose their sovereignty. The last observation is that, although Jerusalem's story is marked by wars over identity, there have been more times when these different identities found a way to live side-by-side in the city, and in that history there is hope.

Notes

1. Article IV of the CE 944 treaty between Byzantine emperors and Russian Varangians (Thayer 1923).

2. Thayer enumerates the following treaties, so called "Capitulations": Italian cities (1540), Sardinia Treaty (1740), France (1535), Austria (1625), England (1675), Holland (1680), Sweden (1737), Denmark (1746), Prussia (1761), Bavaria (1870), Spain (1782), Russia

(1783), United States (1830), Belgium (1838), Hanse Cities (1839), Portugal (1843), Greece (1855) and Brazil (1858).

3. The Europeans powers did not strive for territorial controls in Palestine but for "influence." The easiest way to establish "influence" was the policy of "protection" of religious minorities. The Russians already has [sic] the Orthodox Christians and the French had the Catholics to "protect." To draw even, England and Prussia (later Germany) has [sic] to find or create their own minorities to be "protected." From 1839 the British took the Jews under their wing, and a small Protestant community was created by way of conversion. The policy of religious-cultural penetration and of "religious protectorates" thus made Jerusalem an arena of European rivalries. (From Alexander Schölch 19th Century, quoted by Dumper [1997])

4. Quoted from Sergio Minervi, "The Vatican and Zionism: Conflict in the Holy Land 1895–1925," in Wasserstein (2001, 75).

Works Cited

Dumper, M. 1997. *The Politics of Jerusalem since 1967.* New York: Columbia University Press.

Friedland, R., and R. Hecht. 1996. *To Rule Jerusalem.* Cambridge: Cambridge University Press.

Harvey, D. 2000. *Spaces of Hope.* Berkeley: University of California Press.

Kushner, D. 1999. "The District of Jerusalem in the Eyes of Three Ottoman Governors at the End of the Hamidian Period." *Middle Eastern Studies* 35, no. 2: 83–102.

New York Times. 1858. "Dissolution of the Ottoman Rule." July 30.

Sharon, A. 1973. *Planning Jerusalem, the Old City and Its Environs.* Tel Aviv: Japhet Press.

Thayer, L. E. 1923. "The Capitulations of the Ottoman Empire and the Questions of Its Abrogation as It Affects the United States." *The American Journal of International Law* 17, no. 2: 207–233.

———. 1914. "Dr. Silverman sees crisis in Palestine: Turkey's declaration of war has removed the last source of income for Jews there." November 9.

Wasserstein, B. 2001. *Divided Jerusalem, the Struggle for the Holy City.* New Haven, Conn.: Yale University Press.

Williams, T. W. 1921. "Palestine is still a land of problems. Moslems and Christians bitterly opposed to colonization by zionist immigrants." *New York Times.* July 10.

2

Imperial Nationhood and Its Impact on Colonial Cities

ISSUES OF INTER-GROUP PEACE AND
CONFLICT IN PONDICHERRY AND VIETNAM

Anne Raffin

This volume examines conflicts within cities through the lens of political institutions and social identities that operate on a variety of scales. Colonial cities of
the French Empire hosted a multiplicity of institutions and identities. This was
not just because most colonial cities were places where interaction among various
ethnic and national groups took place, but also because the requisites of urban
governance in cities of the imperial periphery required attention to a multiplicity
of local legal and social institutions that preceded colonial dominion (Coquery-
Vidrovitch 1988).

For such culturally diverse cities where governance practices were imposed
from outside, and where loyalty among local populations sustained imperial rule,
the politics of identity served as a field of contested claims. Indeed, linked to the
recognition of individual and group identity were issues of access to social or political power and resources, as well as the struggle to gain self-respect and valida-
tion of one's identity. Playing with identity and the allegiances it entailed was a
tricky game that could lead to conflicts. In the cases at hand, the French colonial
power in Pondicherry (Pondichéry in French; here referred to in its Anglicized
spelling), India from the 1850s to 1914, and the Vietnamese cities of Saigon and
Hanoi from the 1850s through the 1920s challenged the existing social identities,
which were often based on kinship group, parentage, religion, and incipient nationalism. While the two Vietnamese cities could be termed cosmopolitan, since
they had inhabitants from different parts of the world (Europeans, Chinese, Indians, natives), I would characterize the city of Pondicherry as provincial, as the

composition of the population was mostly made up of locals and a small European community.

What conditions make cultural diversity a source of tension and possible violence for cities under colonial rule? According to Iris Young, in her study of federalism among the various Native American groups that made up the Iroquois Confederacy, a sovereign state exercises "central and final authority" over all political and legal subjects within a bounded territory (Young 2000, 247). For our case, French territorial sovereignty over its colonies raises the issue of the imperial power's legitimacy. On the one hand, France and its discourse of the "civilizing mission" promised to "uplift" the locals who were not yet as fully "civilized," "modern" and "rational" as the Europeans. Colonized subjects were promised that over the long term, they would become a sovereign entity which would be "an independent, self-determining agent" (Tanner 2007). On the other hand, racial hierarchy characterized the everyday life of the colonial world.

Along with the other pieces in this volume, this essay analyzes inter-group dynamics through a focus on individuals, institutions, and the built environment. However, this chapter differentiates the imperial state from the colonial state. The imperial, or metropolitan, state oversaw the *metropole* (the territory of the capital itself) and its empire. The colonial state was built by representatives of France in order to manage a specific overseas territory. The limitation of the empire's power resulted from overlapping sovereignties of the imperial state and the colonial state, which could have conflicting agendas about the implementation of new Republican policies and laws regarding how to maintain the balance of power.

French sovereignty over foreign territory also introduces the problem of identification. Which territorial entity gave the local inhabitants their main identity— the motherland and its empire, the colony, or a given community? The fragility of the imperial state's authority became apparent when this transnational institution imposed new values, institutions and demands on colonial inhabitants, who responded by taking into account their own interests, sense of place, and identity.

This chapter argues that state policies created in France but implemented in colonial settings—such as universal suffrage for male Indian natives, decentralized local councils in Pondicherry, and repatriation of Frenchmen from Vietnam to the motherland for the war effort—served to promote the conditions for conflict in Vietnam and India. These various policies acted to reinforce the discrepancy between the promise of the civilizing mission, and the reality of a racialized social order.

Did natives' responses to these policies undermine the sovereignty of the imperial state? And what lessons can we learn regarding the process of fostering and maintaining peace in a plural urban environment? The authority of the imperial state was undermined in Pondicherry, since the colonial law was used by social actors as a system of resources against the authorities' projected goal. More precisely, high-caste Indians led by the leader Chanemougam were able to take over newly created local political institutions and reinforce existing social differences in a mainly Hindu society, even though the law of universal suffrage aimed at undermining the hierarchy of the caste system.[1] High-caste individuals resisted the Republican empire's attempts to impose a sense of imperial nationhood. They did not perceive themselves in terms of a "nation," but as belonging to a religious and exclusionary community defined by the caste system, a system based on the notions of pollution, purity, and space and sanctioned by an embedded stigma. While they did tolerate French political sovereignty, members of the religious elite refused to embrace French cultural sovereignty based on universal republican ideas. High-caste individuals accepted a position of subordinated subjecthood in the colonial order as long as their dominant position was maintained within their own religious community. These conditions gave rise to a divergence between the imperial state with its ostensible goal of a "civilizing mission for all" and a local state at the urban level, where administrators often chose to implement an ideology of respect for cultural and religious differences. In India, such disparate policies resulted in escalating tensions that eventually led to caste warfare.

In the case of Vietnam, new state policies and changing conditions in labor and housing markets led to demands among the local Vietnamese for more ethnic integration, all of which played a role in intensifying inter-ethnic conflict. Nevertheless, the authority of the imperial state was not diminished. Long-distance control continued to be maintained even after Frenchmen were sent back to the metropole to serve in World War I. In addition, local state bureaucrats in Hanoi were able to protect the "dual city," as Hanoi was run almost as two cities in one, the colonial and the indigenous. The distinction between the two halves of the city was enforced by a law pertaining to the built environment, which required that all houses in European neighborhoods comply with a European architectural style.

Later conflicts between Vietnamese and local Chinese also failed to challenge the colonial order in Saigon. In his newspaper articles in the early twentieth century, Vietnamese journalist Gilbert Chieu and his companions supported the idea of Vietnam as a partner of the imperial power. They promoted the idea of economic nationalism, which entailed the economic emancipation of Vietnam from the Chinese community. They pressed for power and authority over the economic resources of their land, in other words, for a "secessionless" economic sovereignty that would be shared with the French.[2] This Vietnamese group based their claim on their relation to the soil. They argued that the Chinese had no sovereign economic rights over Vietnam since their legal status was as foreign Asians who did not belong to the French imperial nation, as did the Vietnamese. The colonial government gave some backing to the Vietnamese as part of the "Franco-Annamite collaboration" and as a means to counteract the growing economic power of the Chinese in the early phase of the 1919 anti-Chinese campaign, but eventually chose to support the status quo for fear of destabilizing the social order. In the case of Vietnam, the status quo did not pose a conflict between the ideas of the metropole and the more immediate concerns of the colonial authorities.

The decision to compare Pondicherry and Vietnam was based on the desire to study the implementation of colonial rule and spatial segregation by a single colonizer in two different colonial settings. The comparison of specific historical instances of inter-group civility and inter-group violence is aimed at identifying conditions that enable the recurrence of such events over time and space. In addition, Pondicherry and Vietnam were chosen because they embody contrasting outcomes, specifically in regards to political participation versus nonparticipation of the colonized entity.

What explains the variations in colonial policy regarding incorporating locals into the imperial political community? Pondicherry, an old colony which France had taken in 1673 before the age of democracy, was an exception in the field of colonial policy, along with the four French communes within Senegal and the colonies of Martinique, Guadeloupe, Guyane, and Réunion (Deschamps 2003, 110). Indeed, unlike Vietnam, the French establishments in India (Pondicherry, Karikal, Mahé, Yanaon, and Chandernagore) benefitted from the Republican proposal to politically emancipate the indigenous male population by granting them universal suffrage in 1848. Universal suffrage was used in these colonies as a means to promote the assimilationist cause through electoral campaigns (Lara 2007, 9–12). Indians indirectly benefited from this ruling, which initially targeted the newly emancipated slaves from Réunion and the Antilles. The extension of these rights (voting and abolition of slavery) was rooted in the French Revolution, which reconceptualized these human rights as universal, creating ideals the French then felt needed to be spread throughout the world (Hunt 1996).

The political decision to expand universal suffrage to the colonies in 1848 was in continuity with an electoral process that had emerged in France during the revolutionary period (1789–1798). While the French colonies were not invited at first to participate in the 1789 States General, a delegation of colonizers from Saint-Domingue (which became the independent nation of Haiti in 1804), *was* able to be admitted to the National Assembly. Three years later, the legislative assembly officially recognized the principle of colonial representation through the Decree of 22 August 1792. Yet, under the reign of Napoleon Bonaparte (Napoleon I), Article 91 of the Constitution of 25 VIII Frimaire (1799) stipulated that the colonies were subject to special laws, which subsequently removed their deputation.

The debate regarding colonial representation resumed during 1840–1850. Lara argues that the 1848 expansion of universal suffrage to the colonies did not initially provoke discussion regarding the compatibility of voting rights with colonization or the issue of whether the natives could be considered citizens when they were not independent. Victor Schoelcher, the principal spokesman at the time who worked for the abolition of slavery, likewise failed to address such fundamental questions (Lara 2007, 19–23). However, this law was withdrawn in French India due to the eruption of violence in July 1848. This involved incidents such as the burning of pariah villages to punish outcastes who began wearing slippers, at the time a privilege of only the upper castes (Weber 1996, 100–102).

In 1871, universal suffrage was again implemented in French India. Indian males were granted the right to vote in national elections. This decision was in line with the Third Republic—the republican parliamentary democracy regime of France from 1870 to 1940—and its universal principals of Republicanism, specifically, liberty, equality, and fraternity. Yet while equality among locals was affirmed, racial boundaries were drawn through the creation of different electoral lists for French and Indian voters. In 1884 a third list emerged for the *renonçants,* meaning Indians who renounced their legal status as Hindus or Muslims in order to subject themselves to the French civil law decree of 21 September 1881. The creation of this three-list electoral system was a response from the colonial Supreme Court (*conseil supérieur des colonies*) to a plea by the *renonçants,* who had asked to have the right to be registered on the first list with the Europeans. This right was not granted even though the *Cour de cassation*—the main court of last resort in France—had decided the case in favor of the *renonçants* in 1883 (Clairon 1926, 95–99; Annasse 1975, 121–124). Shared sovereignty associated with different forms of statehood (imperial state versus colonial state) had thus resulted in disagreements among different layers of political authorities and institutions.

Local political participation was extended in French India with the emergence of the local council and the colonial council in 1872. The latter was supplanted in 1879 by a general council elected by universal suffrage, in which the colonizers would hold the highest number of seats (Clairon 1926, 105). French predominance was also maintained by having the members of both councils elected by a voting pool that was fifty percent French and fifty percent Indian despite the French's numerical minority status (Weber, August 1987, 7; Closets d'Errey 1934).

Pondicherry was a miniscule colony in which the French lacked the means of coercion to dominate the population. Instead, the colonizers had to adopt an ideology approving differences in order to be tolerated by the natives. Respect for local customs became the norm. As the decree of 6 January 1819 stated: "The Indians either Christians, either Moors [Muslims], or gentiles [Hindus] will be judged, as in the past, according to the laws, practices, and customs of their castes" (*Bulletin officiel des établissements français de l'Inde*, 1877, 539).[3] Despite the imperial state-centered assimilationist policy of the 1870s–1880s, respect for difference was still, at the local level, often implemented as a way to maintain peace among different local groups and the interests of the high castes.

In contrast, Vietnam, where the French arrived in 1858–1859, did not benefit from such an assimilationist perspective, nor do the local elites seem to have demanded laws stating a respect for social and cultural differences. Despite the creation of chambers of representatives at the provincial level in the colonies of Tonkin and Annam under Sarraut (governor-general 1911–1914 and 1917–1919), political participation was only consultative and confined to a tiny proportion of the local population (Brocheux and Hémery 2001, 292–295). Sarraut was the apostle of the "Franco-Annamite collaboration," a motto presented to the Vietnamese elite as the path to a liberal evolution of the colony. In his speeches, Sarraut asserted the need for Indochinese people to take part in running the federation "in a liberal collaboration, for the benefit of the common (public) domain." Otherwise, as he stated, it would be unworthy of France and its civilizing mission, while by the same token French legitimacy in the eyes of the locals would be endangered (Larcher 1995, 398). In addition to this discourse of partnership was the rhetoric of a "civilizing mission" to uplift the uncivilized natives by assimilating them into European culture. However, the Vietnamese had very limited opportunity to take advantage of European civilization through education or professional positions offering training and promotion (Aldrich 1996, 228). The colonizers were interested mainly in economic gain (Duiker 1995, 32).

Such varying legal and cultural conditions attest to the influence of an imperial state on ethnic/racial and caste relations. I argue that these ethnic/racial and caste conflicts, resistance, and collaboration were not caused by inter-group tensions per se; rather, they were more often the result of colonial policies that brought such tensions to the fore. This piece will first discuss the impact of the French state on urban design in colonial settings as a tool to propagate the notion of a "greater France." By the end of the nineteenth century, France had acquired a vast empire that demanded a reconfiguration of the notion of national identity in order for these new territories to become part of French nationhood. The rise of a "greater France," encompassing the country's overseas territories, obliged leaders to reflect on the role and status of France as an imperial nation as well as to boost an "imperial mentality" among its citizens and subjects (Cooper 2004, 131). French rhetoric promoted the idea of closely linking the colonies with the mother country and the universal ideals of republicanism (Baycroft 2004, 149). In 1885, Jules Ferry at the Chamber of the Deputies in Paris stressed one of the goals of colonization: to augment the greatness (*grandeur*) of the French nation. Part of displaying such grandeur was the alteration of the face of the colonial city, which consequently altered the forms of urban conflict, as we will see in the second part of this chapter.

Colonial Sovereignty and Its Impact on Urban Design

Vietnam

Mamdani has described the colonial state in the African context as a "bifurcated state" that rules through race and direct rule in the cities, and through tribes and indirect rule in rural areas. Related to these methods of governance was the issue of firmly establishing foreign sovereignty (Mamdani 1996, 3). He further argues that the universal aspect of the colonial state is its "organization and reorganization" as "a response to a central and overriding dilemma: the native question" (1996, 16). Following his argument, we will see how urban design was perceived as one of the means to the "pacification" of the locals—which often translated into the urban segregation of racial groups in both colonial settings—and how colonial authorities channeled racial identities into geographical locations as a means to maintain administrative power.

In the early days of colonialism in Asia, building an imperial identity was similar to the process of consolidating a national identity in France, since the goal was to export France to the colonies in order to propagate French culture overseas. The French colonial experience, in contrast to the British one, was far more linked to the metropole and subsequently influenced by the domestic political life of France (Bayly 2000, 585). With regard to urbanism, such a unilateral vision led first to a policy of assimilation in Vietnam. An example of assimilation in urban design was the physical demolition of Saigon in 1859, replaced by a French city with a European architectural style. At the turn of the century, the American Jasper Whiting, visiting the city, wrote:

Saigon . . . is Paris on a small scale. The streets and boulevards are broad and immaculate. The public buildings are handsome, dignified structures, standing well back from the thoroughfare, and surrounded by gardens laid out with great taste. There is a miniature Champs-Élysées, a miniature Bois de Boulogne, and a miniature Avenue de l'Opéra, and each is adorned with statuary such as only French artists can produce. There is, too, a twin-spired cathedral, the Notre Dame of the city, and a beautiful Opera House, of which every resident is justly proud. As in Paris, this latter building stands at the head of a grand boulevard in the very heart of the city. (Edwards 2003, 91)

The implementation of direct rule—where the colonial power did not negotiate governance with the local elites and their indigenous institutions—guided the urban reconstruction of Saigon. Western aesthetic ideals were the norm, and centralized politics did not rely on local elites' thoughts on the matter (Mamdani 1996, 16–17). Thus sovereignty became associated with a particular set of cultural and political practices defined by the French, to the exclusion of the ones designed by the colonized subjects (Anghie 2004, 7).

Similar was the later project of turning Hanoi into the "Paris of Tonkin." An urban architecture would emerge symbolizing the power of France over the locals and having little respect for Vietnamese heritage. The Bao Thien Pagoda, constructed under the Ly Dynasty (1009–1225), was replaced by the Cathedral Saint-Joseph in 1887. Monsignor Puginier, bishop of Hanoi, had the capacity to convince the local colonial state to endorse such projects, and in this case Vietnamese Catholics also supported the construction. Here, there was not a simple division between the colonizers and colonized; rather, a religious entity superseded this binary division. However, in general, local elites did not play an intermediary role in the remaking of the urban design—since the buildings were Franco-French projects, local elites were not viewed as valid participants.

Other ancient pagodas were demolished to make way for a city hall, the central post office and, later, the school Collège du Protectorat, all institutions embodying the colonial power. Many Vietnamese homes were also destroyed in the effort toward colonial urbanism. Under Governor General of Indochina Paul Doumier (1897–1902), the architect Auguste-Henri Vildieu changed the profile of Hanoi by creating buildings such as the edifices of the résidence supérieure, the law courts, etc., all in a neoclassical style embodying power as well as durability. The iron bridge, Pont Doumier, whose construction lasted three years and cost six million piastres to the budget of Indochina, epitomized the display of French superiority (Van Ky 1997, 57–60). The center of Hanoi was conceived as a visual representation of the sovereign Republic at its best. As Mamdani has pointed out for other contexts, it was a colonial practice to exclude native institutions from the new "civilized" urban setting (1996, 16–18).

Assimilationist urban development was not only about exhibiting the superiority of the French. Colonial urban design was also molded by security issues, what Mamdani refers to as the native question. In 1862, Colonel Coffyn, the Lieutenant-Commander of the Engineers, was given the assignment of rebuilding the city of Saigon. Inspired by the architect of modern Paris, Baron Georges-Eugène Haussmann, he transplanted his ideas of large boulevards and public spaces to Saigon. In both cases, numerous chaotic, small streets were replaced by wide, straight boulevards. Wide streets addressed not only Haussmann's sense of aestheticism, but also security concerns. Indeed, wide, long streets allowed the military to charge more easily against opposition movements and to monitor and control the population more efficiently. Such considerations were very much part of Coffyn's thinking. He viewed the alteration of the physical space as a means of dealing with the native question, hence a tool to consolidate French sovereignty over the city.

The notion of "respecting differences" became the cornerstone of French colonial policy by the twentieth century. After World War I there emerged an urbanism based on the notion of association. Colonial authorities came to the conclusion that transplanting French culture into the newly conquered territories was unrealistic since colonies often had too few French administrators to implement such projects. In addition, the colonial theorist Jules Harmand, who supported a policy of association, claimed, "the social standards of the Native inhabitants were too remote from those of France for assimilation to be practicable" (Mamdani 1996, 83). According to Mamdani's model, the colonial European experience witnessed a shift from "rejuvenating to conserving [colonial] society" (1996, 286). Part of this shift relevant to our subject was a new respect for different local cultures, including preservation of historical monuments and local aesthetics, which became the motto of the politics of association. For instance, under Sarraut, indigenous decorations began to appear on public buildings, such as the Provincial Treasury (Wright 1991, 73–84, 190–191). According to Wright, such urban policy mingled with other socially oriented policies, such as the building of more hospitals and schools, likely would have curbed opposition to the greater colonial project and reduced the need for coercion. From eradicating the built identity of the Vietnamese, now the French were trying to preserve aspects of the native urban culture.

In keeping with the trend of bringing architects and urban planners from France rather than using local ones, the urbanist Ernest Hébrard came to Hanoi in 1923. He continued the practice of mixing Western and Asian decorative elements, but he was inclined to incorporate more traditional Vietnamese style than his predecessors (Logan 2000, 101). Hébrard represented the "limited opening" of colonial institutions to local influence in the 1920s and 1930s as a means to counteract indigenous reformist movements as well as to incorporate the Vietnamese more concretely into greater France. During this period, a slightly larger number of Vietnamese were able to obtain low-level entry jobs in the local administration; the University of Hanoi was built in 1926; and the colonizers officially acknowledged the existence of a Vietnamese culture. However, evidence of Vietnamese representation eventually receded after the colonial project was well established (Pédélahore 1986, 132–133). As Vietnamese society lost its sovereignty to France, it also lost, in the eyes of the colonizers, its capacity to produce its own culture under the colonial order. Hébrard was a product of his time and culture. In his formative years he became interested in the concept of a universal city that could be applicable everywhere. Tensions between universalist and assimilatory standards lay at the heart of his perception of urbanism, and mirrored the contradiction of the French imperial discourse on greater France (Cooper 2001, 48–49).

Though architectural miscegenation was allowed, when it came to town planning the dual city was the norm. As Abu-Lughod points out in her classic study of Rabat, Morocco, we should understand "dual city" not in the sense of the creation of parallel cities, but in the fact of introducing "a new dominant structure, to which the preexisting cities became increasingly subordinate. The French system was not side-by-side and apart. . . . It was above the Moroccan system" (Abu-Lughod 1980, 151). In terms of town planning, Hébrard realized master plans for Hanoi, which were completed by 1924. One major critique of the project was his treatment of racial segregation. He strongly pleaded for a spatial separation of races: "Specialization of residential districts is necessary, especially in relation to the native districts which for a variety of reasons must not be mixed with European districts" (quoted in Logan 2000, 104).

According to Hébrard, since interracial interactions would occur due to economic necessity, such movements needed to be organized. Thus, he endorsed a mapping of the city segregated by race and class, with native quarters encompassing workers and shopkeepers separate from residential areas, which he called "bourgeois neighborhoods." However, Hébrard neglected the suburbs, where the majority of the locals lived; nor did he pay attention to the building of cheap dwellings for Vietnamese. Indeed, "greater France" was primarily French and defined by French officials, as Hébrard emphasized during his teaching at the Hanoi College of Fine Arts. As his lectures reveal, he never thought of Vietnamese architects and planners as developing a national style free from Western influence

(Logan 2000, 104–105). Hébrard's recognition of Vietnamese culture translated into cultural subordination, not into native cultural sovereignty.

Further, as seen through the lenses of Mamdani's formulation of colonial governance, "a calculated preoccupation with holding power" was a key element in defining colonial state policy (Mamdani 1996, 286). Cities had to be racially organized in order to function smoothly. Such social separation between races was grounded on ideological discourses based on the fear of moral contamination. The discourse of state authorities in Indochina warned French administrators not to move in with local women, since it would "degrade the magistrate . . . which [would] compromise . . . his honor" (Saada 2002, 99). Such discourses were replicated in the French literature. Dürrwell, who wrote his memoirs in 1911 after living thirty years in Vietnam, supported an essentialist description of the Vietnamese mistress (called *congaïe*), pointing to her "degraded morals":

> Loves jewels and adorns herself with them immoderately, but loves gambling even more, and doesn't hesitate to sacrifice them to her favorite passion. Wheedling and cuddly; but deep down, deep down in her little Annamite soul, vindictive and unconscionably mean, like the vicious child that she is. (Edwards 2003, 104)

In addition, a concern for the presumed Vietnamese lack of hygiene prompted European populations to ask for racial segregation due to fear of physical contamination. The extension of the sovereign French state over Vietnam was spatially limited due to a hygienic gap between the "civilized" colonizers and the "uncivilized" locals. Medical authorities supported such separation along all dimensions of the colonial experience. For instance, Dr. Marcel Léger presented this indigenous society as a bed of disease, therefore strongly advising segregation between the colonized and colonizers. As he wrote in the early twentieth century:

> The indigenous are, indeed, for certain illnesses, reservoirs of viruses and it is right to keep them away. We know the important role they play in the maintenance of the paludal endemic [*endémicité paludéenne*]. (Cooper 2004, 150)

Pondicherry

While the colonial power forcefully implemented its own physical boundaries over the cities of Saigon and Hanoi, French officials in Pondicherry did not so obviously use divide-and-rule tactics, since a societal segregation was already in place due to the caste system. Despite the Third Republic's discourse of integration and assimilation of colonized populations, in practice separation of the races was often the norm, especially at the urban level. In fact, state employees would often underline in official documents the attraction of Pondicherry as a dual city: having a canal that clearly separated the "white" town from the "black" one. This 1868 note was sent to the Minister of the Marine and Colonies:

> Pondicherry is a pretty city which is very noticeable and visited by our opu-lent neighbors. If it does not have the development and the wealth of the great capitals of British India, it is nevertheless true that its buildings, walks, and its beautiful roads, the regularity of its layout, its separation from the black town, its property, its salubrity, and the relative safety of its harbor (*rade*) give it its own physiognomy, a particular importance, and in sum with the historical memories which are attached to its name, it is a space where the French flag can be deployed without fear. (Inde, FM, SG, box 470, file 635, Centre des Archives d'Outre-Mer, France [hereafter CAOM])

As Mamdani has shown in other contexts, a state-enforced segregation among ethnic and racial populations was at work (1996, 5–6).

The physical separation of the races also had to involve the descendants of mixed-blood people, often the result of relations between local women and Por-tuguese men. This intermediary group, the *topas,* was spatially located between the European and local populations. Being a transitional group between the white population and the locals, they lived in the white part of the town near the canal (Huillet 1867, 83). Pre-existing segregation remained in the black town along caste lines, while the outcastes were settled far away from the rest of society. Since the primary reason for colonialism was commerce, the French authorities, lacking physical force, did not disturb the organization of the indigenous people. In this way they sought to maintain friendly relations with the local population (Chopra 1992, 115–118).

Deloche's research confirms that both Pondicherry's gridiron plan and the separation of black and white towns was the work of the Dutch, who had earlier ruled this enclave according to a politics of divide-and-rule. In addition, Deloche shows how the Dutch relocated the Indian community to a distinct area, west of the settlement, and retained for themselves the old town along the seashore, which benefited from the breeze coming from the sea (2004, 41–44).

In addition to spatial separation, the representation of attachment to the mother country, France, in the form of public art was another tactic for dealing with the native question. As a tool for developing transnational patriotism toward the im-perial nation in the locals, Napoleon III's wife, in France, expressed her desire "to see honored by lasting tokens the names of men [in France and in the colonies] who have left noble examples to follow, in order to develop through this public tribute the feeling of patriotism and duty in all the classes." Accepting this request, the local administration installed a commemorative plaque for Desbassyns de Richemont, the nominated governor of Pondicherry in 1826, at the colonial secondary school of Pondicherry, a typical example of colonial architecture that he established during his governance.

With the support of the Minister of the Marine and Colonies, the local authorities also decided to erect a statue in honor of Dupleix's achievements in the colony. Joseph Dupleix, who was the governor of Pondicherry from 1742 to 1754, was able to conquer and control a vast Indian territory. As one official observed: "The name of Dupleix is inseparable from the one of Pondicherry in the history of French colonies: it is the highest personification of the influence that France has formerly exercised over the destinies of India" (Inde, FM, SG, box 349, file 226, CAOM).

An imperial "imagined community" was based on the glorification of French heroes such as Dupleix, and it aimed at developing a feeling of love among locals toward the French empire. On June 20, 1870, the civil and military authorities of Pondicherry inaugurated the statue of Dupleix, located in Dupleix Square, in the white town. A guard of fifty men was guided by musicians escorting the procession to the square, where fifteen cannon shots were fired when the statue was revealed to the public. This theatrical inauguration was a rehearsal for the later commemorations of the Dupleix's contribution to French India, all an attempt to feed an imagined collective memory based on nostalgia for Dupleix's grandiose schemes to expand French sovereignty in India.

Thus French sovereignty was being promoted through the installation of such cultural symbols as statues and plaques in the colony. While this collective memory was expressed through collective art, the spatial layout of Pondicherry continued to reflect the subordinate position of the natives. Locals complained of the dual city where the two racial enclaves received different treatment. For instance, the newspaper *Le Messager de l'Inde* in 1901 lamented the lack of efforts and resources deployed by city hall to improve the hygiene in the black town, where cases of cholera appeared:

> The dead don't complain, and the majority of the deceased persons are in the black town! We assist impassively in an organized death—we are saying an organized death, because the causes of insalubrity in the black town are known by everybody: insalubrious housing, the vast majority of people living in crowded conditions, permanent refuse dumps, and infection of the surface of the soil. ("L'hygiène et la salubrité publique," *Le Messager de l'Inde* 71, September 4, 1901)

In the same vein, local authorities were criticized for living only in the white town and barely spending time in the Indian quarters:

If the authorities of the town, instead of only living in the few streets which make what we call the white town, were established indiscriminately in both parts of the town, they would see, then quite obviously, the sources of infections which desolate the section of the town where live the Natives. ("Bulletin," *Le Messager de l'Inde* 76 and 77, September 20 and 24, 1902, p. 569)

The strategy of racial division was also manifested in the authorities' worry over the climate and the issue of hygiene, which limited French manifestations of "everyday sovereignty" since the environment first needed to be "civilized." The months of April to June were extremely hot, accompanied by winds called *souffle de feu* (blow of fire), which carried sand and insects (Weber 1996, 198). Such climatic characteristics were often perceived as physically debilitating for the colonizers. As the colonial engineer in charge of the department of civil engineering noted in 1870: "We are struggling constantly against . . . the ardors of a climate which makes us age faster and wears out, mercilessly [and] in a very short time, the most robust constitutions" (Inde, FM, SG, box 470, file 633, CAOM). One of the main concerns of the French during this season was therefore to protect themselves from the weather.

Some solutions were suggested by the colonial state. One of them, proposed by the governor in 1860, was the periodic watering of the white town's streets and the bazaar, located in the black town and close to the canal, as well as the streets surrounding this large market. Since "coolness" was thought to be a required element for the health of the colonizers, their quarters required such treatment, as did the bazaar where they purchased their goods. The colonial space needed special care. While the governor anticipated resistance from the Indian population—the people working and living near the bazaar would have to water the street in front of their stand or dwelling—he was confident that in the long term they would see how this method of cooling was "useful and agreeable," and would appreciate a method put forward to tame and uplift the environment (Inde, FM, SG, box 476, file 690, CAOM; *Le Moniteur official des établissements français dans l'Inde,* n. 428, 14 May 1858).

Cholera was an endemic problem, especially in the black town. In 1901, a French pharmacist warned of the risk of an epidemic if one area in the indigenous quarters was not cleaned up rapidly, adding that the local administration should prohibit the natives from throwing their refuse outside and using this dump as a site for latrines (Inde, FM, SG, box 532, file 990, CAOM). Such unhygienic habits among the Indian community reinforced the demands for urban segregation as a means of self-preservation for the white society.

In the cases of both Vietnam and Pondicherry, we see similar motives and techniques of domination in separating groups as a means to maintain France's sovereignty over its colonies and in remaking the built environment along aesthetic lines symbolizing the political and cultural sovereignty of the French. This had an impact on the politics of identity at the local level.

Colonized Subjects' Responses to Various Sovereign Policies

Hanoi

While similarities emerge across French-held colonies regarding the colonial state's urban policies of divide and rule and expressions of French cultural sovereignty through urban design and public art, the local responses to these imperial initiatives were more complicated. Native responses were molded not only by the local culture, but also by the capacity of different networks of people to challenge the colonial initiatives. More precisely, various ethnic/racial, caste, and transnational groups competed for different forms of sovereignty at the city level. These examples give us information regarding the colonial mechanisms that triggered either peaceful or conflict-oriented relations in colonial cities.

Inspired by Craig Calhoun's work on the politics of identity regarding how to interpret the notion of difference between individuals, groups, and nations, I argue that different applications of the notion of a "greater France" and its civilizing mission affected how colonial authorities managed their colonies and the indigenous responses to such projects. These dynamics highlight the gap between the civilizing mission's promise and the reality of a hierarchical and racial social order, a discrepancy that could provoke inter-group tension. In the cases at hand, colonial intervention included a concrete political incorporation of the Indians into the imperial nation by giving them the right to vote and new local political institutions. In Vietnam, the actions of the French led to conditions that redefined the balance of power between the colonizers, the Vietnamese, and the Chinese. Comparing colonies of two distinctive time periods shows how the metropolitan power's idea of an imperial nation influenced the way the French handled Pondicherry and Vietnam. Following Calhoun's steps, tensions between [trans]nationalism and other forms of collective identity will be explored, in line with his observation that there is no identity or collective "unmarked by difference" (1995, 192).

In Vietnam, the Chinese community had been organized in *bang* or associations as a means of self-organization since the time of Emperor Gia Long (1802–1840). Such organizations encompassed Chinese who spoke the same dialect and shared a common place of origin. During the colonial period, each *bang* was responsible for its members' behavior and payment of taxes to the state. This system separated the natives from the Chinese. In addition, ethnic Chinese benefited under the French from a special status that permitted them to own land; travel freely within the Indochinese federation; create commercial businesses in rice, opium, and alcohol; and transfer wealth to China (Chang 1982, 6–8; Leveau 2003, 121). This colonial divide-and-rule strategy was applied as a means to control the Chinese and Vietnamese, and inter-group divisions between both communities meant that neither group could assert itself as a real political threat to the colonial regime (Cheung 2002, 39).

Some Vietnamese, such as Gilbert Chieu at the beginning of the twentieth century, started advocating that Vietnamese business replace Chinese predominance in industry, banking and commerce. In the same vein, newspapers such as *Thoi Bao* and *Co Minh Dam* propagated the idea of "economic nationalism." Before World War I, some Vietnamese businessmen tried to break into professions traditionally held by Chinese, such as in commerce and rice trade (Goscha forthcoming, 11–12). These Vietnamese wanted a bigger and more important role to play within the sovereign imperial French nation. Nguyen Phu Khai, founder of the newspaper *Tribune Indigène,* strongly supported the idea of economic emancipation for the Vietnamese. Embracing the same beliefs was Bui Quang Chieu, who created Vietnam's Constitutionalist Party, and it was this organization that promoted the anti-Chinese campaign in Vietnam in 1919 (Brocheux 1972, 454).

This campaign started on 1 August 1919, when two Chinese-owned cafés on Hamelin Street in Saigon increased the price of a cup of coffee. Their regular customers, mostly Vietnamese civil servants, decided to boycott these establishments. On 9 August, the newspaper *L'Opinion,* while recounting the event, called for a boycott and stressed the power of boycott as a bargaining tool when used collectively ("Boycotteurs, Boycottés," *L'Opinion,* 9 August 1919). This article provoked many indigenous newspapers to discuss the economic situation of the Vietnamese in the colony and to ask for a boycott of all Chinese products as a first step toward economic emancipation (Indo, GGI, Série F, box 39827, file 6, CAOM). Appealing to the nationalism of the Vietnamese, the newspaper *Thoi Bao* urged:

> Go compatriots, boycott all in one élan the café, pork [*xieu-mai*], food sold by the Chinese. We will see to whom they will sell their products. That will teach them to increase (as they like) the prices and to despise us.
> This is why I cry out: in view of the augmentation of the price of a cup of coffee, every Annamite [Vietnamese] in a Chinese café is not an Annamite ("Tang gia tach ca phe," [Cup of coffee's rising price] *Thoi Bao* 54, 1 August 1919).

When the Vietnamese and Chinese accused one another in the press, the situation became further inflamed. In the *Courrier-Saigonnais,* the Chinese author Ly-Thien compared Vietnamese to "savages" and reminded them of their subaltern position: "idiotic inhabitants, your country is conquered and you still pretend to be able to open your mouth. It is a joke, aren't you afraid that we laugh at you!" ("Aux petits Annamites Sauvages," *Courrier-Saigonnais* 5–290, 29 August 1919).

Rumors that the Chinese were putting crushed glass in rice and cakes began to spread through the city and increased anti-minority feelings. Violent incidents occurred between the two communities, and Chinese merchants were frequently attacked. Even though the French authorities preferred to support the economic development of the Vietnamese community to the detriment of the Chinese, they finally had to intervene in order to maintain peace. As a means of restoring order, the colonial state started censoring local newspapers. According to local officials, by October peace was restored in Saigon (Inde, GGI, Série F, box 39827, file 6, CAOM).

Ultimately the boycott movement did not weaken Chinese enterprises in any significant way, and it died out by the mid-1920s. However, it did allow some Vietnamese to enter into commercial activities (Smith 1969, 132–136). French authorities tried to limit their intervention in the conflicts, as long as they did not lead to racial demonstrations. They were reluctant to hold back the Vietnamese in their struggle against Chinese economic power, since the former had by now been elevated to the rank of partner in the building of a "Franco-Annamite collaboration," as part of Sarraut's political plan for Indochina after World War I (Goscha forthcoming, 13). The reality of colonial group juxtapositions—the Chinese businessmen versus a disproportionately rural Vietnamese population—rankled some politicians in Paris who wished to strengthen the Republican ideal of unity and equality in the colony. However, the Vietnamese were not asking for economic parity; the issue, rather, was nationalism.

The friction between the Chinese and Vietnamese illustrates how the place of the Chinese in greater France was a point of contention. For instance, the newspaper *Cong Luan Bao* stressed the different status of the Chinese, who "receive hospitality in our country due to their commerce," unlike the Vietnamese, who were defined as French subjects and therefore legitimate members of the community. Chinese living in Indochina were legally defined as "foreign Asian." Thus, as this article implies, they were not part of the imperial nation, but rather only an economic partner of the colonial state, which tolerated them in the territory ("Encore les Chinois," *Cong Luan Bao* 242, 5 August 1919; Goscha, forthcoming, 8). However, the Chinese did not see their situation as precarious, since they perceived the Vietnamese as a backward community and believed that the colonial state needed their economic skills and expertise in order for the colony to function properly.

As one group of Chinese merchants claimed, "The life of the Annamites is between our hands. They won't be able to do anything against us because the French government will listen better to us than to the conquered and ignorant Annamites" (Letter published in *Courrier-Saigonnais* 5–295, 4 September 1919). Calhoun notes how nationalist rhetoric often emphasizes the commonalities of the nation's members and rarely stresses the highly differentiating features of its constituents (1995, 259). Since membership in the nation was defined legally, the Chinese were relegated to the role of outsiders; thus, a boundary emerged between "us," members of greater France, versus "them," aliens. The Vietnamese identity became linked to the territory to protect the Vietnamese economic sphere against the Chinese. They asserted that the Chinese had no sovereign economic rights over Vietnam due to their status as foreign.

In addition to economic emancipation from the Chinese, some Vietnamese were seeking fairer treatment from the white community who controlled the administration of Hanoi. More precisely, demographic changes among the European community in Hanoi during World War I and the war's economic consequences affected the power relations among racial groups and translated into inter-group tensions.

In his classic work on *Community and Conflict*, Rex coined the term "housing classes" to describe low-status immigrants' disadvantaged position in the housing system of Great Britain (Rex 1967). Confining subordinated groups to unattractive neighborhoods was also common in the colonial context. During World War I, Hanoi's housing market became a site of struggle over racial segregation. More precisely, Vann presents how the recalling of Frenchmen to the motherland during World War I allowed some Vietnamese merchants to take over the superior economic positions that the French had left. As their revenues grew, some Vietnamese bought property in white areas of the city, where they built houses in the local architectural style (Vann 1999, 175–182).

Economic improvement for this new Vietnamese elite led to a demand for higher living standards, in this case, access to colonial neighborhoods. Rather than being limited to an ethnically partitioned space, they demanded a "republican" space that would be accessible to all, hence the right to enjoy the prestige of belonging to the imperial nation and the proper recognition of their economic success. However, even if the economic barrier between the colonizers and colonized were erased—and these natives could bear the cost of housing in white neighborhoods—the ideology of racial superiority would still prevail. The French community reacted by asking local state institutions to enact a law requiring only European architectural style for housing in certain streets. In 1915, Article 55 stated that in various streets, the height of the façades, the ledges, the gable roofs, and so on would be determined by decree, and the owners would have to follow the instructions given to them by the town council ("Réglement de Police, construction diverses: article 55," Hanoi, 19 May 1915, in reference 26172, GGI, CAOM). As Calhoun shows, the politics of identity that emerged in response to the Republican ideal of being treated as equal could not supersede the essential izing discourse of race. The skin color of the Vietnamese limited their choice of identity in the eyes of others, and a racist ideology maintained them in an inferior position (Calhoun 1995, 200).

Pondicherry

In India, the identity of belonging to a greater France promoted by the imperial state in the 1870s could not easily supplant an identity rooted in longstanding cultural practices (for example, the Hindu identity and its caste system, the latter a form of social organization adopted by local Christian converts and Muslims as well).[4] Yet, access to privileges and resources was also very much at the heart of the politics of identity.

In Pondicherry a battle took place between supporters of a secular public space, and those wishing to maintain religious rules, with each side fighting for sovereignty at the city level. For instance, in an effort to preserve the heritage and improve the physical appearance of the city, a committee for historical monuments was created in 1879. However, due to religious considerations, it was difficult for state officials to gain sufficient access to temples or mosques, thus obstructing the task of restoring such buildings. The law made it even more difficult for authorities to monitor religious establishments, since a decree of 13 January 1855, prevented the colonizers from interfering in "the administration of the properties of the temple (*pagoda*)" (Conseil général de l'Inde française 1879, 315–316; *Bulletin officiel des établissements français de l'Inde* 1879, 642–644). However, the Third Republic's rhetoric of *mission civilisatrice,* that is, bringing the "superior" French civilization to the indigenous populations, provided context for the local newspaper *Le Progrès* to complain that the politician de Lanessan was not allowed to visit a temple—considered first as a tourist curiosity by the newspaper—located in the district of Pondicherry ("M. de Lanessan, devant la déesse Koguillamballe de Villenour," *Le Progrès* 221, 23 January 1887, p. 1004). According to the religious texts, there was no injunction against non-Hindus entering temples. Since temples were built by caste/community, the restriction was based on a politics of purity/pollution. If whites were denied entry to temples, it was because they were perceived as outcastes, not because of being white. As Calhoun notes, mobilization for large new political projects—in this case a transnational Republican greater France—led to disputes over which identities would remain or become salient. In this case, a secular identity was trying to overshadow a religious one (Calhoun 1995, 232). In the end, respect for local customs and therefore racial separation based on religious lines was the path chosen by the local state officials in order to be peacefully tolerated by the indigenous population.

Under this Republican regime, which groups would define the social organization of this public sphere in the colony? Would it be the coalition supporting a religious identity or the one embracing a secular and rational principle of governance? For some colonial authorities, security and local order were in jeopardy when local testaments had to be executed after someone had died, as in the case of the will of Souprayapoullé, a shopkeeper who died in 1878. His will was to leave "all his fortune, to the manes [soul] of his [late] daughter; he wanted to deify her." As such, his sole legatee—in this case the colony—had the duty to complete the construction of a little temple (*pagotin*) on top of the grave, where ceremonies would be performed every day in the name of the deceased. Next to it, a pond would be dug for the ablutions. Finally, interest from financial investments would serve to feed the poor every day with cooked rice at the grave.[5]

Turning a burial place into a cult-oriented space was perceived by some officials as a danger since it would encourage "wandering" and "begging" through the city and thus challenge the colonial authorities' desire to run the city in an orderly manner. Even worse, it could give birth to "a cesspit of all vices and impurities, a deleterious center of unhealthy contaminations," bringing Indians who embodied a biological fear for the Europeans. Wanting to respect local customs while avoiding the possibility of crowds, the majority of the council members decided to have the food distributed in different places (Conseil général de l'Inde française, 1878, 196–212, RCP).

From the 1870s till World War I a more participatory approach was chosen, allowing the different racial groups to have their voices heard. Greater France was adapting to local pluralism. Such a peaceful solution echoes Varshney's research on India since independence, which finds communication and civic associations cutting across ethnic and cultural groups diminish the possibility of ethnic/racial violence (2002). Calhoun points out that a nation is thought of as a unitary and integral entity; therefore, nationalist ideas run counter to the notion of diverse identities. Such thinking does not tolerate independent subnational discourses or movements that are perceived as divisive (Calhoun 1995, 243). Respect for a subnational perspective was perhaps a forced choice on the part of the French, since the memory of Indians leaving the city as a means of protest was vivid in the colonizers' collective memory. This memory was built around two specific events.

First, the superior council of Pondicherry decided in 1711, under pressure from the Jesuits, to prohibit pagan feasts on Sundays and during celebrations of Catholic feasts. Second, due to this decree, the important Indian Pongal feast could not take place in February 1714. In protest, almost all the local population left the city. Without the Indians performing many essential tasks for the colonizers, the city could not function and this showed how limited the expression of French sovereignty was. To convince the natives to come back, the officials had to promise that such a prohibition would never again be implemented (Esquer 1870, 339).

Divisions took place not only regarding public space, but also within civic space. Only Brahmins could be employed in the court system, since the locals could not swear before a judge, but only before a Brahmin (Conseil local de Pondichéry 1888, 42–43). However, the latter were allowed to leave the room when an outcaste entered it (Weber 1988, 643). The same measure was applied to Muslims, who took their oath to a mullah. Respect for differences was an Indian characteristic, as one *procureur général* noted: "I come from a country, the Reunion Island, where there are around 40,000 Indians; never have we thought of Indians taking an oath in a special manner" (Conseil général de l'Inde française 1881, 460–461). Again, religious authority prevailed over political authority and demanded this separation in order for justice to function properly. Indians had been able to impose their sovereignty over the judicial procedure in the city, and subsequently to preserve a non-colonial state sphere of influence that encompassed civic spaces as well.

By putting caste members and outcastes on an equal footing, universal suffrage as a legal practice challenged social identities and practices. Treating both outcastes and caste members as voters was a way of redefining how they should be treated, and caste members strongly resisted the practice. For instance, "in 1878 . . . 'the strange fact' was noted that, at the time of the first elections, 'the entrance to the polling halls was forbidden to pariahs because of their low status'" (Weber 1991, 293).[6] This desire among the caste members to be physically separated from the outcastes was based on "the notion of impurity [which] is at the basis, theoretically at least, of the caste society" (Dumont 1980, 44). This universalistic identity encompassing all Indians triggered a coordinated defense against the assimilationist denial of the caste system's social organization. As Calhoun has pointed out for other European contexts, the state has often forced cultural assimilation on its citizens (1995, 234).

In our case, people of the high castes tolerated their position of subordinated subjects in the colonial order as long as their position remained dominant within their own religious community.

At the heart of identity politics is the issue of cultural recognition. For instance, some Indians wanted to be recognized and treated as an assimilated group that had received a French education. Encouraged by the decree of 1871, which gave them the right to participate in political life, their leader Ponnoutamby entered the civic space of the court wearing socks and shoes rather than going barefoot. The magistrate told him that he was an Indian and could not dress in a Western manner. He refused and was punished for his boldness. In retaliation, he appealed to the Supreme Court of Justice in France and won. Indeed, France respected local customs but did not force people to conform to them. Those who clustered around Ponnoutamby included mostly local Christians, and, later on, *renonçants* who wanted to be emancipated from the caste system. These examples illustrate the rivalry among local coalitions. In one case the colonizers sought to differentiate themselves from the locals; in the other, a group of natives demanded to be assimilated into the culture of the dominant group (Poulain 1894, 5–6).

As the Republican experience did alter the cultural allegiance of some locals, the politics of identity played out not only between groups, but also within groups: those who wanted to obey the customary laws and local habits, and those who wished to follow the French civil laws. Further, Indians who embraced the Republican ideal needed the support of the existing Republican institutions in France, which led to their indirect participation in the Republican coalition trying to gain sovereignty over the city. Indeed, for some Republicans in the mother country, Pondicherry was one site for testing Republicanism overseas. Here shared sovereignty between the imperial state and the colonial state, each with its own authority and institutions, led to heightened tensions.

Debates in local and general councils led participants to resolve the situation through containment measures, not only to preserve their advantages, but also as a means of preventing further turbulence within the society. Nonetheless, these republican political reforms eventually resulted in provoking a "war of castes" from the 1890s onwards. For instance, during the municipal election of 1890, Chanemougam and his supporters lost the communes of Villenour and Oulgaret in Pondicherry due to the secession of the Vannia caste (farmers), which represented more than thirty percent of the population. Exasperated by the arrogance of the high-castes, the Vannia caste leader Sadassivanaïker made an alliance with the progressivist French party leader Henri Gaebelé. Far from being a "true progressivist," Sadassivanaïker's decision demonstrates how caste identity could become politicized, and how alliances could be created out of caste rivalries as well as personal rivalries. The roots of political tension were not only due to ideological differences among groups (Weber 1996, 36, 251–253).

Another example involves members of the Chetty caste (powerful bankers and merchants), who were won over by the French party during the renewal of the 1897 General Council. At the time, the high-caste leader Chanemougam and his supporters did not support public works, which usually brought big money to the Chetty. Opposing any form of equality between the castes and the outcastes which would pose a threat to their privileges, the *choutres* [upper-caste Indians who converted to Christianity] generally voted for Chanemougam, who also received the support of the French Catholic *missions étrangères* and Muslims during the first municipal election in Pondicherry on 30 May 1880 (Weber 1996, 233–234). Even in electoral politics, then, communal identity and castes' interests were not easily displaced by a Republican identity.

In addition, electoral fraud became a regular practice, with voting registers including many names of those who were already deceased. A lack of civil registration facilitated such irregularities. During the 1893 legislative election, the French Party and the Indian Party ran in opposition, with the latter seeking to maintain the status quo. Violence spread throughout different parts of Pondicherry including Ariancoupam, where the Vannia attacked their adversaries: "Twenty-five houses were entirely razed, domestic animals' throat cut, children beaten, the women [and] the girls [were] assaulted and injured." The day before this incident, the candidate Henri Gaebelé had been wounded by a bullet (Weber 1996, 256–257).

In the above examples violence was limited to election day, but for the 1906 legislative elections, a caste war, between the upper castes on the one hand and the Vannias and the outcastes on the other, lasted several weeks and resulted in many wounded and dead. Electoral fraud and violence became part of the political repertoire in Pondicherry during various elections between 1891 and World War I. As social scientists have stressed, democratic behavior is not only a display of inter-elite political competition; it also involves a specific form of social organization that precludes the likelihood of electoral fraud and violence (Avritzer 2000, 59).

Conclusion

Battles over sovereignty—that is, competition over who rules the city and how such struggles are resolved—are at the heart of explaining the mechanisms that can enable peaceful governance of diverse societies. In the cases at hand, different groups fought to impose their power over colonial cities, while decisions formulated in France challenged the identity of these groups and determined their access to resources and privileges. More precisely, the implementation of limited political rights in Pondicherry and Sarraut's discourse of a "Franco-Annamite collaboration" for the management of the colony in Vietnam were intended to "uplift" the natives to the rank of the Europeans, with the promise of enabling the colonized to become sovereign agents in the future. Such an ideal clashed with the actual hierarchical social order of the colonies, as well as with the existing legal and social institutions.

In Pondicherry, the high caste coalition led by Chanemougam fought against the Republican empire's endeavor to impose a sense of French nationhood. New political laws promulgated in the metropole challenged the prestige and access to privilege of the native elites by making them the equal of the outcastes. While members of the higher castes could accept the French running the colony, they could not tolerate the imperial power imposing a Republican ideal on their every-day life and challenging their communal and religious identities.

The majority of the indigenous populations in French-held India and Viet-nam linked their political claims to the existing social hierarchies. Exceptions in-cluded the *renonçants* in the Indian case, the new elite in Hanoi, and Vietnamese businessmen in Saigon. These three groups put their aspirations behind the "civi-lizing project" of France. However, their collective desires for a more egalitarian integration within the French nation were not fulfilled; instead the outcome had a negative impact on the ability of urban groups to coexist peacefully.

Conflicts emerged when there appeared to be a mismatch between reform and existing interests: on the one hand, a transnational imperial state imposing po-litical reforms in the 1870s (India), the repatriation decision during World War I (Vietnam), or a new politics of "Franco-Annamite collaboration" after World War I (Vietnam); and on the other, a local administration of the colonial cities often de-fending the interests of the upper castes in Pondicherry, the interests of the col-onizers in Hanoi, or the interests (law and order) of the colonial authorities in Saigon.

Meanwhile, other sections of the local communities reacted differently to such decisions coming from the metropole. In Pondicherry, an identity-based group, the upper caste, used the new local institutions as a tool to fight against the im-perial state and its assimilationist project of a greater France. In contrast, the In-dians who sought to be assimilated and treated as equal to the French used old, existing institutions located in France, such as the Supreme Court of Justice, to support and implement their demands. Overlapping sovereignties between the imperial state and the colonial one created ambiguous situations regarding which entity was the relevant authority.

In Vietnam, the new local elite in Hanoi did not have access to political insti-tutions. Denied access to the city machine, they decided to speak through their actions at the community level by attempting to settle in white neighborhoods. Participants saw this as a way of indirectly fighting against the existing discrimi-natory state and demonstrating their new social status resulting from economic success (Katznelson 1981).

In 1919, the city of Saigon witnessed fighting between two identity-based groups competing over control of the local economy within the imperial state. Both the

Chinese and the Vietnamese communities relied on the colonial state to defend their interests. In Saigon, the local authorities first backed the economic aspirations of the Vietnamese as part of the "Franco-Annamite collaboration" but then switched to a more restrained support when law and order were jeopardized and Chinese merchants went on the offensive. This policy change indirectly supported the existing economic status quo in Saigon.

In all these cases, the intervention of the state led to inter-group tension. These experiences offer a lesson on how such turbulent governance might be avoided. The evidence here suggests that under imperial authority, the maintenance of a segregated ethnic/racial status quo was more peaceful than an integrated society. In Vietnam, the repatriation of Frenchmen to the motherland during World War I disturbed the triangular relations between French, Vietnamese, and Chinese, and provoked friction among these communities regarding access to jobs and housing in Hanoi. The balance between the racial groups was disrupted when the new Vietnamese elite bettered its economic position and asked for access to white neighborhoods, while the white community fought back by using local institutions.

In addition, sovereignty, understood in terms of social inclusion, weakened the existing social hierarchies—Hindu and colonial—by spreading the ideas of republican equality and Franco-Annamite collaboration. Such ideals allowed for the redefinition of individuals' self-identity, and unsettled the coexistence among groups by redefining their access to social and political power and resources. At the same time, the existing partition of space did not always lead to tension and polarization. In Pondicherry, the partition of space was linked to the caste system and perceived by the majority of the population as promoting stability. Interdependence among various castes performing different tasks in specific areas was part of a belief system that allowed society to function properly. Similarly, the racial partition of space and its ethnic architectural representations in Vietnamese cities generally served to maintain peaceful coexistence. Only when equalitarian ideals drove some groups to contest such divisions did it led to conflicts and competition among urban subpopulations.

In the case of Vietnam, the first steps toward economic integration of the Vietnamese after World War I led to numerous attacks against Chinese merchants and fueled anti-Chinese rumors in Saigon. The aim of replacing Chinese businessmen with Vietnamese provoked social tension. In contrast, the colonial government's actions to neutralize the press and maintain occupational specialization of the natives and Chinese in Saigon quickly restored peace to the city. Again, the geographical separation of ethnic and racial groups allowed the city to run more harmoniously, compared to attempts to racially integrate neighborhoods. However, such a policy could easily lead to a sense of humiliation among groups that did aspire to integrate.

Thus communal harmony was likely to be maintained when the various groups were divided along racial, ethnic, and religious lines, and did not compete with one another economically or in terms of status, social legitimacy, and cultural recognition. If members of each group functioned in a different cultural world and were firstly concerned with their community affairs, interactions took place not only in the marketplace, but also in the public and civic spheres. In order for the interests of each identity-group to be taken into account and for peace to prevail, it was sometimes necessary, as Varshney argues (2002), for some communication and civic associations to exist that could cut across ethnic and cultural groups (see the case of Souprayapoullé).

In Pondicherry, the Republican ideal of a greater France was quickly abandoned when it came to the everyday ruling of the colony. Rather, respect for existing norms was the chosen approach of the local authorities. However, colonial state intervention did reallocate power among the various groups in society. It strengthened the power of the upper-caste Indians who took over local institutions designed by the Third Republic, which in turn weakened the power of the white community. Lower castes often supported the upper-caste leader Chanemougam, who stressed the saliency of their collective religious identity over a detached and individualistic Republican identity.

Regarding the colonial state's actions on access to resources and privileges, it was probably unwise for authorities to implement equity laws and grant universal suffrage before fully enforcing the rule of law, as electoral fraud became a serious problem. Trying to carry out democratic practices in a democratically unaccountable political system was unworkable. Furthermore, individual identities could not be easily erased by a new large-scale identity. Therefore, societal changes needed to take place before Republicanism was adopted by a large portion of society.

Rather than promoting equality among locals, then, these measures ended up reinforcing stratification according to Hindu religious distinctions and racial differentiation. Yet this situation permitted local officials to maintain a hierarchical but peaceful status quo until around 1905, when events in Pondicherry resulted in the "caste wars" due to the politicization of caste. Respect for local customs rather than cultural assimilation permitted different cultural groups to live peacefully side by side and seems to have reduced conflict.

This study suggests that in comparing the French-held urban colonies of India and Vietnam, the maintenance of spatial and cultural separation led to more

peaceful conditions than attempts at an integrated society, a conclusion that reinforces Calhoun's point:

> In the cosmopolitan cities of empires . . . citizens . . . could coexist in toler-
> ance not because they liked each other, or shared some lowest common de-
> nominator of common culture. They could coexist in large part because they
> were not called upon to join in very many collective projects. They were not
> called upon to join together in democratic self-government, most crucially, or
> to share their universities, or their neighborhoods. Though they met each other
> in commerce, the peace among them was maintained in part because they were
> otherwise separated into enclaves concerned with their internal affairs. (Cal-
> houn 1994, 2)

However, such tolerance came with a high price to pay for groups which attempted
to change the status quo. They often faced a situation of humiliation, in which
they had to accept the will of the majority and were hence refused basic rights. For
instance, the Vietnamese elite in Hanoi were barred from their project of sharing
the prestige associated with living in a white neighborhood beside the colonizers.
Similarly, in Pondicherry the Christian lawyer Ponnoutamby, a strong believer in
the Republican assimilationist policy, was denied full cultural assimilation into
French culture by the local court system.

Here we see how group identity and self-definition may affect urban cooperation or conflict. When existing social hierarchies began to lose some of their legitimacy, this leads groups to redefine their identity, which may in turn have a negative impact on their ability to coexist peacefully with others. The propagation of
the Republican ideal of equality in Pondicherry, and the spread of the ideas about
Franco-Annamite collaboration, acted to weaken hierarchical Hindu and colonial orders. These ideals also intensified feelings of humiliation for "people [who]
resent their ill-treatment even more when it loses the patina of time-honored
normality," and who were thus led to reject their existing identity for a new one
(Smith 2001, 539). At the same time, these developments also challenged the identity of various privileged groups, such as the colonizers, the Chinese, and the upper castes, and resulted in conflicts between ethnic/racial groups in Vietnam, and
between caste and racial groups in Pondicherry.

Alongside identity issues, the colonial built environment also had consequences
for the urban social order. What was the impact of the city on group identity and
members' capacity to coexist with one another? Again, colonial-imposed urban
spatial patterns created competition among identity groups in both settings. The
universalist ideas promoted by the metropole were undermined by the function-

alist division of space, in which each ethnic/racial group and caste was assigned a specific residential and, in many cases, occupational niche. Some locals and colonizers attempted to defy religious spatial segregation in Pondicherry, while in Indochina, a Vietnamese elite demanded access to white neighborhoods. In Hanoi, the forced ejection of local inhabitants from particular urban spaces, as well as the building of Western architectural representations, conveyed the message that the Vietnamese did not belong in such "high-status" built environments.

Generalizing from the examples discussed here, we can observe a degree of continuity between how state officials apprehend and deal with inter-group tensions in contemporary occupied territories, and how these issues have been managed in imperial environments in the past. Watching the Iraqi case today, in parallel with the historical context, we may look back at the French imperial experience as a universal lesson on how, and how not, to consolidate and enforce structures of peaceful governance over a plural population. Reflecting on historical examples to derive a more complete, universal, and perhaps more interactive framework regarding urban conflict management, those in charge would do well to consider the mechanisms of a caste or ethnic/racial status quo, the legacy of humiliation processes, and the role of communication across caste and ethnic/racial groups as a means of cultivating peaceful coexistence among urban groups in cities with diverse populations.

Notes

1. In the case of Pondicherry, there were few Brahmins, and no Kshatriyas or Vaishyas. The Vellaja caste, "the aristocracy of the Shudra," prevailed over the colony. The Vellaja usually lived in the city of Pondicherry and often engaged in liberal professions (law, trade). They built relationships with the colonizers earlier than the other castes, and many converted to Christianity. Jacques Weber, *Pondichéry et les comptoirs de l'Inde après Dupleix. La démocratie au pays des castes* (Paris: Editions Denoel, 1996), 34–36; Pierre Girod, *L'Agriculture et l'Hydraulique Agricole dans l'Etablisement de Pondichéry* (Pondichéry: imprimerie ?, n.d.), 3. In Record Centre of Pondicherry, Jeewanandapuram, Lawspet, Pondicherry, India (hereafter RCP).

2. I borrow the term "secessionless sovereignty" from *Political Theory and the Rights of Indigenous Peoples* (Ivison et al. 200, 14).

3. All translations from French to English are mine, unless otherwise noted.

4. In 1830, 87.6% of the population was Hindu, 1.9% Muslim, and 10.4% Catholic (Weber 1996, 31).

5. In the context of death, food had to be served cooked since cooked food is considered to be nonpolluting, unlike uncooked food, which is thought to pollute. Since the father's

wish was to transform his daughter into a deity, he had to attend to her ritually through the offering of food. Deities' needs in Hinduism are similar to those of human beings and as such are treated in the same way as individuals' wants. However, Hindus are not just feeding the god, but people are getting blessed by eating the leftovers of the deity.

6. In Hinduism there are four Varna according to the textual model: Brahmin (priests), Kshatriya (kings and warriors), Vaishya (businessmen), and Shudra (the service group performing menial tasks, including barbers, etc.). The outcastes are out of this caste system, and their role is to serve these four castes. In practice, there is not a single and universal model since every place has its own caste organization.

Works Cited

Abu-Lughod, J. 1980. *Rabat Urban Apartheid in Morocco*. Princeton, N.J.: Princeton University Press.

Aldrich, R. 1996. *Greater France: A History of French Overseas Expansion*. London: Macmillan Press Ltd.

Anghie, A. 2004. *Imperialism, Sovereignty and the Making of the International Law*. Cambridge: Cambridge University Press.

Annasse, A. 1975. *Les Comptoirs Français de l'Inde (Trois siècles de présence française) 1664–1954*. Paris: La Pensée Universelle.

Avritzer, L. 2000. "Democratization and Changes in the Pattern of Association in Brazil." *Journal of Interamerican Studies and World Affairs* 42, no. 3: v–76.

Baycroft, T. 2004. "The Empire and the Nation: The Place of Colonial Images in the Republican Visions of the French Nation." In *Empire and Culture: The French Experience, 1830–1940*, ed. M. Evans, 148–160. New York: Palgrave Macmillan.

Bayly, S. 2000. "French Anthropology and the Durkheimians in Colonial Indochina." *Modern Asian Studies* 34: 581–622.

Brocheux, P. 1972. "Vietnamiens et minorités en Cochinchine pendant la période colonial." *Modern Asian Studies* 6, no. 4: 443–457.

Brocheux, P., and D. Hémery. 2001. *Indochine: La colonisation ambiguë 1858–1954*. Paris: Editions la Découverte.

Calhoun, G., ed. 1994. *Social Theory and the Politics of Identity*. Cambridge, Mass.: Blackwell.

———. 1995. *Critical Social Theory: Culture, History, and the Challenge of Difference*. Cambridge, Mass.: Blackwell.

Chang, P. 1982. *Beijing, Hanoi, and the Overseas Chinese*. Berkeley: Institute of East Asian Studies, University of California.

Cheung, M. 2002. "The Legal Position of Ethnic Chinese in Indochina under French Rule." In *Law and the Chinese in Southeast Asia*, ed. M. Barry Hooker, 32–64. Singapore: Institute of Southeast Asian Studies.

Chopra, P. 1992. "Pondicherry: A French Enclave in India." In *Forms of Dominance: On the Architecture and Urbanism of Colonial Enterprise*, ed. Nezar AlSayyad, 107–137. Aldershot, U.K.: Avebury.

Clairon, M. 1926. *La renunciation au statut personnel dans l'Inde Française.* Paris: Société Annonyme du Recueil Sirey.

Closets d'Errey, H. de. 1934. *Précis chronologique de l'histoire de l'Inde Française (1664– 1816) suivi d'un relevé des faits marquants de l'Inde française au XIX siècle.* Pondichéry, India: Imprimerie du gouvernement.

Cooper, N. 2001. *France in Indochina: Colonial Encounters.* New York: Berg.

———. 2004. "Making Indo-China French: Promoting the Empire through Education." In *Empire and Culture: The French Experience, 1830–1940,* ed. Martin Evans, 131–147. New York: Palgrave Macmillan.

Coquery-Vidrovitch, C. 1988. "Villes coloniales et histoire des Africains." *Vingtième Siècle* 20: 49–73.

Deloche, J. 2004. *Origins of the Urban Development of Pondicherry according to Seventeenth Century Dutch Plan.* Pondicherry, India: French Institute of Pondicherry.

Deschamps, D. 2003. "En attendant le vote des indigènes." *Outre-Mers* 90, nos. 338–339: 109–131.

Duiker, W. J. 1995. *Vietnam: Revolution in Transition.* Boulder, Colo.: Westview.

Dumont, L. 1980. *HOME HIERARCHICUS: The Caste System and Its Implication.* Chicago: University of Chicago Press.

Edwards, A. 2003. *Saigon: Mistress of the Mekong.* Hong Kong: Oxford University Press.

Esquer, A. 1870. *Essais sur les castes dans l'Inde.* Pondichéry, India: Imprimeur du government.

Goscha, Christopher E. "'Did anyone ever ask our opinion?' Intra-Asian Debates and Legal Categories in French Colonial Indochina." In *Songs at the Edge of the Forest: Essays in Honor of David Chandler,* ed. Anne Hansen. Madison: Center for Southeast Asian Studies Monograph Series, University of Wisconsin Press, forthcoming 2010.

Huillet, Le docteur. 1867. *Hygiène des blancs, des mixtes et des indiens à Pondichéry.* Pondichéry, India: E.V. Géruzet imprimeur du gouvernement.

Hunt, L. 1996. *The French Revolution and Human Rights: A Brief Documentary History.* New York: Bedford Books of St. Martin's Press.

Ivison, Duncan, Paul Patton, and Will Sanders, eds. *Political Theory and the Rights of Indigenous Peoples.* London: Cambridge University Press, 2000.

Larcher, A. 1995. "La voie étroites des réformes coloniales et la 'collaboration Franco-Annamite' (1917–1928)." *RFHOM* 82, no. 309: 387–420.

Leveau, A. 2003. *Le Destin des fils du dragon: l'influence de la communauté chinoise au Viêt Nam et en Thaïlande.* Paris: L'Harmattan; Bangkok: IRASEC.

Logan, W. S. 2000. *Hanoi: Biography of a City.* Singapore: Select Publishing.

Mamdani, M. 1996. *Citizen and Subject: Contemporary Africa and the Legacy of Late Colonialism.* Princeton, N.J.: Princeton University Press.

Pédélahore, C. 1986. "Constitutent elements of Hanoi City (19th–20th centuries)." *Vietnamese Studies* 12 (New Series): 105–159.

Poulain, C. 1894. *Notes sur l'Inde française, n. 2: le régime politique.* Chalon-sur-Saône, France: Imprimerie de L. Marceau.

Rex, J. 1967. *Race, Community and Conflict: A Study of Sparkbrook*. London: published for the Institute of Race Relations by Oxford University Press.

Saada, E. 2002. "The Empire of Law: Dignity, Prestige, and Domination in the 'Colonial Situation.'" *French Politics, Culture & Society* 20, no. 2: 98–120.

Smith, D. 2001. "Organizations and Humiliation: Looking beyond Elias." *Organization* 8, no. 3: 537–560.

Smith, R. B. 1969. "Bui Quang Chieu and the Constitutionalist Party in French Cochinchina, 1917–1930." *Modern Asian Studies* 3, no. 2: 131–150.

Tanner, M. 2007. "Pathologies of Sovereignty: History and (Post)Colonial Domination." http://www.allacademic.com/meta/p_mla_apa_research_citation/1/9/8/2/0/p198201 _index.html (accessed 15 May 2010).

Vann, M. G. 1999. "White City on the Red River: Race, Power, and Culture in French Colonial Hanoi, 1872–1954." Ph.D. diss., University of California Santa Cruz.

Varshney, A. 2002. *Ethnic Conflict and Civil Life: Hindus and Muslims in India*. New Haven, Conn.: Yale University Press.

Van Ky, N. 1997. "Le modèle français." In *Hanoi 1936–1996: du drapeau rouge au billet vert*, ed. G. Boudarel and N. Van Ky, 56–81. Paris: Editions Autrement.

Weber, J. 1987. "Les Etablissements français en Inde au XIXè siècle (1816–1914)." *Le Trait-D' Union* (August): 1–3.

———. 1988. *Les Etablissements français en Inde au XIXe siècle (1816–1914)*. Paris: Librairie de l'Inde.

———. 1991. "Chanemougam, 'King of French India' social and political foundations of an absolute power under the Third Republic." *Economic and Political Weekly* (9 February): 291–302.

———. 1996. *Pondichéry et les comptoirs de l'Inde après Dupleix. La démocratie au pays des castes*. Paris: Editions Denoel.

Wright, G. 1991. *The Politics of Design in French Colonial Urbanism*. Chicago: University of Chicago Press.

Young, I. M. 2000. "Hybrid Democracy: Iroquois Federalism and the Postcolonial Project." In *Political Theory and the Rights of Indigenous Peoples*, ed. Duncan Ivision et al., 237–258. Cambridge: Cambridge University Press.

3

Confessionalism and Public Space in Ottoman and Colonial Jerusalem

Salim Tamari

For many observers, Jerusalem epitomizes a "city of identities"; an ultimate geography defined by sharp ethnic and religious divisions, where distinct social groups worship and live in separate quarters.[1] While the city does contain a plethora of holy sites worshiped by the three Abrahamic traditions, civic identities and spatial logics have not always fallen into such broadly cast categories drawn around religious lines. An examination of the early twentieth century transition from the Ottoman Empire to the British Mandate yields a complex local narrative of seemingly increased fluidity of agency and norms, and the simultaneous beginning of a profound redefinition and administration of space and society. As sovereignty arrangements shifted and the incoming British sought to legitimize and consolidate their governing authority, colonial administrators continued the process of institutional and secular modernization begun under the Ottomans. But they also took significant legal, physical, and conceptual steps which recast citizenship and the physical form of the city into larger and less flexible categories of religion and ethnicity.

In particular, through physical planning and municipal regulations, the British Mandate authorities projected a modernist discourse that was heavily framed by orientalist and biblical narratives, leading to a process of what I call here confessionalization of public discourse. In contrast to the Ottomans, whose modernizing schemes focused on the provision of public institutions and secular civic spaces throughout the city, the British newcomers viewed the city as two separate and opposing pieces: the old city, home to key religious sites and monuments, and the modern perimeter. Because of its historic value, as seen through colonial eyes at least, a key objective for British administrators was to preserve the old city and its built environmental character in terms of its pre-Ottoman "biblical" past. Physical manifestations of the old city's religious and symbolic identity were the sole important characteristics to be conserved for visitors and pilgrims, while residents in both old and new parts of the city—and the logic of urban planning practice more generally—were themselves subject to divisions based on the newly asserted primacy of ethnic and religious groupings as a marker for Jerusalem's larger identity and importance as a world historic city.

This chapter examines the colonial transition from Ottoman Empire to British colonial rule and how it manifests in the physical spaces of Jerusalem and the confessional identities of its residents. Drawing on biographic narratives of the city's transformation during this crucial juncture, the analysis fleshes out details of urban planning practice and citizen response, supplementing a more institutional history of Jerusalem during the Mandate period. In contrast to traditional portrayals of transition in the city from Ottoman to Mandate administration, which suggest a clean rupture occurring in 1917, this chapter shows that the colonial process did not follow the guidelines of a single master plan, but one with multiple actors navigating through spaces of ambiguous negotiability. In making this argument, the chapter draws directly on primary resources dating to the transition period, particularly the diary of Wasif Jawhariyyeh, a local artist and civil servant. In addition to adding nuance and detail to the analysis, Wasif's diary shows that he benefitted from a somewhat inadvertent proximity to key actors in the Mandate period, creating a view that is at once subaltern while maintaining proximity to the world of power-holders.[2] The diary thus accommodates the subjective experience of an urban resident living through the transition as well as an interpretation of urban life as seen through the lenses of both the ruler and the ruled.

Three Crucial Decades

One often forgets that the British Mandate over Palestine occupied barely three decades of the country's modern history. In scholarly literature and Palestinian popular imagination, the Mandate has acquired a colossal, if not mythical, impact on the formation of modern Palestinian society and perceptions of its destiny. A quick list of the Mandate's oft-cited achievements (and disasters) drives home this point: the creation of modern institutions of government, including a new civil service and police force, and the centralization of the national bureaucracy in Jerusalem; the modernization of the land code and the taxation system; the creation of a legal corpus to replace (and supplement) the Ottoman code; the conduct of a national census (1922 and 1931), and the creation of the population registry; the creation of the rudimentary features of citizenship and icons of unfulfilled sovereignty (currency, stamps, passports); a modern secular educational system; and finally an infrastructure of roads and communication system, including a broadcasting authority (the Palestine Radio in 1931). A major consequence of these administrative changes was the separation of Palestine from greater Syria. All this happened in thirty years (less if we deduct the years of initial military rule). But the Mandate is also remembered—retrospectively—for one major accomplishment: laying the grounds for partition and the creation of the state of Israel (Wasserstein 1995, 29–41).

Between the surrender of Jerusalem to General Allenby's victorious army by the Ottoman Governor Izzat Bey and Mayor Hussein al Husseini (December 1917) and the commencement of the British Mandate (1920), Palestine witnessed three years of administrative and legal flux. Although British intentions for the country were already defined by the commitments to their French allies, through the Sykes Picot Memorandum, and to the Zionist movement with the Balfour Declaration, these formal policy statements did not translate into clear policies on the ground. The bulk of the British military establishment in Palestine, including General Moony, the first military governor, were either hostile to the prospects of a Jewish national home, or ambivalent toward it, on the grounds that it violated British promises to Sherif Hussein and his Syrian allies, or—more importantly—because it provoked Palestinian-Syrian yearning for independence, and made the control of the street problematic (Huneindi 2003, 42–66). Many local administrators and field officers clearly opposed the idea of a Jewish national home, like Brigadier General Clayton, Allenby's chief political officer, and Sir Walter Congreve, who commanded the British troops in Egypt and Palestine. A legion of philo-semites and supporters of Zionism stood against their position, including Louis Bols, Palestine's chief administrator, General Storrs, Military Commander of Jerusalem, and the first High Commissioner, Herbert Samuel.

Inside the larger framework of contested visions of sovereignty, the British are also remembered for laying the foundation of urban planning in Palestine, and hence for creating the modernity of urban space. The memoirs of Ronald Storrs (1881–1955) based on his letters and diary, are elegant, informed, and highly perceptive of Palestine's Ottoman and Islamic heritage, and constitute an excellent exposition of the ideology behind the liberal colonial hegemonic discourse. The memoirs also crisscross fruitfully with Jawhariyyeh's witty comments on the activities of the Pro-Jerusalem Society—Storrs's pet program for the preservation of the city's public monuments and architecture. The two narratives, Jawhariyyeh's and Storrs's, present us with two divergent discourses—native and colonial—on Jerusalem's modernity.

The conventional wisdom is that the Ottomans had no contributions to urban planning in the Levant, and that it was the British who introduced it to Palestine. Ruth Kark suggests:

> Until the end of the Ottoman period, there was no overall planning of the built-up area in Jerusalem. The Sublime Porte and the local authorities limited their operations to supervision. For security reasons a law prohibited the construction of any edifice beyond a distance of 2,500 cubits (about 1.4 km) from the wall of a city. Because of this restriction, Acre failed to expand beyond its walls until the turn of the century, and had the law been strictly obeyed in Jerusalem as well, the fate of that city would have been similar. (Kark 1991, 58–59)

However, spatial planning and regulation was a local priority to late Ottoman rule of the Syrian Provinces (Lebanon, Syria, Palestine, and Transjordan), and these general laws were not strictly applied as suggested above. The main provincial centers of the Ottoman Levant (Damascus, Beirut, Jaffa, and Aleppo) all had degrees of planning of their public spaces. Jerusalem received planning guidelines of sorts after the passage of the Ottoman Municipalities Law in 1877, which regulated building permits, building material, and height of buildings (Khamaisi and Nasrallah 2003, 298). Historian Hala Fattah notes how

> the increased attention paid to the urbanization of Jerusalem, the spread of communications and the growth of the population forced the Ottomans' hand, so to speak. In the middle of the 19th century, the administrative redevelopment of Jerusalem was a key aspect of the Ottoman centralization of Palestine. As a result of the institution of municipal and administrative councils, Jerusalem's political life was revitalized. (Fattah 1999, 1)

A symbolic feature of Ottoman public monumental planning for the period was the creation or expansion of public squares to commemorate the twenty-fifth anniversary of Sultan Abdul Hamid II's ascension to the throne in 1900–1901. These plazas with their iconic watchtowers became central public spaces in regional cities like Izmir, Tripoli, Jaffa, and Jerusalem. The Hamedian clock tower in Jerusalem became the subject of considerable controversy later when the British military government had it forcefully removed from the Jaffa Gate plaza for "aesthetic reasons," as we shall see.

Aside from Ottoman municipal buildings and *takaya* (soup kitchens), the first important urban buildings were established inside the old city by English and German Protestants in the 1840s, and outside the city walls with the completion of the Russian compound in the late 1850s. According to Alexander Scholch these three schemes triggered the urban modernization of Ottoman Jerusalem, "the new construction, alterations, and expansion of churches, monasteries, hos-

pices, schools, hospitals, hotels, and consulates subsequently continued unabated"
(Scholch 1993, 121). This was followed, in the 1870s, with the creation of neigh-
borhoods for Muslim notables outside the walls, in Sheikh Jarrah and Bab al
Sahira, and by Jewish residential suburbs in Yemin Moshe and Me' She' arim
(Scholch 1993, 121–122).

Ottoman urban expansion schemes and city building regulations did exist, but
were either haphazard or overwhelmed by construction activities undertaken by
autonomous religious endowments, private construction, or foreign public projects. Kark suggests that even though "overall plans for the city of Jerusalem did
exist during the Ottoman period . . . they were not implemented, even partially,
until 1920" (Kark 1991, 59). But it was on the basis of that Ottoman vision that
many successive planning schemes were carried out during the transitional period of the OETA[3] and the early Mandate (Khamaisi and Nasrallah, 296).

Spatial Foundations for Identity Shifts

Planning by the British, however, took a more aggressive approach to restructuring the city into two distinct zones, each with separate areas for the different
religious groups. Against the backdrop of Ottoman planning, Ronald Storrs introduced a scheme in 1918 for urban renovation and preservation, through a confessionalized elite appointed to the Pro-Jerusalem Society. The Society's declared
aims were "to preserve the city's antiquities, develop modern cultural functions
such as museums, libraries, theatre, etc., and foster the education and welfare of
the city's inhabitants" (Gilter, n.d., 31). Storrs was able to assemble an impressive
array of the city's ruling elite to constitute the society's administrative board, including the Mayor of Jerusalem, Musa Kazim al Husseini; the British Director of
Antiquities; the Mufti, Kamil al Husseini; and eventually Haj Amin; the two Chief
Rabbis; the Orthodox, Latin, and Armenian Patriarchs; the Anglican Bishop; and
other leading members of the community (Storrs, 322). One is struck again here
by Storrs's vision of Palestinian society as composed of confessional elements
added to the local aristocracy (a'yan)—a perspective which clashed head-on with
the emerging national movement and its secularized intelligentsia.

Although Storrs was the key figure behind the new idea for the city and its execution, a discussion of the early planning of Mandate Jerusalem cannot be complete without including the participation of two innovative urbanists, William
MacLean and Charles Ashbee. The first, MacLean, then the town planner of Alexandria and Khartoum, was invited by Storrs in 1918 to design the first modern
master plan for Jerusalem, which he accomplished in a record two-month period. Followed by later ground-breaking achievements, his plan ". . . prohibited

new construction within the boundaries of the Old City, mandated that the area around the walls be kept clear, and ordered the leveling of structures abutting the wall from the outside. New buildings, permitted only to the west and north of the Old City, would rise to a maximum height of eleven meters so as not to compete with the skyline of the Mount of Olives. Jerusalem was to be built of stone; industrial structures were banned" (Roman 2001, 24). Almost all of these regulations were Ottoman in origin and British in implementation.

In terms of a conceptual paradigm for an urban future, however, it was Charles Ashbee who provided the bifurcated vision of the new/old Jerusalem. A disciple of William Morris, Ashbee belonged to a generation of socialist romantic thinkers finding themselves in the service of the British colonial enterprise. Although he was brought in by Storrs to survey and revive local handicrafts, his work stretched beyond his original charge (Storrs 1937, 323–326). Officially, he held the position of Civic Advisor to the City until 1922. In addition, he served as the Secretary and the primary coordinator of the Pro-Jerusalem Council, the Society's administrative board. Given his close association with the powerful Storrs, Ashbee made significant contributions of his own in proposing solutions to "the city's modern problems while conserving its ancient holy sights and unique character" (Gitler, n.d., 31).

Ashbee took pains to reconcile his dual conception of the city—the romantic-visionary, and the conservationist-revivalist. He resolved this contradiction, according to Inbal Gitler, by dividing the city into two zones of future redemption: one was the city within the walls, which he saw "in a secular way as an historic monument marked for archeological preservation"; and the new city, which was marked for modern expansion and development (Gitler, n.d., 45–46). The linkage between the two cities relied on a networking of landscaping schemes, which surrounded the city walls and utilized concepts of the English garden combined with a series pavilions invoking an "Oriental style." One of Ashbee's original contributions was an attempt at uniting the city with its rural and agricultural hinterland. This was achieved by "planting endemic natural vegetation, and by leaving part of the park area in state of wilderness or under development by local agrotechniques"(Gitler, n.d., 40). Ashbee's planning of Jerusalem was a labor of love and contradiction, in which he tried, through imaginative landscaping and revived local crafts (which he had introduced as an employment scheme), to synthesize an orientalist vision of the holy city.

By sheer coincidence Wasif Jawahriyyeh, who was toiling at the same period in the Central Registry of the Military Government, caught the attention of Colonel Storrs. Wasif's performances on the oud (a stringed instrument) brought him close to the Governor, who was fond of oriental music from his long stay in Egypt.

Storrs seconded Jawahriyyeh to work as an assistant to Ashbee in the newly established Pro-Jerusalem Council.

In his position as secretary to Ashbee, Jawahriyyeh relates the first incidence
of conflict between the architectural vision of the Pro-Jerusalem Society and the
Jerusalem Municipality. In 1901 the Ottomans had constructed a clock tower inside Jaffa Gate during the tenure of Mayor Faidallah al Alami to commemorate
the twenty-fifth Anniversary of Sultan Abdul Hamid's reign (see above). Jerusalem architect Pascal Affendi Sarofim, the municipal architect at the time, designed the tower in the Baroque style (Jawhariyyeh *Memoirs* manuscript [here-
after Jawhariyyeh ms.], 49). When Ashbee became secretary of the Pro-Jerusalem
Society he took a decision to remove the clock tower, since, according to Wasif
"it did not fit well with the image of the historical wall."[4] The tower was removed
overnight despite protests from the Municipality. Jawahriyyeh, however, concurred with Ashbee's aesthetics. "The design was an elaborate hybridity of styles,
and reminded me of Abdel Wahhab's Franco-Arab music, although I must say
that it should have been moved to another location, perhaps in the vicinity of the
new municipality by Barclays Bank" (Jawhariyyeh ms., 49). Years later Jawahriyyeh had a wooden model of the removed clock tower and the adjoining plaza, destroyed by Storrs, made for the benefit of those who wanted to see what Ottoman
Jerusalem looked like on the eve of the Mandate (Jawhariyyeh ms., 50).[5]

Jawhariyyeh spent months accompanying both Ashbee and Richmond in their
field trips on renovation work at al Aqsa compound, and in the restoration of the
city's ancient wall. Of these trips he said:

> As secretary to Mr. Ashbee I was privileged to observe the restoration work in
> al Haram area, and in other archeological sites of the city. The famous archi-
> tect George Shiber, who later became renowned, was also involved in the reno-
> vation of al Haram as a technical expert under Mr. Richmond. Unfortunately I
> was not to stay long with Ashbee. One winter evening I was considerably drunk
> when I entered the Registry, and started teasing my colleagues. I climbed on the
> desks and was clowning around on the worktables just as Mr. Ashbee entered
> the room and began staring at me.
>
> "Well Hello. Hello Mr. Ashbee," I shouted. Everybody was laughing their
> bellies off, except Ashbee, who went to his office and wrote an angry memo on
> my behalf. That was the end of my career with him. I must say however, that I
> benefited greatly from working under Ashbee, which increased my knowledge
> of Jerusalem historical and architectural heritage. (Jawhariyyeh ms. 2–48)

Wasif goes out of his way to indicate that his expulsion by Ashbee did not diminish his admiration for his work. He also makes a clear distinction between

Storrs the "colonial-orientalist," and Ashbee the architect and planner (Jawhariy-yeh, 48).

These diaries also help us to rethink the changes in the urban landscape of Jerusalem not only as a lived experience by a contemporary observer, but also in an alternate narrative challenging the idea of a clean rupture between Turkish rule and English rule. It undermines the notion that the Ottoman regime and the British regime were opposites, one representing oriental despotism and the other modernity. Jawhariyyeh reminds us that many of the celebrated reforms of the Mandate Administration were already in place during and before World War I. But the tragedies of the war, and disastrous consequences of conscription (*safar barlik*) in poisoning the relationship between the Turkish rulers and the subject Arab population in Syria and Palestine wiped out the memory of these features of Ottoman modernity from Palestinian collective memory.

Here, by contrast, the presumed creation of these institutions of colonial mo-dernity are seen not as an innovation over the "decrepit" Ottoman system, but as an elaboration on the foundations already introduced by Ottoman reforms, such as secular education, the civil service, constitutional reform, and urban planning. In certain areas the British political plans constituted retrogression over the Ot-toman system.

This was the case, for example, with the confessionalization of quarters in the old city. The four-quarter scheme, mentioned in abundance in European travel literature to the holy city, now became an official administrative boundary of the city. The quarters replaced the *mahallas,* the smaller unit of governance employed by the Ottomans, and further enhanced religion as a marker of national identity (Tamari 2002).

Underwriting the Confessionalization of the City

From the beginning of the Mandate, the British began a series of actions to cre-ate a new base, disassociated with pilgrimage, for the city's economic activities, and to reinsert religion as the primary source of social identity. Jerusalem differed from many of the other provincial centers in that its economic base was consider-ably based on religious charities and endowments as well as services to pilgrims. Sharing the fate of many medieval holy cities, such as Canterbury and Lourdes, religion in late Ottoman Jerusalem had become the main commodity of the city, and was seen as the source of livelihood. In spite of this permeation, or perhaps as a result of it, religion was not taken as seriously as a guide to behavior or a norma-tive form of governance. According to Ashbee, the city "maintained a large para-sitic population—priests, caretakers, monks, missionaries, pious women, clerks, lawyers, and a crowd of riffraff—who all had a vested interest in maintaining the status quo" (quoted in Roman 2000). Despite the antisocial texture of this statement, it seems that Ashbee, given his populist credentials, was expressing here a negative assessment of the lopsided occupational base of the city's economy, rather than outright prejudice.

Ashbee combined a romantic vision of the "oriental ideal" of the city with a practical, down-to-earth approach to the unique predicament of Jerusalem. In the 1920 annual report of the Society he defined the city's unproductive base ("riffraff and priests," described above) as the main problem facing the planner. He attempted to overturn this "parasitic" occupational structure through the revival (and introduction) of the traditional crafts in the city's building trades: weaving, tiling (with Armenian ceramic experts brought in from Kütahya), and glasswork from Hebron. Among the projects undertaken and finished in this period were the renovation of the cotton market, Suq al Qattanin, in the old city, the tiling of the Dome of the Rock along with the authorities of the Waqf, or religious endowment, the restoration of the ancient wall ramparts built by Suleiman al Qanuni, and the Citadel of the City. All of these projects involved the establishment of apprenticeships based on the guild system. Storrs set up an annual academy of fine arts at the Citadel where exhibitions on Muslim art, Palestinian crafts, and town planning were held (Storrs 1937, 326–327).

The honeymoon with the colonial authority did not last long. One of the first government acts was to conduct the General Census (1921) in which Palestinians were divided into the three confessional categories of Muslims, Christians, and Jews. The Jerusalem leadership of the national movement saw the census not as part of the planning instrument as it was heralded, but as a prelude to the realization of the National Jewish Home project. A call to boycott ensued, but was not entirely successful.[6]

In the later part of the Mandate, public ceremonials became the lynchpin of confrontation with the British, in contrast to the situation in the late Ottoman period, when the authority was the main sponsor (and patron) of these ceremonials. The main focus of clashes between demonstrators and the military government was the procession of Nebi Musa, or Moses. These clashes began in the spring of 1919 and intensified over the following two years.

Colonel Storrs, in his capacity as the new military governor of Jerusalem, began to regulate the Nebi Musa processions and place them under government supervision—partly as a measure to control the crowds, but also as a plan to regulate religious ritual within the new civil administration of Palestine. In this effort he was acting in collusion with Haj Amin al Husseini, the rising star of the nationalist movement (who in this regard also saw himself as a successor of Salah al

Din, who liberated Jerusalem from the Crusaders in the twelfth century) and recently appointed Mufti of Jerusalem. Both the nationalist movement and the British saw in the control of religious ceremonials a mechanism for realizing their objectives.

Along these lines, the Nebi Musa processions, which under the Ottomans had been one of many syncretic public celebrations, suddenly became an official festival sponsored by the colonial authorities. Haj Amin himself also played a critical role in "nationalizing" the Nebi Musa celebrations under his authority as the Mufti (Jawhariyyeh ms., 131). Similarly, Easter Sunday and the rituals of Good Friday and Fire Saturday were also given state sponsorship. All of these actions were part of the process of confessionalization of popular religious ceremonies that conceived of Palestine as a land of three ancient religious communities, rather than a national community freeing itself from communalism.

Storrs, the orientalist who played a crucial role in inventing this tradition, was succeeded by the fiercely anti-Arab commander Edward Keith-Roach. Jawhariyyeh knew both governors personally and contrasted their personal style of administration, in favor of the wily and cultured Storrs. But he is also fully aware of Storrs's conscious manipulation of religious celebrations, as can be seen in this description of early clashes with the police in 1921:

> The army brought a large armed contingent and placed them at Jaffa Gate, reinforced by heavy cannons and tanks. Sir Ronald Storrs riding his horse in full military attire headed the force. All were facing the great procession of Nebi Musa arriving from Hebron, with the objective of diverting the crowds from clashing with the Jews. . . . It took fully six hours for the procession, which included singing bands, sword players, musical bands with drums, and horsemen representing each village in Mount Hebron with their banners, to arrive from the Sultan's Pool to the edge of Jaffa Gate.
>
> I was standing there with the throngs when the procession found the gates to the old city blocked by the army. With a signal by Storrs half the procession moved east towards Jaffa Road, but then in a sudden move the leaders of the procession turned back and attacked the British troops defying the machine guns and the tanks. It was an unforgettable sight. And what did Sir Ronald Storrs do on this occasion? He suddenly sprung out as a Qahtani Arab, and addressed the crowds in eloquent Arabic: "Greetings to the heroes of Nebi Musa . . . I welcome you according to the honoured tradition which dictates that you go through the gate of the old city towards the Haram." By doing this he avoided a bloody clash with army. The processionals in turn did not clash with the soldiers when they saw that Storrs himself was greeting them, which is exactly what he had aimed at—namely, to re-route the procession inside the walls away from Jaffa Gate. (Jawhariyyeh ms., 20–21)

Keith-Roach, however, lacked both the finesse and the cunning of Colonel Storrs. He described the Palestinians as "a naturally indolent people . . . pleasant to live among [with] their long loose garments covering a multitude of sins" (quoted in Segev 2000, 168). But by that time (1926) it is also more likely that clashes between the national movement and the Zionists became too severe to be contained through logistic manipulations as described in the incident attributed to Storrs.

Local Responses to Deprivation

The period of transition to the Mandate, in essence a time of military rule, is a neglected phase in scholarly studies. The nature of this transition was characterized by political and legal ambivalence, and most Palestinians were not yet committed in their political allegiances. For Jerusalemites in particular, it was a time of constant adjustment, repositioning, and new formulations of future plans based on an evolving present. Over time, however, the broader "communitarian" and localist affiliations began to dwindle, and the new, religion-based nationalism grew.

Palestine in particular was one of the provinces in which anti-Ottoman sentiments were least pronounced at the turn of the century. Even after the proclamation of the Constitution of 1908, when separatist movements in the Arab regions began to add their weight to Greek and Armenian movements asserting themselves against Istanbul, the Palestinian street remained relatively pro-Ottoman. Adil Mana' notes that Palestine was distinguished among the Syrian provinces by its lack of enthusiasm for the constitutional reform. In Nablus and other northern areas, the street demonstrated *for* the Sultan, and against the reformers (Mana' 2003, 243–244). Only in Jaffa and Jerusalem was the Movement of Union and Progress able to attract limited support (ibid., 243 and 249). It was only after Union and Progress began their Turkification program, following the removal of Sultan Abdul Hamid from power, that Palestinians began to join Arab nationalist groups en masse (ibid., 247).[7]

Naturally the British administration is recalled as the conscious instrument (through the Balfour Declaration) which laid the foundation for the displacement of the Palestinians in 1948, and much of Jawhariyyeh's narrative is permeated with this foreknowledge (since he was writing in a later period). It explains to a large extent his ambiguity about the liberation of Jerusalem from the Ottoman yoke, even as Jerusalemites were dancing in the street and as he and his brother Khalil were burning their Turkish military uniforms (Tamari and Nassar 2002, 253–254).

The years preceding the fall of Jerusalem were particularly harsh. Major social dislocations and ruthless suppression of the urban population in the major cities of the region accompanied the devastation of war. The last three years of Ottoman rule were also the years of famine in Syria and Palestine. But hunger was not induced by draught or any other natural cause, but through the confiscation and forced diversion of wheat supplies to the Fourth Army, under the command of Jamal Pasha (Tannous 1988, 35). To compound these disasters Palestine was subjected in the middle of 1915 to a severe attack of locust swarms that compelled a massive relocation of coastal populations inland (Manaʾ 2003, 84-85). Lebanon was first hit by famine in the spring of 1916, and the famine soon spread to the other urban centers of Syria and Palestine. In his memoirs, Dr Izzat Tannous, a Jerusalemite medical student (and later officer) in the Ottoman army, described the devastating impact of the famine when he was stationed in Beirut:

> Walking from Ras Beirut down to the Burj, the centre of town, it was a common affair to step over ten or fifteen dead bodies lying on the sidewalks for the municipal cart with one horse to pick them up and bury them. I fretfully stepped over these corpses many a time but it became routine. Children cried day and night: "Jouʾan!" (hungry), and rushed at every garbage can for anything to eat. . . . babies were left at hospital gates at night to be taken in the morning to be fed. (Tannous 1988, 36)

In Jerusalem the scarcity of food supplies was associated in the people's mind with the conscription. In his sardonic way Jawhariyyeh composed a ditty revolving around popular obsessions with missing dishes. He jointly wrote the lyrics with Omar al Batsh—his teacher and oud master in the Ottoman army:

انشودة المجاعة

بيضات بيضات بيضات مشوية   كرشات كرشات كرشات محشيه

واسكب واشرب وغني واطرب   يا سمك يا سمك يا سمك مقلي

ما على الإنسان من مهرب   بادر بادر بادر واشرب

منه لا تفزع   فالسكر أنفع

An Ode to Hunger
Tripe tripe, stuffed with rice, Eggs eggs, eggs in the oven
Fish. Oh fish fried in batter. Pour the wine, drink, sing and be happy
Be daring and drink, For being high is the only way
Refrain
Qabwat, qabwat fried Kubbeh, kubbeh cooked with yogurt
Carrots, carrots oh stuffed carrots. Come and settle in my stomach
Zucchini with meat, kishk with lard
Aubergine ala yakhni with fluffy rice
Refrain
Oh Kunafeh, do not desert me. Oh pudding you are my destination
Almond hariseh you come first. The queen of deserts after the stuffings
Pistachio cracking, taqqish faqqish. Fill you narghileh and get stoned
After the qatayif, pick your teeth
After all these helpings you will need a bath   (Jawhariyyeh 2005: 29–30)

Wasif first performed this song at the table of the *Mutassarif* (Governor) of Jerusalem and his Turkish officers as evening entertainment. "I kept thinking all the time of how my family and friends outside were not only deprived of these foods, but did not even have the chance of looking at them" (Jawhariyyeh, 2:30). Paradoxically this macabre "ode to hunger" had a hallucinatory effect and spread like wild fire in Jerusalem. Masses of people sang it as a way of invoking the famous "stuffed" (*mahashi*) dishes of the city that had disappeared from their lives. But as the wording shows, it went beyond the evocation of food toward adopting an attitude of licentiousness and abandon. It continued to be a popular ballad for years after the war.[8]

And despite the devastation, or perhaps as a result of it, several writers were able to look back at those years as signaling a major restructuring of Palestinian and Syrian society. A contemporary observer refers to the radical impact of the movement of population and the war economy on the normative aspects of daily life: villages coming to the city on a regular basis, women going to school and removing their veils, the emergence of café culture, and the decline of religiosity in Nablus and Jerusalem (al Barghouti 2001, 192–193). The decline of religiosity, it should be added, went along with the rise of confessionalism, as we also witness for Lebanon in the same period. A derivative development of these normative changes was the decline of local affinities and the strengthening of Syrian and Arab nationalism.

The space opened by the transition allowed, at least briefly, for new local agency, in political as well as individual and social life. Jawhariyyeh recalls the three years of transition as the days of chaos—both in the country as a whole and in his private life, as if one condition mirrored the other. But the "chaos" here is also seen here as a period of "creative anarchy."

In his personal life, those were the "precious" years of bachelorhood before he got married and settled down. They were also ushered by the death of his patron, the mayor of Jerusalem, Hussein Effendi al Husseini. He describes his condition then as one of "vagabondage" (*tasharrud*):

> I roamed around the city as if in a trance. I would spend all night partying, and then sleep all day, then spend another evening in neighboring villages of Jerusalem. I paid no attention to anybody or anything, and would only go home to change my clothes, sleeping mostly at my friends' homes until my body was completely depleted from intoxication. One day I am celebrating in the Bab Hatta neighborhood, and in the next morning I am having a picnic with the families of the top notables (*a'yan*) in the city. Then I would have a "session" with some of Jerusalem's gangsters (*zuran* and *qabadayat*) in a city alley. (Jawhariyyeh ms., 23)

But these episodes of hedonism, which lasted most of 1918 and part of the next year, reflected a mood that engulfed *the city as a whole*. Jawhariyyeh provides us with numerous episodes of public celebrations of freedom in the streets of the Old City, marked by musical processions and open consumption of alcohol. In one such fantasia involving hundreds of revelers, the celebrants started in Damascus Gate, moved out of the old city through Musrara, to the Russian Compound, back into the old city from Jaffa Gate, to the Austrian Hospice and ended in the Sheikh Rihan neighborhood of *Mahallat al Saadiyya* (Jawhariyyeh ms., 40–46). "Why did we have these orgies of celebration the likes of which we have not seen since then?" asks the author. He proceeds to answer himself: "The people were hungry for a moment of release, after the years of humiliation, disease, hunger and dispersal during the war and Ottoman despotism. When the British arrived we began to have a breath of freedom. Unfortunately our joy was short lived, for they brought us catastrophe which was several times more disastrous than the Turkish yoke." (Jawhariyyeh ms., 41–42)

These outbursts of street merriment soon found an outlet during the years of military government through the mushrooming of local cafés and café-bars.[9] They were places where Jerusalemites could meet at leisure, listen to gramophone music, drink *araq* and cognac, and smoke an *arghileh*. Two outstanding cafés from this period were Maqha al arab in Ain Karim (owned by Abu al Abed Arab) which stayed open all night, and the Jawhariyyeh café-bar—which featured live entertainment by visiting musicians from Cairo, Alexandria, and Beirut (Jawhariyyeh ms., 44–45).

The departure of the Turkish troops also encouraged some of the secret anti-Ottoman societies that had been active as literary or sports organizations to surface. Most notable among those associations were the Society for Arab Amity (*Jamiyyat al 'al Arabi*), established in Istanbul in 1908 after the proclamation of the new constitution; The Arab Forum (*al Muntada al arabi*) (1909), with branches in many Syrian cities; the Arab Maiden (*al Jamaiyyah al arabiyyah al Fatat*), 1912, based in Beirut; the Qahtani Association (*al Jam'iyya al Qahtaniyya*), and The Green Flag Society (*Jam'iyyat al 'alam al Akhdar*), both in Istanbul in 1912 (Sidqui 2001, 196–197). Among these quasi-secret groups in Palestine was the Literary Club (*al Muntada al Adabi*), whose membership included Fakhri al Nashashibi (who became later the leader of the Defense Party militia against the Husseinis and the Palestine Arab Party), Saliba al Juzi (brother of Bandali, the Marxist historian), Khalil Sakakini, Musa Alami, and Is'aaf al Nashashibi (Jawhariyyeh ms., 26 and 86–87; Sakakini 2004, 128). Sakakini's Vagabond Party (*Hizb al Saaleek*) was an early precursor of the literary club and his circle included leading figures from Jaffa and Jerusalem intellectual circles such as Nakhleh Zureiq, Adel Jaber, and the Issa brothers (founders of the *Filasteen* newspapers in 1909). The Literary Club became the nucleus of the Christian-Muslim Associations during the Military Government. We have a record of a mass rally held in early 1918 just outside Jaffa Gate in which the main speakers were Fakhri Nashashibi and Saliba al Juzi; both spoke against the Balfour Declaration and in favor of Syrian unity (Jawhariyyeh ms., 26).

Urban Chaos, Liminal Space, and Military Rule

Local political actors also enjoyed greater agency during the transition period. The Jawhariyyeh memoirs shed significant light on the critical postwar years during which much political ambiguity about the future direction of Palestine prevailed. These were the years of cultural liminality in Palestine, when questions of sovereignty still prevailed because the colonial system was not yet ushered in—despite the military collapse of the Ottoman system. "We lived in a state of ignorance" Colonel Storrs, military governor of Jerusalem, later confessed—"and my word was the law" (Storrs 1937, 272–273). Under the administration of General Moony all civil laws were suspended in favor of the military administration. Suddenly in Palestine, according to Mandate historian Bayan al Hut, there were no lawyers, no judges, no courts, and no newspapers (al Hut 1981, 66). The northern part of Palestine was still under Turkish control in 1918, and the British were mobilizing resistance in the name of Sherif Hussein against the fledgling Ottoman army. But even after the defeat and final consolidation of British rule over the country, the borders between Transjordan, Lebanon and Syria with Palestine remained "Ottoman," with fluid boundaries and a common cultural outlook.

While the legal vacuum was filled in the countryside by a reversion to common law (al qanun al urfi) and tribal law, the situation in the big cities allowed appointed judges and senior administrators—both British and Palestinian—considerable leeway to exercise their discretion in applying the law at the local level. These discretionary powers are illustrated by a number of recorded cases in 1919 at the Jerusalem Court of Appeals, presided over by Judge Muhammad Yusif al Khalidi, widely known for both his eccentricity and fairness. In one of those cases a well-known Old City prostitute was brought before him on charges of "disturbing the peace." Judge Khalidi apparently had been drinking heavily the night before, and was still in a daze when the woman was ushered screaming into the court.

> Judge Muhammad al Khalidi: "Shut up, you whore (ya sharmuta), and control yourself."
> Prostitute: (enraged by the insult) "My lord, I may be a prostitute at home, but here I am a citizen in the court of the state."
> Judge Khalidi: (sobering and taken aback) "You are absolutely right."

The proceedings were temporarily halted and the judge addressed the court secretary Jamal al Salahi:

> "Write this down: In the new case of slander, brought by the plaintiff fulaneh the daughter of fulan (i.e. so and so),[10] against the accused, Judge Muhammad Yusif al Khalidi, the court judges for the plaintiff. I hereby fine the accused [myself] five Palestinian pounds."

He then took five pounds from his wallet, handed it to the court secretary, who issued him with an official receipt. The judge then entered the case into the court protocols, and apologized to the prostitute; he then proceeded with the original charges against her (Jawhariyyeh ms., 13–14).[11]

Another feature of both cultural and sovereign liminality was the porousness of the new borders with Lebanon, Transjordan, Syria, and Egypt, which still reflected the old domains of Ottoman greater Syria. In the summer of 1922 Wasif goes on an excursion with his brother Khalil to Syria and Lebanon through the northern borders. Khalil had spent three years of the war as an Ottoman soldier stationed in Beirut. The passage through Ras al Naqura, which within ten years had become a formidable frontier post, is hardly recorded in the memoirs, as if one passed from one district to another (Jawhariyyeh ms., 30). Three years later Wasif repeats the same trip with his wife Victoria, passing again with hardly any formal procedures (Jawhariyyeh ms., 161). The two stories illustrate the fluidity of frontier areas on the eve of the British and French protectorates delineating the borders of new states in a move that consolidated notions of citizenship, exclusion and separation. The new Mandate regulations ended when northern Palestine and southern Lebanon were constituted subdistricts of Bilad al Sham (greater Syria), which, under Ottoman rule, had open borders and shared cultural and social affinities.

Another important realm where citizenship became increasingly confessionalized was the new Mandate bureaucracy. One example of this was the civil service and land registry. The phasing out of border fluidity and the establishment of a new, more circumscribed territorial unit for administration corresponded to the growth and consolidation in Palestine of the governing apparatus of the colonial state: the army, the police force, the civil service, and the corpus of the new legal system. As such, these spatial and administrative developments derived from and reinforced British efforts to consolidate their sovereign authority, even as they led to changing relationships with the citizenry. But in establishing sovereignty and citizenship, colonial authorities were equally hamstrung by prior efforts to confessionalize the city, and their spatial and social consequences. This is clear with a closer look at civil service activities and the land registry. Within every sector of the new state, the British had to balance a system of appointments that took into account the representation of the native Palestinian population and the emigrant Jewish population. But while native representation was individual and direct, taking into account social status and confessional considerations, Jewish representation was mediated through protracted negotiations with the Jewish Agency and Zionist Executive. During the crucial formative stage of British rule, when the new civil administration was installed in 1920, Jewish representation was overwhelming, even though they constituted less than twelve percent of the population. Segev writes: "The Palestinian Jews in senior positions were prominent principally during Samuel's tenure. Together with the British Zionists, they held key positions in his administration, complained Lieutenant Colonel Percy Bramely, the director of public security in Palestine. In fact, Bramely wrote, Samuel's was a 'Zionist-controlled government'" (Segev, 167).

Jawhariyyeh himself was a direct witness to and participant in the formation of the new civil service. Within the latter Wasif became a senior staff member in the National Registry (*Qism al Tahrirat*) and then (in 1919) in the Land Registry, whose main task was to complete the codification and commercialization of the land tenure system that was initiated by the Ottomans in 1858. He was later promoted to the position of director of the financial section in the Land Registry, and became head of the Property Committee and a member of the Appeals Committee (for people who felt they were assessed unjustly) (Jawhariyyeh ms., 2:21). The memoirs constitute a rich record of this transformation in his time. In the summer of 1920 he made this entry: "The core of the new civil administration is made up of the heads of security, education, finance, customs, justice, and agriculture—all English; the heads of the departments of Immigration, Passports, and Land Administration are British and Jews. Mr. N. Bentwich, a Zionist, was appointed as legal advisor to the government. Is this the initial implementation of the Balfour Declaration in Palestine?" (Jawhariyyeh ms., 2:21).

His work in the Land Registry for over two decades (with Sami Hadawi and Stephan Hanna—both of whom later became prominent writers in their own right), provides us with a detailed record of the manner in which the new laws were geared to facilitate the transfer of urban and rural property to the Zionists. This process included the abolition of the tithe and the *werko*.[12] Both were Ottoman land taxes that were aimed at bringing in state revenue from landowners without regard to its quality or productivity; the institution of the new graded land-tax based taxation on use, location, and quality. Finally, it included the expediting of the Land Settlement, whose main objective was a comprehensive cadastral registration of land plots to enhance and simplify the operations of the *Tapu* (Land Registry).

As with efforts to recast and divide confessional identities in space, Mandate changes in bureaucratic structuring and policy were not automatically internalized and reproduced by Jerusalemites. It is paradoxical, given their later nationalist credentials, how Sami Hadawi and Jawhariyyeh were critical instruments in this process of land alienation, initially unaware of its significance, and certainly unwilling to perform these tasks. But Jawhariyyeh's rendition of the process is typical of the early hedonistic years in Jerusalem: passive resistance through delaying work, bureaucratic sabotage, and creating a jovial atmosphere of idyllic celebration in one of the most critical departments of the colonial government. While his colleagues, Jews and Arabs, were struggling with the intricate book entries of the new land registration system during Keith-Roach's administration, he composed the following ditty lampooning the system of recording agricultural statistics:

ترتيب القواعد   واللي أدهى من كل ده

كرسنه وحنطه وفول   والله تجنن نفضل نحسب ونقول

أعشار وويركو على طول   وتحصل وتنزل وتدور لغاية شهر أيلول

وأدخل بالأستاذ وآتي باليومية   من حسابات عام ومفردات شخصيه

وواردات وصادرات   من سابقه وحالية

وتحويل العملة ألمصريه   للداهية الفلسطينية

في الشطب الدكمات   وتعداد الحيوانات

من حيث وليت   وإحنا صابرين

Homage to Double Bookkeeping
Worst of all is to establish these Rules
We are going mad with these calculations: barley, and wheat and fava beans
Tithes and Werko all year round . . . round and round till September ends
Go to the books and enter the numbers,
for public accounts and personal liabilities
Imports and Exports past and present
And converting Egyptian Lira
to the impossible Palestinian Pound
Deleting mistakes and animal census
From where we come, we grin and bear it.   (Jawhariyyeh ms. 4–59)

These mundane anecdotes, satirizing the daily routine of the colonial bureaucracy during the period of the military government, draw a cumulative broad picture of an emerging liminal identity. A legal vacuum filled by administrative fiat defined this period, along with a hedonistic street culture that celebrated the loss of tyranny, but filled it with new uncertainties, and porous borders that still retained the texture of an older sense of a continuous Levantine (*Shami*) culture. What "cemented" these three elements together was a strong sense of the local— of Jerusalem being the center of the country's shifting boundaries, and an anchor against the schemes engineered by the new colonial enemy, which drove many Palestinians into nostalgia for the "accursed" Ottomans.

In addition to the use of processions for protest as described above, another striking turn within the nationalist discourse related to the manner in which British by now openly posed as sponsors of the scheme for a Jewish National Home, and the reversal of their early promises for Syrian independence. This made people—initially exhilarated by the end of Turkish rule—nostalgic toward the Ottoman era, and even toward the "Turanic" regime of Mustafa Kamal Ataturk, despite his openly anti-Arab credentials. Wasif narrates a performance by the Egyptian-Jewish composer Zaki Murad (the father of singer Leila Murad) in which he sang a tribute to Ataturk in 1921, which became widely popular in Jerusalem:

الفؤاد مخلوق لحبك

والعيون على شان تراك   الفؤاد مخلوق لحبك

والنفوس تحيا بقربك   والملوك تطلب رضاك

اشفي صبك من لماك   راعي ربك رق قلبك

دور

والقمر محسوب ضياك   الجمال منسوب لشكلك

وانت في باهي علاك   من يطلول في الملك وصلك

مين يليق لك في سماك   مين يماثلك مين يعادلك

Ode to Ataturk

The heart beckons to you in adoration
and the eyes are cast towards your beauty
Royalty seeks your concord
the soul is enlivened by your presence
[...]
Nobody is your equal
Nobody radiates in your brilliance   (Jawhariyyeh ms. 84–85)

Although the song was ostensibly composed for King Fuad the First by Ibrahim Qabbani, it was nevertheless seen in Syria and Palestine as a tribute to Ataturk's victory over the allied troops. The record of this song was in constant demand for some time after the war, especially when Palestinians began to feel "the pernicious objectives of British rule." The Abu Shanab Music store in Damascus Gate, the main importer of Egyptian records, could hardly keep up with popular demand (Jawhariyyeh ms., 84–85).

New Public Spheres

Beyond the new confessionalization of space and society, war and social dislocation created new conditions of individualistic urban lifestyles and practices on the eve of the British Mandate in Palestine. Famine, disease and exile contributed to the disruption of the social fabric of whole communities. In Jerusalem, as well as in other cities in the area, both new public spaces and new behavioral patterns began to emerge. A substantial state sector gave rise to an enlarged civil service, and investments in the national economy invigorated the mercantile strata in the coastal regions. The urban changes included the extension of residential communities outside the old city walls. Secular education, cafés, social clubs and recreational centers catered to the growth of new bourgeois tastes and sensibilities, and private writings of this period reflect a sense of individualism and escape from familial and communitarian bonds.

City planning during the Mandate period, drawn by MacLean, Geddes, and Ashbee—and local architects such as George Shiber—contributed to the development of these urban sensibilities. At the heart of Ashbee's garden landscaping schemes, which separated the old walled Jerusalem from its new suburbs was the creation of a designated route through a sequence of experiences that elicited differing emotions and aroused varied associations. According to Gitler, the new scheme was specifically planned "to arouse in its visitors emotional or religious sentiments for the city and its walls, which bear so many centuries of evocative history. Similar to the English picturesque garden, benches were also added in locations offering both rest and enjoyment of the view" (Gitler, 39). To what extent did these intentions succeed in evoking these subjective associations, while creating a sense of privacy in public space? The answer is difficult to ascertain, except for those limited candid disclosures in the narratives of contemporary native writers.

Wasif Jawhariyyeh's memoirs, in common with a large number of Arab autobiographies, are infused with the spirit of individualism that prevailed in Arab literature of the late nineteenth century, but suffer from an absence of personal intimacy. This judgment may sound paradoxical given the detailed disclosures Wasif offers about the private lives of himself and his contemporaries. The memoirs are especially valuable because they expose, ridicule and celebrate the conventional, the hidden, and the unmentionable. These include the insular goings-on of the Jerusalem upper classes, the foibles of Ottoman and British military and political leadership, and the hilarious heroics and scandals of ordinary people. It dwells on the mundane and helps us to see it with fresh eyes. Nevertheless these events are more *anecdotal* and *expository of human foibles* than they are *intimate*.

Once set in motion, confessionalization as both a social and spatial process appears to have been almost impossible to reverse. In the case of Jerusalem, as in the country as a whole, the manner in which British planning and administrative policies contributed to the enhancement of confessional identity made it very convenient for Zionism to create a secular nationalism—ultimately based on the principle of a putative Jewish ethnicity. Palestinian nationalism also was fed by contradictory secular and religious motifs. On one hand, a secular streak emphasized "Muslim-Christian brotherhood" as a central component of national identity, while on the other, a religious component used Islamic affinities as a mobilizing factor in building a revived Palestinian (that is, non-Syrian) nationalism. With confessionalization acting as a critical factor in British governance and urban planning practice, the religious motifs of Jerusalem became the galvanizing iconography of opposing nationalist movements, rather than the source of syncretic celebrations, as in prior periods. This in turn changed the nature and goals of struggles over sovereignty. The historic dichotomy between a secular Zionism hostile to Jerusalem as Judaism's central cultural domain and a conservative Jewish orthodox tradition that was Jerusalem-centered gave way to a new nationalist split between Jewish and Arab Nationalisms. In this struggle, the "holy city" of "parasites and beggars" became the most important symbolic contested territory.

In the case of the Palestinian national movement, despite its secular character, exemplified by the political platforms of its main parties (Istiqlal, Palestine Arab Party, Defense Party, and the Communist Party) and the secular ideological persuasion of its leadership (perhaps with the exception of the followers of 'Iz ad-Din al Qassam in the north of Palestine), religious motifs had become essential in formulating its outlook. This can be seen in the uses of religious ceremonials, such as Nebi Musa processions, in nationalist mobilization—which had hitherto been a syncretic folk festival; and the location of religious sites (the Wailing Wall/Buraq and al Aqsa) as loci of clashes between Arabs and Jews. It is also exemplified by the increased use of religious language in nationalist slogans and exhortations, for example, "*Seif ed-Din al Haj Amin!*" ("Haj Amin [Husseini], the sword of religion!"). For Jews both secular and religious the loss of the old city in 1947 was a loss of Zion, and the capture of Jerusalem became a rallying cry for secular Zionism.

Notes

1. This essay is a modified version of an earlier essay entitled "Years of Delicious Anarchy." I am indebted to Bernadette Baird Zars and Diane Davis for their critical reading and helpful editorial suggestions.

2. Wasif Jawhariyyeh's memoirs contribute significantly in conveying the spirit of emancipatory anticipation that engulfed Jerusalem (and Palestine) during the critical three years of military rule. Wasif himself was maturing as a musical performer, and reached an age where he was able to reflect on the future of Palestine and Jerusalem from the momentous events that he witnessed. He also occupied a strategic vantage point in these events: as an entertainer to members of the city's notable elite, as well as his enhanced position in the nascent British civil service in the capital of the country.

3. The Occupied Enemy Territories Administration (1917–1920).

4. Henry Kendall, in his Jerusalem City Plan, refers to the incident as "permission was tactfully obtained to remove a hideous clock tower with dials showing the time according to both Western and Arab reckoning." He claims that the tower was erected to commemorate the thirty-third anniversary of Abdul Hamid's reign, not his twenty-fifth.

5. Fifteen years later Prof. T. F. Meisel, the Hebrew University archeologist, visited Jawhariyyeh and wrote glowingly about this model in an article published in the *Palestine Post*, on 10 August 1945.

6. In Jawhariyyeh's memoirs the national movement was already divided on the issue of census boycott, with Fawzi Nashashibi—a cousin of Raghib and a future leader of the opposition (pro-British) faction—already counseling support for the census.

7. Manaʾ notes also that considerable differences exist between Palestinian historians (e.g., Bayan Nweihid al Hut) and Israeli ones (e.g., Y. Porath) on the degree of Palestinian support for Arab anti-Ottoman groups, with the latter emphasizing its limitations. Al-Hut suggests that Palestinian representation in Arabist groups was considerably higher than their demographic weight in the Arab provinces (see Manaʾ 2003, 248). But these differences are more likely to be due to their stress on different time periods.

8. Although we have the words for this ballad, unfortunately the melody is lost. Jawhariyyeh never studied the musical notation system and therefore did not record it.

9. For a description of these café-bars and their clientele, see my "The Vagabond Café and Jerusalem's Prince of Idleness."

10. Her name is withheld, presumably because her status as a prostitute is not certain.

11. This case is among several court cases cited by Jawhariyyeh, ms. section 3: 13–14.

12. The *werko* was originally a land and real estate tax levied on *Zaʾamat* (*sipahis*, or feudal estates). With the abolition of feudal estates the *werko* became a land tax imposed by the state, together with the tithe. For details, see Doukhan 1938, 98–99.

Works Cited

al Barghouti, O. S. 2001. *al Marahil, Tarikh Siyasi*. Beirut: al Muʾassasah al Arabiyyah lil Dirasat wal Nashr.

———2003. *al Quds al Uthamaniyya fil Mudhakkarat al Jawhariyyeh*. Ed. S. Tamari and I. Nassar. Beirut: Institute for Palestine Studies.

Doukhan, M. 1938. "Land Tenure." In *Economic Organization of Palestine*, ed. Said Himadeh, 98–99. Beirut: American University of Beirut Press.

Fattah, H. 1999. "Planning, Building and Populating Jerusalem in the Ottoman Period."

Jerusalemites Forum. www.jerusalemites.org/jerusalem/ottoman/7.htm (accessed December 2008).

Gitler, I. B. Undated. "C R Ashbee's Jerusalem Years: Arts and Crafts, Orientalism and British Regionalism." *Assaph Studies in the Arts, Tel Aviv University* 5: 31–32

Huneindi, S. 2003. *A Broken Trust: Herbert Samuel, Zionism and the Palestinians,* Arabic edition. Beirut: Institute of Palestine Studies.

al Hut, B. N. 1981. *Al Qiyadat wal Mu'assasat al Siyasiyya fi Filasteen, 1917–1948* (Leadership and Political Institutions in Palestine). Beirut: Institute of Palestine Studies.

Jawhariyyeh, W. 2003. *al-Quds al-Uthmaniyah fi al-mudhakkirat al-Jawhariyah: al-kitab al-awwal min mudhakkirat al-musiqi Waṣif Jawhariyah, 1904–1917,* ed. S. Tamari and I. Nassar. Jerusalem: Al-Quds, Muassasat al-Dirasat al-Maqdisiyah.

Jawhariyyeh, W. 2005. *al-Quds al-intidabiyah fi al-mudhakkirat al-Jawhariyah: al-kitab al-thani min mudhakkirat al-musiqi Waṣif Jawhariyah, 1918–1948,* ed. S. Tamari and I. Nassar. Beirut: Institute for Palestine Studies.

Jawhariyyeh, W. *Memoirs (1904–1948).* Manuscript in four volumes. Ramallah: Institute of Jerusalem Studies.

Kark, R. 1991. *Jerusalem: Planning and By-Laws (1855–1930).* Jerusalem: Magnes Press.

Kendall, H. 1948. *Jerusalem City Plan, Preservation and Development during the British Mandate, 1918–1948.* London: Her Majesty's Stationery Office.

Khamaisi, R., and R. Nasrallah. 2003. *The Jerusalem Urban Fabric.* Jerusalem: International Peace and Cooperation Center.

Mana', A. 2003. *Tarikh Filasteen fi Awakhir al ahd al 'Uthmani 1700–1918.* Beirut: Institute of Palestine Studies.

Roman, Y. 2001. Jerusalem's Wall. *Eretz Weekly.* www.eretz.com/NEW/images/Contents. pdf (accessed 12 April 2010).

al Sakakini, K. 2004 *Yawmiyyat,* vol. 2. Ramallah: Institute of Jerusalem Studies.

Scholch, A. 1993. *Palestine in Transformation, 1856–1882.* Washington, D.C.: Institute for Jerusalem Studies.

Segev, T. 2000. *One Palestine Complete.* New York: Metropolitan Books

———2001. *Mudhakarat Najati Sidqi.* Ed. H. Abu Hanna. Beirut: Institute for Palestine Studies.

Storrs, R. 1937. *Orientations.* London: Nicholson and Watson.

Tamari, S. 2003. "The Vagabond Café and Jerusalem's Prince of Idleness." *Jerusalem Quarterly* 19: 23–36.

———. 2002. "The Modernity of Ottoman Jerusalem." Introduction to *Ottoman Jerusalem,* by W. Jawhariyyeh. Beirut: Institute of Palestine Studies.

Tannous, I. 1988. *The Palestinians: Eyewitness History of Palestine Under the British Mandate.* London: I. G. T. Co.

Wasserstein, B. 1995. "The British Mandate in Palestine: Mythos and Realities." In *Middle East Lectures* 1: 29–41. Tel Aviv: The Dayan Center for Middle East and African Studies.

PART 2

Scales of Sovereignty and the Remaking of Urban and National Space

4

Sovereignty, Nationalism, and Globalization in Bilbao and the Basque Country

Gerardo del Cerro Santamaría

What role does Bilbao, a key urban node in the economic prosperity of the Basque region, play in the over 100 years of history of politically organized Basque nationalism and its fight for independence? How have the structural features of the Basque region's political economy and its multiscalar linkages with the Spanish nation-state been molded or influenced by urban policies in Bilbao? Further, does it make sense to examine these questions just within the "imagined community" of the city, the region, or even the nation-state and their workings? Or, should we take a transnational and globalist approach, assuming that periods of intense global interconnectedness significantly influence the attitudes, strategies and actions of political and economic leaders regarding urban, regional, and national political dependencies? This chapter questions the extent to which the complex of identities and networks of sovereignty that lead to urban and regional violence in the Basque country are understandable primarily from a local perspective, suggesting instead that Basque nationalism is embedded within a multiscalar context of allegiances and competing sovereignties. With this point of departure, the chapter assesses the impact of the complex and multilayered globalization process—and the reemergence of subnational and transnational tensions it is causing—upon what we could call "the spatialities of nationalism" and the prospects for Basque sovereignty in the twenty-first century. Stated differently, it questions whether there is a causal relationship between the territorial basis of nationalist struggles and the ongoing transformation of nation-states under conditions of contemporary globalization—including spatial changes in the built environment—and seeks to answer by exposing the nexus between Basque urban and territorial structure, the features of Basque nationalist struggles, and the impact of these struggles upon the Spanish nation-state.

This chapter proceeds from the assumption that the interplay and shifting focus between geopolitical scales can transform the nature and dynamics of competing sovereignties, as my analysis of the evolving strategies of confrontation between Basque nationalism and the Spanish state will show. In light of the questions posed in the introductory chapter of this book, I try to establish a link between the evolving nature of Basque nationalism, the multiscalar features of globalization, and the role of urban mega-projects in sustaining Basque identity and struggles for sovereignty. The paper establishes a historical context that will help the reader understand the roots of current conflicts and divergence of interests between the Basque city-region and the national sovereignty claimed by the Spanish state. It begins with an analysis/summary of the historical evolution of confrontations between Basque nationalists and the Spanish state, the fight of *Euskadi Ta Askatasuna* (ETA or Basque Homeland and Freedom) for independence and socialism, and then focuses on recent transformations of Basque attempts to exert political influence vis-à-vis Madrid during the current wave of increased global interconnectedness. These transformations include a largely successful attempt to control important segments of civil society by the regional state apparatus through clientelist strategies, and with the launching of a quasi-developmental strategy of urban-led economic growth with the two-fold objective of economic efficiency and political visibility in the global arena. A major example of the noneconomic strategies implemented by Basque nationalist leaders can be seen in the negotiations to bring the Guggenheim Museum to Bilbao, as well as in the commitment to use this urban mega project for strengthening the economic and political foundations of the city-region vis-à-vis the national state. The paper concludes with an reflection on the recent (March 2006) ETA ceasefire, the ongoing negotiations with the Spanish government, and the potential consequences of an end to ETA's fight for Basque sovereignty.

Identity and Sovereignty in Historical Perspective

A combination of globally induced political economy factors and their materialization in both the national and regional domains shaped the ways in which Basque nationalism emerged to play a fundamental role in the evolving networks of competing sovereignties within the Spanish nation-state. Not every sector of the Bilbao and Basque societies was in favor of the transformations brought about by industrial capitalism in the mid- to late nineteenth century. In fact, Basque nationalism politically took shape in Bilbao during the last third of the nineteenth century as an immediate reaction against the new industrial society. According to Díez Medrano, whose work provides the main source for this section, "it had been the breakdown of Spanish state finances, worsened by the loss of most of the American colonies, that laid the groundwork for nationalist thinking by contributing to state initiatives toward economic liberalization and political centralization in early nineteenth-century Spain" (Díez Medrano 1995, 36). Economic liberalization drastically modified the structure of real property, of forms of relations of production, and of mechanisms for the distribution of goods. Combined with a secularization ideology, these changes antagonized broad sectors of traditional society, including the lower rural nobility, the clergy, the peasantry, and the petty bourgeoisie. Díez Medrano suggests that "although liberalism created some of the conditions for conflict between the forces of change and the forces of reaction, and between both of these and the Spanish state, uneven development at the Spanish level promoted conflict between the Basque socioeconomic elites and the Spanish state" (Díez Medrano 1995, 38). As it is known, modern industrial and commercial capitalism centered mostly on the Basque Country (and Catalonia, which was the other industrial region in Spain), especially in the last third of the nineteenth century, while the rest of the country remained anchored in an agrarian system with low productivity levels.

> Although big landowners, who largely controlled the state apparatus, and peripheral capitalist elites agreed on the need to liberalize the economy, they faced entirely different social and economic problems and had very different views about how to conduct government. Since for most of the nineteenth century the industrial and commercial bourgeoisie represented only a very small social group, it was the agrarian bourgeoisie who had the greater influence on state policy, thereby transforming class conflict between the agrarian elite and the commercial and industrial elites into conflict between the state and these commercial and industrial elites. (Díez Medrano 1995, 46)

The structural roots of Basque nationalism are to be found not only within the Basque Country, but also in the multiscalar articulation and interplay of political and economic developments taking place globally, nationally and regionally.

Centralization measures adopted by the state during the nineteenth century greatly intensified conflict between the state and the traditional and capitalist groups of the Basque Country. The local reaction in the Basque Country was class-based, and had to do with the articulation of interests of various class and power groups. Indeed, "as class conflict between traditional and capitalist social groups intensified within the Basque Country, and as conflict between the state and Basque society heightened, the control and extension of local power mechanisms became more important for Basque traditional and modern economic elites" (Díez Medrano 1995, 52). These mechanisms became important both as a means to impose a particular socioeconomic structure at home and as a counter-power to the state. "For the traditional elites, local autonomous institutions were seen as mechanisms for isolating their region from changes taking place in the rest of Spain, whereas for capitalist elites the local institutions were seen as a mechanism for fostering regional industrial development independently of transformations taking place in the rest of Spain" (Díez Medrano 1995, 54). Centralization, by precluding these possibilities, "exacerbated conflict in the region, and class differences within the Basque Country and between the Spanish state and the Basque Country became harder to reconcile. Because Spain was by now exposed to ideological influences originating in other European countries, the presence and memory of political autonomy, complemented by the cultural distinctiveness of the Basque Country, eventually facilitated the transformation of these internal and external class struggles into nationalist struggles" (Díez Medrano 1995, 56).

Like the Basque capitalist elite, the local Basque bourgeoisie had a disinclination to support a nationalist program based on the defense of the *fueros* (local laws) and cultural revival, and had little influence in the development of Basque nationalism. This was due to the elites' traditional orientation toward Spain, the political ascendance of the Spanish-oriented oligarchy and, especially, ideological conflict between the local bourgeoisie and the old middle classes, the latter of which formed the social base of Basque nationalism. "The calls for decentralization made by the few local capitalists who turned to nationalism can be seen as a strategy employed by those who had been excluded from state-level political institutions, to increase their power share. Such a strategy may be inherent in the expansion of peripheral capitalism, because of the lack of opportunities for upward mobility for some members of the local capitalist class" (Díez Medrano 1995, 60). There were also ideological motivations on the part of the local bourgeoisie, whose imagined community was the Basque Country. It was the traditionalist nationalism of Sabino Arana, founder of the Basque Nationalist Party (*Partido Nacionalista Vasco*, PNV), that would succeed in articulating the politics of nationalism in the Basque Country. The social base of the PNV was the lower middle class. "Although the early nationalist organization included some members of the working class and some members from well-to-do bourgeois families, most of the early adherents were artisans, salaried workers, clerks, salesmen, and small-scale merchants. Instead of powerful capitalists, what one finds among the nationalist leaders are pharmacists, doctors, engineers, lawyers, clerks, and accountants: educated members of the Basque middle class" (Corcuera 1979, 84). Some of the ideological principles of the PNV were clearly anti-Spanish, because Spain meant the introduction of liberalism in the Basque Country. Arana's nationalism, which pervaded Basque nationalist discourse until the Civil War (1936–39), was a defensive reaction against what he viewed as the corrosive influence of liberalism in Basque society. This explains, for example Arana's negative reaction and attitudes toward Spanish immigrants, whom he saw as a threat to the established social order. The targets of his attacks were also the economic, political, and cultural elites of Vizcaya, groups that held pro-Spanish attitudes.

Social and electoral support for the PNV grew between 1890 and 1930. By 1936, Basque nationalism had become the most powerful political force in Vizcaya and Guipúzcoa by attracting substantial support from traditionalist forces and the local bourgeoisie. "Basque nationalism remained a predominantly traditionalist movement aimed at establishing a society of small-scale industrial and agrarian producers in which religious principles would inform most aspects of life. It was therefore the program of a conservative middle class whose most radical members placed independence from Spain at the forefront of their program" (Díez Medrano 1995, 88). Demands for independence were shelved during the years of the Second Republic (1931–39), and the PNV sought to obtain an *Estatuto de Autonomía*, or Statute of Autonomy, similar to the one the Catalans had extracted from Spain. One can also discern another form of nationalism, led by segments of the local bourgeoisie, which worked from within the PNV to turn the party away from separatist goals, but without great success.

Bilbao's Three Identities

This volume suggests that identity-based differences among citizens in cities do not in and of themselves produce conflict. Such is the case in Bilbao up to the 1960s, and especially during the period 1900–1937. This period saw the configuration in Vizcaya (the Basque province of which Bilbao is the capital) of three political cultures with deep roots in the local society, and clearly differentiated them from each other: Spanish right, Basque nationalism, and democratic left. This triangle of options was polarized in the peaceful confrontation (particularly in 1918–23) between the idea of a Basque national identity maintained by the growing nationalist movement and the affirmation of the "Spanishness" of the Basque Country by the ideologies of both the right and the democratic left. It is important to note that none of the three political alternatives was ever hegemonic. On the contrary, in the eleven elections held in Vizcaya between 1900 and 1923 political representation was in the hands of a variety of political parties and ideological tendencies. This pattern continued during the Second Republic (1931–37). In the 1933 elections, the Spanish right got 11 percent of the vote in Bilbao; the PNV got 32 percent, and the left got 28.8 percent. In 1936, the percentages were respectively 16,

23.5, and 37.7 (Fusi Aizpurúa 1984, 22). Bilbao is the city that best represented the triangular configuration of Basque politics, a tendency still visible today. The city was the birthplace of both Basque nationalism and Spanish socialism.

Bilbao had a deep-rooted liberal tradition, a legacy of and symbolic link to anti-Carlist resistance of the nineteenth century. The roots of this tradition can be found in the mercantile activities of the city. The commercial urban bourgeoisie, developed during the nineteenth century, was the social base of liberalism. This never became a clearly defined doctrine or a set of well-delineated principles, but rather remained a collective conscience of civic behavior and political tolerance. Politically, Bilbao's liberalism was expressed in the Liberal Union, which sent representatives to the Spanish Parliament and captured the majority of the municipal vote between 1876 and 1903. Liberalism cannot be equated with democratic principles during those years. In fact, the political expression of Bilbao's liberalism was rather a conglomerate of interests connected to the local oligarchy, acquiescent to the political status quo, which tolerated electoral corruption. After the decade of the1880s, local liberalism became a spirit or a conscience that would influence other movements, in particular the republican and socialist movements (Fusi Aizpurúa 1984, 149).

The republican tradition of Bilbao has to do with the profound anti-Carlist sentiment of the city and the degeneration of liberalism. The growing urban middle classes during the first third of the twentieth century formed the support base for republicanism. The socialist movement, on the other hand, grew as a result of the transformation of Bilbao into an industrial powerhouse since the 1880s. The abilities of local socialist and trade union leaders created a sentiment of loyalty toward the Socialist Party among the working classes; the Party would become the hegemonic voice of workers in Bilbao for many years. Instead of anarchist, like other cities such as Barcelona, Bilbao was decidedly socialist from the very beginnings of the industrial revolution. In fact, Bilbao's socialism has been one of the foundations of the Spanish socialist movement, providing leaders and ideology during the twentieth century. As the party of migrant workers in Bilbao, the PSOE (*Partido Socialista Obrero Español,* Spanish Workers Socialist Party) was detached from any nationalist aspiration. The values of solidarity and egalitarianism contradicted the efforts at regional and ethnic differentiation. The labor movement was a universal revolutionary ideal whose ethics went beyond the ideas of race and homeland. The ethnic and linguistic tenets of Basque nationalism in its origins could do little for the workers in Bilbao, who were interested in improving their living conditions and becoming integrated into the new society. Around 1912, the Spanish left became sympathetic to the nationalist aspirations of the Basques, based on a liberal-democratic interpretation of the *fueros* as the foundation of a modern representative system based on popular sovereignty. Later on, in 1930, it was the Basque socialists who introduced the concept of Basque *autonomía*, based on liberal and lay principles, and convinced the Spanish left to accept it. Similarly, the first *Estatuto* in 1936, which made possible the formation of the first Basque Government, was the product of Basque socialists (Fusi Aizpurúa 1984, 155).

An urban phenomenon from its beginnings, Basque nationalism was born in the city of Bilbao, and during many years Bilbao was the only nationalist bastion in the Basque Country. The nationalist movement was a reaction against the massive societal changes triggered by the industrial revolution in Bilbao, which (the nationalists thought) threatened a Basque cultural identity based on ethnicity and tradition. Commercial Bilbao, the liberal professions, small industrialists, and employees constituted the social base of nationalism in Bilbao, a base not so different from the one supporting liberal Bilbao. "This shows that nationalist Bilbao was not simply the embodiment of a distorted image of an ideal Basque past, but rather the affirmation of a cultural identity that had never disappeared and that was always very sensitive to its own historic singularities" (Montero 1998, 53).

Bilbao and Basque Nationalism during the Franco Years

It was during the Franco years that confrontations about Basque identity and sovereignty turned into political conflict and violence with the birth of the armed group ETA. It is tempting to find the roots of Basque violence in the existence of an authoritarian government in Spain, but this does not explain the timing of the conflict, that is, it does not explain why political violence around Basque sovereignty claims had not existed between Franco's rise to power in 1939 and the inception of violence in 1960. The causal factors of conflict must be found, at least partially, somewhere else: in the socioeconomic transformations brought to the Basque Country by the prosperity of the 1960s and the spatial transformations that it caused in the built environment of Bilbao. As Basque society experienced an important wave of reindustrialization and development in the late 1950s and 1960s, and as the urban built environment of Bilbao was reshaped by the influx of tens of thousands of immigrants, regional and local sovereignty claims exacerbated competition among identity groups. However, in order to understand what happened during the 1960s, we must begin earlier in time.

In October 1936, just weeks before Madrid fell under siege, the government of Spain's Second Republic approved a Statute of Autonomy for the Basque Country. In the context of the breakdown of the central state caused by the war, the approval of the Statute greatly empowered the newly created Basque government. In its short but active life the Basque government, presided over by José María de Aguirre, enacted legislation to promote the Basque language, established law and order, and ensured food distribution to the besieged population. The highly religious character of the PNV ensured that there would be no religious persecution in the Basque Country, in contrast to other Spanish areas under republican control. Consequently, Franco's justification of his uprising as a crusade against communism and atheism did not have the same legitimizing effects in the Basque Country as it did in other regions of Spain (Maravall 1978; Pérez Agote 1982).

The PNV was active in its opposition to the Franco regime, particularly until 1950. But the most significant political event in Basque nationalism during the Franco years was the founding of ETA in 1959, born out of a faction of PNV militants who asked for a more active stance against Franco. ETA, always more militantly nationalist than the PNV, soon evolved into a revolutionary movement that used military tactics against the Franco regime and advocated the end of capitalism. From 1959 to 1968, ETA was a small oppositional group "whose patterns of political mobilization were comparable to those of other anti-Francoist organizations across Spain" and was the only organization in the Basque Country that led an effort to fight for labor relation issues or organized and mobilized workers with resolve and efficacy (Jáuregui Bereciartu1981).

Initially, ETA differed from the PNV only in its more militant attitude and its more uncompromising attitude toward the goal of independence from Spain. The fundamental goal of nationalism for the early leaders of ETA was to preserve Basque culture and especially the Basque language. If immigrants were viewed with suspicion it was not because they corrupted the Basque race (as Sabino Arana, the founder of the PNV, thought in the late nineteenth century) but rather the Basque culture, although ETA leaders, and later the representatives of the nationalist left, have always claimed that Basques are those who live and work in the Basque Country, without ethnic distinctions. In addition, ETA "did not emphasize religion as a defining concern of the Basque nation, nor did it proclaim any programmatically religious goals" (Jáuregui Bereciartu 1981, 47). Finally, ETA's socioeconomic views were much more progressive than those of the PNV, advocating for the socialization of basic economic sectors, state planning and the promotion of cooperatives. "Its vision was critical of capitalism but not anticapitalist" (Jáuregui Bereciartu 1981, 48).

Between 1960 and 1968, ETA went well beyond its radical predecessors, moving toward socialist political positions and, for the first time, advocating the use of violence against the Spanish state. The figure who most influenced this shift was Federico Krutvig. In 1963, he fulfilled the request of a Basque friend to "publish a book that would be very nationalist, and which at the same time would be very progressive and leftist" (Beltza 1976, 32). The result was *Vasconia,* which "outlined a way of reasoning and a political program borrowed from Third World national-liberation movements" (Beltza 1976, 34). According to this ideology, the situation of the Basque Country was one of colonialist—later imperialist—oppression "that could only be redressed through a revolutionary war and the strategy of the 'action-repression spiral'" (Beltza 1976, 37). The goal of this strategy was to trigger a series of political and social reactions that would eventually lead to direct confrontation between the Basque people and the Spanish state. In addition, ETA's revolutionary rhetoric increasingly included among its goals the creation of a socialist society (Ibarra 1987).

In the late 1970s and 1980s, especially, ETA frequently put into practice its military strategy against the Spanish state, which continues today. The ascent of ETA's bloody fight for independence and socialism in the Basque Country coincided in time with the transition to democracy in Spain after Franco's death, and with the world energy crisis of 1973. These were all major events that dramatically influenced the course of history in the Basque Country and Bilbao. While Basque political leaders bargained for regional autonomy with the new democratic leaders of Spain, Bilbao's years as an industrial power were numbered. A new era began for the city after the irreversible decline of Fordist Bilbao in the 1970s: an era of economic restructuring, first, and urban revitalization, later.

Sovereignty and Political Turmoil in Democratic Spain

Basque confrontation with the Spanish state and Basque political violence around sovereignty claims did not cease with the end of Franco's dictatorship and the establishment of a new democratic regime in Spain. In addition to ETA's violence, there was the attempt by Basque politicians to try to find a political solution to Basque historical claims. Legitimized by its historical role as the leading representative of Basque interests, the PNV was the chief negotiator with the Spanish government over the status of the Basque Country in the Spanish constitution and the content of the future Statute of Autonomy for the Basque Country. These negotiations, which took place in the context of an ever-tightening spiral of violence by ETA and repression by the Spanish security forces, were fraught with tension. Because ETA threatened the PNV's hegemony in the Basque Country, and because Spanish democrats feared an involutionist insurrection on the part of the military, violence constrained both the PNV's and the Spanish government's ability to negotiate (Montero 1996). In these negotiations the PNV demanded the right to self-determination for the Basque Country, a Statute of Autonomy granting as much power devolution as the state might relinquish, fiscal autonomy, and the inclusion of Navarre in the Basque Autonomous Community, the creation of which was being negotiated. Although the PNV was very dissatisfied with the way these issues were treated in the new Spanish Constitution and called for Basque Country voters to abstain in the December 1978 constitutional referendum, the Basque Country would end up obtaining a generous Statute of Autonomy that granted the region a level of political autonomy not matched by any other region in Europe, and which includes the local collection of taxes and the issuing of bonds.

Controversy over the Basques' right to self-determination persisted during the 1979 negotiations for the approval and implementation of the Basque Statute of Autonomy. "Disagreement on this issue was the underlying factor in other conflicts, such as the PNV's demand to gain absolute control over the police forces in the Basque Country, its desire for fiscal autonomy and its demand for institutional mechanisms to ensure the future entry of Navarre into the Basque Autonomous Community" (Díez Medrano 1995, 132). The Statute granted more autonomy to the Basque Country than it had ever enjoyed before, but this was not enough for Basque nationalists, who insisted on the right of Basque people to self-determination. The functions the Statute delegated to the Basque Autonomous Community included the administration of justice, of some aspects of economic policy, and of police, culture, and education. "Statute provisions also authorized the creation of a Basque public-television channel, declared Basque language the official language along with Castilian, established a Basque government and a democratically elected Basque parliament, and granted ample fiscal autonomy to the Basque Country" (Díez Medrano 1995, 134). Fiscal autonomy meant that the Basques would be in charge of collecting their own taxes, and they would negotiate with the Spanish government a quota to be paid annually to the Spanish treasury.

This political agreement about Basque sovereignty claims, important as it was, did not end ETA's fight for independence by violent means. Since 1975, and as a result of many splits, ETA became "progressively dominated by groups who spent little time debating ideological issues and saw military confrontation as the only way to achieve their goal of independence for the Basque Country" (Díez Medrano 1995, 141). This militaristic trend within ETA had resulted in an escalation of violence following Franco's death. The number of persons killed by ETA rose from no more than three between 1968 and 1973 to seventeen in 1976, sixty-seven in 1978, and eighty-eight in 1980. Throughout the 1980s, ETA maintained fairly high levels of violence, accounting for between thirty and forty deaths per year.

Overt war between ETA and the Spanish state, complicated by anti-ETA violence exerted by far-right groups financed by the Spanish government, created a terrible climate of violence (Clark 1984) and was one of the reasons for a coup d'état led by a small group of pro-Franco military officers in Spain in 1981. In more recent years, however, general public condemnation, more efficient police actions, and the collaboration of French police forces have led to a sustained decline in the number of killings during the 1990s and beyond.

ETA's concentration on military activities was complemented in the political sphere by the activities of *Herri Batasuna,* a political party it created in 1978, and KAS (*Koordinadora Abertzale Sozialista,* Independentist Socialist Party), a closely connected social movement that encompassed many diverse associations. Both *Herri Batasuna* and KAS espoused ETA's separatist and anticapitalist goals while denying formal ties with the separatist military organization. *Herri Batasuna* has over the years changed names into *Euskal Herritarrok,* first, and *Batasuna,* later, without changing its strategic objectives and support of ETA's military fight. In 1998, ETA announced a truce but resumed its violent activities shortly thereafter. In 2006, ETA officially announced a "permanent ceasefire" and its desire to find a "democratic" solution to the Basque conflict.

The public opinion during the democratic years reflects the division between nationalist and non-nationalist tendencies within Basque society, and the relationship between the Basque Country and Spain, as can be evidenced in the following tables.

New Regionalism, Developmentalism, "Project-based" Globalization, and Sovereignty

In addition to being a result of the configuration of power structures within Spain and the Basque Country, determination on the part of Basque nationalist groups to continue their fight for power and control of Basque society and the evolution of domestic political confrontations between Basque nationalism and the Spanish state after 1980 obeyed a transnational logic in which the resurgence of nationalist movements worldwide and the restructuring of capitalism in advanced economies play a significant role. Globalization, indeed, has transformed the geopolitics of state structures, especially in the case of multinational states such as Spain, where the balance of power between the central state and the regions has shifted by virtue of devolution and federalization, and by a resurgence of Spanish nationalism and the global reach of Spanish corporations in the 1990s. This phenomenon illustrates the idea that the multiscalar nature of globalization is not

Table 4.1. Trends in Support for Independence in the Basque Country

YEAR	Percentages and Ns
1976	9 (404)
1979	25 (777)
1982	25 (916)
1988	20 (722)
1991	15 (428)
2003	28 (797)
2005	27 (777)

Sources: Jiménez Blanco et al. 1977; Gunther et al. 1986; Shabad 1986; Análisis Sociológicos, Económicos y Políticos 1988; Centro para la Investigación sobre la Realidad Social 1991. Sociómetro del Gobierno Vasco, October 2003 and 2005.

Table 4.2. Poll: What Would Be the Economic Consequences of Independence for the Basque Country? (1991)

Response Option	Percent of total response
Much better	5.5
Somewhat better	27.6
The same	1.5
Somewhat worse	17.9
Much worse	13.5
Don't know	33.5
N	(525)

a zero-sum game in which regions rise because nation-states shrink, but rather a much more complex articulation of forces at various domains of social action which brings about very uncertain and unstable outcomes.

Besides globalization (or as a manifestation of it), another major factor influencing the development of political violence around sovereignty claims in Bilbao and the Basque Country has to do with urban spatial transformations taking place in Bilbao during the late 1980s and 1990s. As this book argues, the interaction between sovereignty status and the urban built environment determines whether identity differences devolve into conflict. The urban built environment, as a concept intended to focus attention on urban space, is to be understood in terms of urban spatial patterns, spatial (and architectural) representations, and urban policies that make or transform space. What we find in Bilbao starting in the 1990s is, almost simultaneously, a major transformation of the built environ-

Table 4.3. Trends in Self-identification in the Basque Country 1979–1991

SELF-IDENTIFICATION	1979			1988			1991		
	Natives	Immigrants	Total	Natives	Immigrants	Total	Natives	Immigrants	Total
Only Spanish	9.7	53.4	25.5	4.3	33.3	13.8	3.8	34.5	14.7
More Spanish than Basque	0.7	6.6	2.8	2.7	16.9	7.3	2.9	13.8	6.9
As Spanish as Basque	24.0	23.9	23.9	26.0	29.1	27.0	22.5	35.6	27.3
More Basque than Spanish	15.0	3.7	10.9	26.6	8.9	20.9	27.0	8.6	20.4
Only Basque	50.6	12.4	36.8	40.5	11.8	31.1	43.8	7.5	30.8
N	543	281	857	489	237	726	315	174	489

Source: Gunther, Sani, and Shabad, Spain After Franco (1986); Análisis Sociológicos, Económicos y Políticos 1988; Centro para la Investigación sobre la Realidad Social 1991.

Table 4.4. Trends in Self-identification in the Basque Country, 1979–2005

	1979	1988	1991	2003	2005
Only Spanish	25.5	13.8	14.7	5	8
More Spanish than Basque	2.8	7.3	6.9	6	4
As Spanish as Basque	23.9	27.0	27.3	35	N/A
More Basque than Spanish	10.9	20.9	20.4	17	13
Only Basque	36.8	31.1	30.8	30	32
N	857	726	489	2848	2879

Source: Gunther, Sani, and Shabad, Spain After Franco (1986); Análisis Sociológicos, Económicos y Políticos 1988; Centro para la Investigación sobre la Realidad Social 1991. Sociómetro del Gobierno Vasco, 2003 and 2005.

ment via revitalization and the gradual decrease of political violence by ETA. It is claimed here that the interactions between sovereignty claims and the transformations in the built environment in Bilbao brought about by globalization in the 1990s created the political opportunity structures that inhibited competition among identity groups. This produced two important outcomes: first, the loss of relevance of political violence to the goal of reaching regional independence, and second, the clustering of sovereignty claims around a peaceful political proposal by the PNV. Let's begin by examining the transnational context of globalization and its impact in the Basque region.

Globalization is not a new phenomenon in Bilbao. All recent Basque efforts at internationalization have historical precedents. Basque economic internationalization can be observed in the sixteenth and seventeenth centuries and then again in the period 1880–1936. Basque political globalization, clearly expressed in the Guggenheim project, also occurred before 1936 through the coordinated foreign action by the PNV and then during the Second Republic (1931–39) by the Basque government (Ugalde 1997; 1999), although never with the public visibility that the museum's operation has had in recent years. Bilbao's globalization may also have extended its reach during the most recent cycle, due to the impact of the foreign investments of Bilbao's global bank, BBVA. The financial globalization of the BBVA had reached unprecedented levels during the 1990s, with a solid expansion into Latin American markets and attempts at consolidation within Europe. Similarly, the projects to enlarge Bilbao's port show the city's unequivocal intention to be incorporated into the growing flows of maritime trade. The significance of the BBVA headquartering in Bilbao can be observed in the fact that, should the Basque government go ahead with its political emancipation projects, the Spanish government might be putting pressure on the bank's management to relocate their headquarters to Madrid. Economic and political globalizations are, therefore, intertwined in the case of Bilbao, re-enacting the regional–national tensions.

Structural adjustments in the local economy, initially triggered by global forces but mediated at the regional and national levels, and the long-standing political tension between the Basque region and the Spanish state shape Bilbao's current urban developments. On the one hand, Bilbao remains a key node connecting large segments of the Spanish economy with the world via its port, which is managed by agencies owned by the Spanish government. On the other hand, Bilbao's industrial base has become increasingly interwoven with the regional economy, and the city is no longer the only industrial center of the Basque Country—although it remains the largest one and also the economic capital of the region. The Basque government places Bilbao at the core of its economic and political agendas, and thus the path from urban restructuring to regional geopolitics is marked by the standing tension between the regional and the national governments regarding control of urban policies and facilities. In this context, deliberate globalizing strategies implemented at the regional level by Europe's only fiscally independent regional government constitute a show of political power vis-à-vis Madrid.

Political Globalization and Sovereignty

As argued above, economic performance is not the only way to measure efforts at globalization on the part of Basque authorities. In Bilbao, restructuring came at the same time as another domestic political process not directly linked with globalization: the devolution of political power to the regions and the organization of a de facto federal state in Spain. So whereas the traditional ties of the city's economy with national development (steel and shipbuilding sectors) vanished, a new set of regulating forces appeared at the regional level. Compounding this complex situation of political and economic restructuring within and outside Spain, globalization discourses are perceived and deliberately used by Basque political elites to advance their sovereignty goals. In fact, globalization can be understood as a political opportunity structure for nationalist forces to seek new arenas for conflict and reidentification in their quest for sovereignty. Globalization is embraced by Basque political leaders as a process by which the Basque Country can be linked to the world, possibly without Spain's patronage and mediation. The best known example of such a strategy is the Guggenheim project, discussed below. This project is not only an illustration of transnationalization of cultural policies, but also an example of how Basque nationalist elites fight for influence in the shaping of *evolving* and *multiple* regional political identities in a time of globalization.

Since 1994, a number of major developments have taken place in Bilbao and the Basque Country, and the chronological proximity of these events (at least if considered from a *long durée* perspective) leads us to think that there might be structural or causal factors at work in current transformations of the Basque city-region. The year 1994 marked first of all a turning point in Bilbao's two-decade-long economic decline, and the beginning of a period of remarkable prosperity for the city and the city-region that continues today. It was also during the nineties when Basque nationalist elites, represented by the PNV, began their slow but firm shift toward a political position clearly committed to achieving independence from Spain, thus distancing themselves from two decades of tacit acceptance of Spain's post-Franco democratic model and its quasi-federal territorial system, or

Estado de las Autonomías. Although the PNV has been a pro-independence political party since the beginning of its history in the late nineteenth century, it became clear toward the end of the 1990s that sovereignty (or *soberanismo*, as it has been called in a recent political plan by Basque President Ibarretxe) was moving to the forefront of the party's short-term political strategy.

Ibarretxe's plan attempts to modify the status of political relationships between the Basque Country and Spain by suggesting a new mode of Basque association with the Spanish state. This so-called *plan para la convivencia* (plan for living together) was first proposed in the fall of 2002, and triggered fierce criticism on the part of Spanish politicians and commentators. The plan was formally approved by a majority in the Basque Parliament in December 2004 and rejected in the Spanish parliament in February 2005. The plan proposes the possibility of free association of the Basque Country within the Spanish state. It is not, therefore, a plan for rupture with the State, but one that aims at the recognition of full Basque political identity and the development of the mechanisms to execute self-government within the context of global capitalism, including an additional set of powers that the regional government does not yet have. The plan's ideological underpinnings are to be found in so-called New Regionalism.[1] In fact, Basque President Juan José Ibarretxe has cited Edward Soja's presentation in Bilbao, and even Manuel Castells's ideas, to suggest that "we live in a regionalized world on multiple levels [in which] the centralized governments of traditional European states no longer have a monopoly on power and decision making. Rather, political power is shared among various levels and through interconnected networks" (Ibarretxe 2002, 6). Not surprisingly, Ibarretxe cited the Guggenheim project as one major and well-known example of the Basque outlook on global matters. By the end of 2005 it was clear that Ibarretxe's *plan para la convivencia* had been superseded by political events, in particular the results of Basque elections in the spring of 2005, which did not give Basque nationalists a mandate to continue with the plan.

State Developmentalism, Globalization, and Identity

In the globalization/sovereignty debate, it is crucial to question "postnational discourses" (Smith 2001). States continue to have a capacity to act independently in the face of globalization processes. Local, domestic politics matter to a degree, which reinforces the argument in favor of various levels of analysis. In fact, the Spanish case shows that states are not really "losing control" in the face of globalization processes. The evolving relationships between the Basque region and the Spanish state show the viability/reality of one of the most economically and politically independent regions in Europe (not to say the world)—although one with unmet sovereignty aspirations—within the context of a nation-state that, in recent years, has not reduced its international role (rather the opposite). Spain's expanded role in Latin America could not have happened without a clearly defined state policy of protecting national industrial champions during the 1980s, which inhibited mergers and acquisitions with foreign companies and made possible Spain's current world economic role. Contrary to Kenichi Ohmae's argument (1995), it is not always the case that regions grow because states shrink. The regional-national relationship is complicated and nuanced. It is not a zero-sum game, but a more complex articulation of forces at both the regional and the national levels—one that is not only economic but also political. In sum, states may gain global control even as regions gain it too (it depends on historical, political relationships between the region and the state), as has happened in a country such as Spain with great regional decentralization. Of course, in the Spanish case, the relationship between such strong state structures, regional and national, is not easy. But, because they have historical roots, such difficulties cannot be explained by exclusively focusing on the present day.

One could argue that the economic policies of Basque nationalism, specifically those of the PNV (in power in the Basque Country between 1980 and 2009), resemble those of a developmental state that "establishes as its principle of legitimacy its ability to promote and sustain development, understanding by development the combination of steady high rates of economic growth and structural change in the productive system, both domestically and in its relationship to the international economy" (Castells 1998, 270–1). A recent illustration of developmental states in the global economy focusing on the Irish case has been provided by O'Riain (2004). The Basque Country is a case of an "old" developmental state, manifested since the fifteenth century in the local growth machine (Logan and Molotch 1987) that sought the promotion of economic development and the retention of local commercial privileges due to the scarcity of food and agricultural resources. This commitment to economic development was reflected in the local laws of *fueros,* which had an important economic component. The priority of regional state action has always been for economic development, defined for policy purposes in terms of growth, productivity, and competitiveness (a recent example is the newly created Basque Institute of Competitiveness, sponsored by local universities and corporations, the Basque government and Harvard's Institute of Competitiveness). Business and politics are almost completely intertwined and political entrepreneurship is common in the Basque Country. This growth and competitiveness agenda is derived from comparisons with external reference economies that provide state actors with models for emulation. In the

Basque case, such external reference has often been Europe rather than Spain. In fact, Spain has often been the anti-reference—the model the Basques (Basque nationalists, to be more precise) had to separate from.

An additional reason explains the strength of regional state action in the Basque case. Because latecomers to the industrialization process, such as Bilbao, invariably face a different set of problems and possibilities than their technically more advanced predecessors, they must forge their own development institutions and ideologies. But equally, less developed regions and latecomers have hidden reserves of labor, savings, and entrepreneurship. Nations and regions wishing to overcome the penalties of late development also seem to require a strong state. The issue is less whether the state should or should not intervene, and more achieving something through intervention. Basque developmentalism addressed industrialization at the city-region level in close relationship with the needs of the nation-state. The economy was viewed strategically with the aim of building an industrial structure that would maximize Basque gains from international trade and export-led development. Fordist Bilbao was an era in which state regulations and nonmarket governance mechanisms were designed to restrain competition so as to concentrate resources in strategic industries and allow the region's industrial growth and its expansion into other areas of Spain.

Bilbao's relationship to the world economy is not driven exclusively by market efficiency, but also by a strategic concern to preserve regional autonomy through international trade networks and global economic power. The city's "global reach" resides in the powerful bureaucracies and political entrepreneurship of regional political policy organizations and ministries, in close connection with regional business elites and their companies. Although attracting foreign investment is a priority for the Basque government, facilitating the foreign trade and investments of Basque corporations is also a major regional economic policy priority. In addition, global political visibility may be yet another important factor shaping the region's involvement in the world economy.

"Project-based" Globalization and Sovereignty

Cities and regions feature their own "pathways to globalization," which consist of various economic and political strategies developed at the regional level to establish flows and transnational connections with the world economy, and of local developments to cope with changes triggered at the global level, together with structural and territorial adjustments to position the city in the context of world cities. The Guggenheim project is the latest of Bilbao's globalization efforts, a case of project-based globalization, and a prime pathway for Basque globalization *and* sovereignty. The motives of Basque political leaders in bringing the museum to Bilbao, after a negotiation process in which coincidences played an important role, were not shaped primarily by "cultural" concerns, but, instead, are better explained by two factors, one global and the other domestic: (i) recognition of the need for regional image change and urban regeneration in Bilbao under conditions of contemporary globalization—which in practice meant participating in a global venture for iconic architecture—and (ii) the long historical insistence on the part of the PNV leaders on political emancipation from Spain, reflected in this case in the realm of cultural politics. In this way, the Guggenheim project was not an isolated case of urban boosterism. Instead it is the latest and most successful example of how Basque leaders managed to bypass Madrid and conduct their own independent international affairs. The role of architecture in globalization has not been comprehensively studied until very recently.[2] As discussed elsewhere (del Cerro 2006), iconic, spectacular architecture—driven in this case by the ambitions of entrepreneurial politicians and cultural managers—plays a fundamental role in the worldwide deployment of contemporary globalization and the creation of large-scale social spaces because it has the power of rescaling the territorial significance (local into regional into national into global) of specific buildings and the cities where they are built.

The Guggenheim Museum has "put" Bilbao on the global map, to the benefit of the city and the Basque region, and has played an important role in the city's entrepreneurial strategies (González Ceballos 2003) and the possibility of thinking about a global transnational museum (Guasch and Zulaika 2005; Fraser 2005). It surely constitutes global Bilbao's best known and, for most people, the only example. In fact, the museum and its impact represent only the latest instance in Bilbao's globalizing process, though undoubtedly the most spectacular in terms of image. As shown elsewhere (del Cerro 2006), Bilbao has a global tradition many centuries old—the city having been founded as a node in trade flows between Castile and the world. The making of globalization in Bilbao owes as much to the city's urban and economic development in the context of evolving world markets as to the politics of local relationships with the Spanish state, the city's contribution to Spain's global expansion, and its persisting defense of local commercial and political rights and privileges in the face of the state's centralizing policies throughout history and up to the present time. This arrangement of forces shaping Bilbao's globalization in the past is also visible in the case of the Guggenheim Museum. With the Guggenheim project, the Basques sent the clear message that the region would link itself to global circuits without Spain's mediation. In this globalization episode there was an added element—the local recognition of a need for image-making through the construction of cultural artifacts, or "flagship projects"—a recognition that came late for Bilbao in the overall scheme of revitalization.

All in all, the discourse on cultural planning and revitalization became well known locally, thanks in part to the activities of consultants and writers on the topic who influenced policy decisions (especially Franco Bianchini—see Bianchini and Parkinson 1993), to the networking efforts of local officials worldwide, and to the recent experiences in image reconstruction of Spanish cities such as Barcelona (with the Summer Olympics), Seville (which hosted the World Fair) and Madrid (which was declared Cultural Capital of Europe) during 1992, the so-called "year of Spain" in the world. The Basques were conspicuously absent from the 1992 events, which symbolized the international presentation of "a new Spain" in opposition to which the Basque political elites wanted to develop a specific political agenda. From the viewpoint of revitalization, the Basques followed a model that had been applied elsewhere, although with not much success in economic terms. From a political stance, the Guggenheim represented the Basque Country's own 1992.

The Guggenheim project was, in fact, considered by Basques to be a regional project (negotiated by Basque government representatives, not by Bilbao's municipal authorities) and its development was due to many different circumstances: inter-city and inter-regional competition within Spain and the possibility of re-opening up the Basque Country to the world with a new image were crucial factors, as was the ruling PNV's regional vision of an increasingly independent Basque Country vis-à-vis Madrid, based on ethnic identity, political autonomy and financial independence. Local/regional politics also played a role—the ruling PNV's loss of hegemony in Guipúzcoa in the regional elections of 1986 and loss of control in the cities of Vitoria and San Sebastian rendered Bilbao "a matter of political urgency" (Juaristi 1997, 2). Although the economic impact of a flagship project such as the Guggenheim museum was not discussed at the time of the negotiations, the Basques were convinced they needed an icon that could change the image of the city and the region abroad.

The entire project was carried out by Guggenheim foundation director Thomas Krens as a global expansion project, and by the Basques as a foreign investment project. The Basques treated Krens as equivalent to the chair of a global corporation or as a head of state who had to be persuaded that investing in the Basque Country was a good opportunity (except that in this case all the investment would come from local, Basque money). The Basques saw themselves as representatives of a sovereign nation conducting international affairs. Coincidence of interests, and similar views about the type of project they were handling, greatly contributed to the final success and the signing of an agreement. Indeed, the Basque representatives (just like Krens himself) embodied the entrepreneurial type of politician/negotiator, rather than the administrative, bureaucratic type (there is a tradition of this overlapping between business and politics in the Basque Country). The negotiations took place between parties with a shared vision on how to conduct business, with a similar *Weltaanschaung* on business matters and with similar self-perceptions about the role each party was to play in the negotiations.

The Controversies

An indication that the Guggenheim project was an extremely controversial case of project-based globalization, and an equally contested effort by Basque political elites to reassert themselves and their region in the global realm and advance their sovereignty aspirations, is the heated debate that the museum brought about in the Basque Country and in Spain. One of Spain's most influential architectural critics, Luis Fernández-Galiano, wrote that

> as a franchise museum, the Guggenheim is an unusual cultural experiment, based on a terrible agreement, and for which the expected economic benefits are uncertain. That the most important Spanish effort in the arts should be an office of an American museum is simply grotesque; the agreement is so disadvantageous for the Basques that it can only be understood as an outcome of hasty and ignorant decisions. The benefits coming from investments and tourism depend so much on Basque political stability that they are uncertain. (Fernández-Galiano 1997, 3)

In fact, the Basque political and economic situation was not optimal to receive the new museum. When the model for the new Guggenheim was presented by Frank Gehry, Krens, and the Basque authorities at the Bilbao stock market, the attendees had to reach the building's entrance through a group of unemployed workers shouting: "Thieves! Fewer museums and more jobs!" (Zulaika 1997, 231)—a dramatic protest voiced by those left behind in the city's industrial crisis of the 1980s. In addition, a few days before the museum's inauguration, in October 1997, the Basque police uncovered a plot by ETA to blow up the building during the opening ceremony to be presided by King Juan Carlos of Spain. One member of the Basque police was shot dead after he suspected that a "group of municipal gardeners" (in fact, ETA activists) had hidden twelve anti-tank grenades within ornamental flowerpots next to the museum. The news circulated around the world.

Basque political instability could not be dispatched. The separatist group *Herri Batasuna,* considered the political arm of ETA and feared because of its influence in ETA's politically violent campaign, sent a letter to Krens's New York office in which the group conveyed their fierce opposition to the Guggenheim project, requesting that it be suspended until there was an open debate in Basque society about the terms of the agreement and the project's overall implications. The letter and the continuous news about killings and kidnappings coming from the Basque Country made the people at the Guggenheim in New York uncomfortable. Krens and his wife had to listen to continuous recommendations from friends not to go to the Basque Country in order to avoid the risk of being kidnapped or killed. The Basque government felt compelled to buy multi-page advertising space in *The Washington Post* and other American newspapers and journals such as the *Harvard Business Review* to promote the museum, highlight investment possibilities in the region based on local financial and industrial power and tax incentives, and stress the idea that ETA was not a real risk because its activity was very limited and the organization was close to its end (Tellitu et al. 1997, 61–64).

Also explosive was the diatribe around the *Guernica*, Picasso's famous 1937 painting that Guggenheim representatives and Basque authorities wanted to move from the Reina Sofia Museum in Madrid to Bilbao for the museum's inauguration. Xabier Arzalluz, the President of the PNV at the time, complained bitterly about Madrid's rejection of the proposal on technical grounds: ". . . for the Basques the bombs and for Madrid the art," he said (*El País* 1997, 26). Arzalluz's words were interpreted by most as an expression of the latent rationale that led Basques to want the Guggenheim in the first place—the creation of a Basque cultural icon that reinforced Basque emancipation from Spain in the cultural realm. To these ends, exhibiting a painting that so tragically portrayed one of the darkest episodes in Basque history in the new Basque state museum would have been a spectacular coup.

Among Basque artists, the most significant voice of protest was that of the late Jorge Oteiza, a Basque cultural icon, introducer of the avant-garde in the Basque Country in the 1950s and, together with Eduardo Chillida, the most world-recognized Basque artist today. Krens and Gehry wanted Oteiza to collaborate in the Guggenheim project, but he refused to donate his valuable legacy of works to the museum or to have them exhibited there. For Oteiza, the project represented the very negation of his life-long work of explaining to the Basques the discourse of art in the twentieth century. Oteiza wrote an open letter to the President of the Basque government, characterizing the project as ". . . authentic double-dealing, something worthy of Disney, totally anti-Basque, and which will cause great damage and paralyze all the cultural activities that could be produced in our country" (*El País* 1992, 24).

Many in the Basque Country saw the project as an unwarranted foreign intervention in Basque culture, the imposition of cultural flows from the core to the periphery (in other words, American cultural imperialism). To see globalization as synonymous with Americanization, as a one-way flow of cultural and financial influence and power, is somewhat one-sided (Berger and Huntington 2003). McNeill (1999) quotes Appadurai (1996) to highlight the fact that foreign cultures become "indigenized" in the process of globalization. In the Basque case, the appropriation of the Guggenheim project by the Basque nationalist elite to advance their own political agenda of cultural and political emancipation vis-à-vis the Spanish state was nonetheless a very clear and prominent aim. As discussed earlier, there was a local context prior to the Guggenheim project that helped the Basques rationalize the high cost and high risk of the museum: "The Guggenheim offered a Basque-controlled flagship which advertised Basque difference (and financial autonomy) to the world, yet which represented the Basque Country not as a primordial backwater but as a society at ease with global modernity" (McNeill 2000, 487). The Guggenheim project, therefore, needs to be understood within the framework of the post-Franco attempts by the regional nationalist elites to regain political and economic identity and sovereignty vis-à-vis the Spanish state. This is not only a quest of the past twenty years, but one of historic dimensions. The international arena has in many cases functioned as a ground for Basque re-identification. The key question is whether and how globalist strategies such as the museum project contribute to shifting the status quo of political identities and conflict in distinctive regions such as the Basque Country. We have tried to show that the interactions between shifts in sovereignty claims and the spatial transformations in Bilbao brought about by globalization have an effect in the development of political violence.

The March 2006 ETA Ceasefire and Prospects for Basque Sovereignty: Concluding Remarks

After three years without causing any death as a result of its terrorist activity, on 22 March 2006, ETA released to the Basque and Spanish public a declaration of "permanent ceasefire" that would become effective on 24 March. With this move, the "Basque socialist revolutionary organization for national liberation" (according to ETA's own definition), which had been fighting for independence and socialism in the Basque Country for over fifty years, killing over 800 people and wounding nearly 2,000, went beyond its own initiative to declare a (short) truce in 1998. According to ETA's 2006 declaration, the purpose of initiating a permanent

ceasefire was to give impetus to a "democratic process" in the Basque Country so
that "through dialogue, negotiation and agreement" the Basque people could re-
alize "the political change it needs." In the document, ETA's leadership notes that
"at the end of the process, Basque citizens must decide about their own future."
In an unprecedented and conciliatory language, ETA observes that "it is time
for compromise" and makes an appeal to authorities in Spain and France to "respond in a positive manner to this new situation," to "leave repression aside," and
to "show a will to negotiate." Finally, ETA reaffirms itself in its determination to
find a "truly democratic solution" and to continue, "until we achieve the rights of
the Basque people" (ETA 2006a, 1–2). On June 24, 2006, three months after the
ceasefire declaration, ETA addressed Spanish public opinion with a three-page
statement in which it discussed the political roots of the conflict, noted that a
new opportunity now existed to solve it, made an appeal to the Spanish government to "express its compromise of respect for whatever decision is made by the
Basque people about its own future," and invited the Spanish public to give support to the process (ETA 2006b, 2).

The reasons ETA had to declare a permanent ceasefire when it did are certainly complex, and are probably rooted in the organization's slow ideological
evolution, as well as in the changing political environment within and outside
Spain, especially after the Irish Republican Army (IRA) put an end to its violent fight for Northern Ireland and decided to negotiate with the British government. According to the former Belfast mayor, Alec Maskey, the Sinn Fein (IRA's
political arm) helped persuade ETA to initiate a new strategy of dialogue and negotiation with the Spanish government (*El País* 2006, 28). The so called "global
war on terror," initiated in the aftermath of 9/11 by President George W. Bush—
whose government included ETA in its list of international terrorist organizations after a request by conservative President Aznar of Spain—also contributed
to the narrowing of strategic options within ETA's reach. The 11 March 2004 Al
Qaeda terrorist attack in Madrid that caused nearly 200 deaths prompted ETA's
political arm, *Batasuna,* to publicly deny any ETA involvement after the conservative government in Madrid targeted the Basque organization as the author of
the carnage.

In addition, it is important to note that ETA's violent strategy never received
backing from a majority of the Basque population. In fact, electoral support for
Batasuna never reached twenty percent when this political group participated in
Basque elections. The two self-declared objectives of ETA's political fight against
the Spanish state (independence and socialism) are supported by approximately
twenty-five to thirty-two percent of Basque citizens in the case of independence,

and probably less in the case of socialism, according to numerous polls. Compounding this situation of minority, albeit extremely loyal, support among the Basque population, ETA's strategy had to face increasingly effective actions by Spanish and French police. In fact, ETA's actions have been decreasing since the early 1990s, whereas the number of ETA militants that have been captured and imprisoned continued to grow over the past two decades and reached approximately 500 individuals in 2006.

After confirming the veracity of ETA's ceasefire, the Spanish socialist president, José Luis Rodríguez Zapatero, drafted an institutional declaration made public on 28 June 2006, to announce the beginning of a dialogue with ETA. The government's statement acknowledges that previous governments (the socialist government of Felipe González in the 1980s and the conservative government of José María Aznar in the 1990s) had already attempted to initiate a dialogue with ETA with no success, proclaims that "the Spanish democracy will not pay any political price for peace," and claims that the government approaches the negotiation process "with determination and caution, with unity and loyalty, and always respecting the memory of ETA's victims" (El País 2006, 18). Zapatero continues by declaring that "the Spanish government will respect the decisions that the Basque people freely adopt, being respectful to legal norms and processes, in the absence of all kinds of violence" (El País 2006, 18). The conservative opposition party, Partido Popular (PP), was the only political group in the Spanish Parliament against such negotiations, and numerous polls show that the Spanish public opinion remained almost evenly divided about this issue, whereas the majority Basque public opinion had been in favor of this process for the past few years (see table 4.5). At the beginning of July 2006, the Basque Socialist Party, a semi-autonomous branch of the Spanish socialists, met with representatives of Batasuna (ETA's political arm), with the declared purpose to encourage them to respect the democratic rules and become a legal political group. In spite of heightened expectations, by the fall of 2006 the peace process came to an end after ETA killed two immigrant workers in a terrorist attack on one of the terminals of the Madrid airport.

The outcome of the process initiated in 2006 (with the ceasefire declaration and the decision of the Spanish government to initiate a dialogue with ETA) was a severe blow to the many who had hoped for a negotiated resolution to the Basque problem. The dialogue between the government and ETA contributed to assess the separatist organization's ideological and strategic flexibility, and tested the government's ability to persuade Spanish opinion that the controversial path taken was the correct one. If the negotiation process had been at least moderately successful, one could have expected an "honorable" dissolution of ETA and improvements to the situation of imprisoned ETA militants. In exchange for a lasting peace, the government might have been willing to make some political concessions, although the official government rhetoric denies it. In any case, peace in the Basque Country would not imply the end of Basque political emancipation claims. On the contrary, the end of ETA, if and when it happens, would bring about a renewed interest on the part of Basque nationalists in pursuing a politically independent future. In any case, if political violence comes to an end and then a referendum on independence takes place—a desirable development in its own right—it is far from certain (according to almost all pollsters) that a majority of the Basque Country's population would actually support the nationalist goals of political emancipation from Spain.

The interplay and the shifting of focus between geopolitical scales, together with major changes in the built environment, can transform the nature of competing sovereignties, as my analysis of the evolving strategies of confrontation between Basque nationalism (focusing on the city of Bilbao) and the Spanish state has shown. In the Bilbao case, the conflict unfolds at various spatial scales showing temporal variability. In fact, relatively new spatial scales (i.e. the global) are utilized by some groups as valid arenas where the struggle around Basque identity and sovereignty can be re-enacted. It is evident that, due to long historical reasons explained in the paper, the regional–national confrontation frames much of that struggle, but one cannot forget the divisions within the region itself, at the city and provincial levels—for these are not always perfectly nested within the regional–national cleavage. Finally, one must note that supranational regions such as the European Union (and not just "the global") have become spaces for political representation of subnational governments such as the Basque government. The PNV, which has controlled the Basque government for the past twenty-five years, uses each opportunity it has in Europe to advance its sovereignty claims and reminds everyone that the only subnational government in Europe with exclusive powers to levy its own taxes should have an independent voice in European affairs. In addition, the Basque nationalist left is well aware that the conflict has added this international dimension, and that the position of international and foreign actors on the legitimacy of political violence has become crucial to advancing their aims. In sum, the issue of scale as it concerns Basque identity and sovereignty encompasses various levels, is overtly political, and shows variations over time. Rather than considering spatial scales as reified units of analysis, the Bilbao case shows that scaling is an ongoing process marked by contestation and uncertainty, which naturally increases the levels of complexity of the political conflict and makes its potential resolution much more challenging.

Table 4.5. Opinion Trends in the Basque Country (2003 and 2005)
(From Sociómetro del Gobierno Vasco, October 2003 and October 2005)
N = 2,848 (2003)
N = 2,879 (2005)

---

1. *Do you think the Basque Country has the right to decide about its future freely and democratically? (2005)*

   Yes 75%
   No 25%

2. *Independence*

   In favor 28% (2003), 27% (2005)
   Opposed 34% (2003), 32% (2005)
   Depending on the circumstances 23% (2003), 31% (2005)
   By province (2003):
   Vizcaya—26% in favor, 35% opposed
   Alava—19% in favor, 45% opposed
   Guipúzcoa—35% in favor, 28% opposed

3. *What would be your vote in a hypothetical referendum on independence? (2003)*

   In favor 37%
   Against 31%
   Would not vote 13%
   Not decided 18%

4. *Dialogue between ETA and the Spanish government (2005)*

   In favor even if there is not an ETA truce 31%
   In favor only after an ETA truce 12%
   In favor only after ETA definitively abandons violence 38%
   Opposed 12%

Political cleavages in the Basque Country around issues of identity and sovereignty exhibit an important regional–national axis, but inter-urban, intra-urban and interprovincial differences are also significant, and their relevance plays itself against the backdrop of a multilevel scale of evolving political and socioeconomic events. While the Basque Country can be seen as a polynucleated and relatively compact city-region, there are three urban centers (Bilbao, San Sebastián, and Vitoria) that concentrate population and jobs. In each of these three centers, the articulation of sociopolitical forces, albeit sometimes obeying regional trends, shows specific characteristics that are a result of the nature and evolution of urban histories. Just to mention the case of Bilbao (the economic capital of the Basque Country and the birthplace not only of Basque nationalism as a political movement but also of both the Spanish Socialist Party and the Spanish Communist Party): the articulation of three main political identities (Basque nationalism, Spanish right, and Spanish left) during the early twentieth century had an undeniable impact on the evolution of political conflicts around issues of identity and an impact on the configuration of such conflicts in the other two cities of the Basque region. In the electoral process, Bilbao (where fifty percent of the Basque population lives) becomes a matter of political urgency for both nationalist and non-nationalist forces because it is the city where local and regional political leaders focus their efforts in the game of economic internationalization, global visibility, conflict reduction, and ethnic/political identity.

The complex of identities and networks of sovereignty that lead to urban and regional violence cannot be understood solely from a local perspective but rather as embedded in a multiscalar context of allegiances and competing sovereignties. In doing so, we have laid out the multiple consequences of the complex and multilayered globalization process—and the reemergence of subnational and transnational tensions it is causing—upon "the spatialities of nationalism" and the prospects for Basque sovereignty in the twenty-first century. As this book argues, there is a causal relationship between the structural and territorial basis of nationalist struggles for sovereignty and the ongoing transformation of nation-states and urban regions under conditions of contemporary globalization. If our hypothesis and analysis are not fundamentally flawed, the shift in the configuration of the networks of sovereignty and the political opportunity structures that have sustained Basque political violence for over forty years may be experiencing a qualitative transformation at the outset of the twenty-first century.

Notes

1. See, inter alia, Aldecoa and Keating 1999; Amin and Thrift 1994; Amin 2002, 2004; Amin and Thrift 1992; Barnes and Ledebour 1998; Benz and Furst 2002; Bergman and Todtling 1991; Charlie 2000; Evans and Harding 1997; Gren 1999; Harvie 1994; Keating and Hughes 2003; Keating 2001; Keating 1998; Keating and Loughlin 1997; LeGales and Lequesne 1998; MacLeod 2001; Markusen 1999; Marston, Knox, and Liverman 2002; Martin 2001; Martin, Sunley, and Turner 2002; Simmonds and Hack 2000; Storper 1997.

2. See Ibelings 1998; Satler 1999; Tzonis 2001; Krause and Petro 2003; King 2004; Umbach 2005; Saunders 2005; Easterling 2005; Knox and Taylor 2005; McNeill 2005; Sklair 2005; 2006.

Works Cited

Aldecoa, F., and M. Keating, eds. 1999. *Paradiplomacy in Action: The International Relations of Subnational Governments*. London: Frank Cass.

Amin, A. 2002. "Spatialities of Globalization." *Environment and Planning A* 34, no. 3: 385–99.

———. 2004. "Regulating Economic Globalization." *Transactions of the Institute of British Geographers* 29, no. 2: 217–233.

Amin, A., and N. Thrift. 1992. "Neo-Marshallian Nodes in Global Networks." *International Journal of Urban and Regional Research* 16, no. 4: 571–87.

Amin, A., and N. Thrift, eds. 1994. *Globalization, Institutions and Regional Development in Europe*. New York: Oxford University Press.

Appadurai, A. 1996. "Disjuncture and Difference in the Global Economy." *Public Culture* 2, no. 2: 1–24.

Azúa, J. 2005. "Guggenheim Bilbao: 'Coopetitive' Strategies for the New Culture-Economy Spaces." In *Learning from the Bilbao Guggenheim*, ed. A. M. Guasch and J. Zulaika. Reno: Center for Basque Studies, University of Nevada Press.

Barnes, W. R., and L. C. Ledebour. 1998. *The New Regional Economies*. Thousand Oaks, Calif.: Sage.

Basque Government Sociómetro, October 1981.

Beltza, J. 1976. *Nacionalismo y clases sociales*. Bilbao, Spain: Nerea.

Benz, A., and D. Furst. 2002. "Policy Learning in Regional Networks." *European Urban and Regional Studies* 9, no. 1: 21–35.

Berger, P. L., and S. Huntington, eds. 2003. *Many Globalizations: Cultural Diversity in the Contemporary World*. New York: Oxford University Press.

Bergman, E., G. Maier, and F. Todtling, eds. 1991. *Regions Reconsidered: Economic Networks, Innovation and Local Development in Industrialized Countries*. London: Mansell.

Bianchini, F., and M. Parkinson. 1993. *Cultural Policy and Urban Regeneration: The West European Experience*. Manchester, U.K.: Manchester University Press.

Calvo Serraller, F. 1997. "Column on the Guggenheim." *El País,* October 17: 25.

Castells, M. 1998. *End of Millennium*. London: Blackwell.

Charlie, J. 2000. "Sub-national Mobilization and European Integration." *Journal of Common Market Studies* 38, no. 1: 1–24.

Clark, R. P. 1984. *The Basque Insurgents. ETA 1952–1980*. Madison: University of Wisconsin Press.

Corcuera, J. 1979. *Orígenes, ideología y organización del nacionalismo vasco (1876–1904)*. Madrid: Siglo Veintiuno de España.

del Cerro Santamaría, G. 2006. *Bilbao: Basque Pathways to Globalization*. London: Elsevier.

Díez Medrano, J. 1995. *Divided Nations*. Ithaca, N.Y.: Cornell University Press.

Douglass, W., and J. Bilbao. 2005. *Amerikanuak: Basques in the New World*. Reno: University of Nevada Press.

Easterling, K. 2005. *Enduring Innocence: Global Architecture and Its Political Masquerades.* Boston, Mass.: MIT Press.

El País. 2006. "El Sinn Fein animó a ETA a que declarara el alto el fuego." March 29: 14.

ETA. 2006a. Declaración de alto el fuego permanente (Declaration of permanent cease-fire). March 22.

————. 2006b. Comunicado de Euskadi ta Askatasuna a la opinión pública española (Declaration of ETA to the Spanish public opinion). June 24.

Evans, P., and A. Harding. 1997. "Regionalization, regional institutions and economic development." *Policy and Politics* 25, no. 1: 19–30.

Fernández-Galiano, L. 1997. "Un pulpo de acero: Guggenheim Bilbao: el arte de la negociación." *Arquitectura viva* 24: 13–17.

Fraser, A. 2005. "Isn't This a Wonderful Place?" In *Learning from the Bilbao Guggenheim,* ed. A. M. Guasch and J. Zulaika. Reno: Center for Basque Studies, University of Nevada Press.

Fusi Aizpurúa, J. P. 1984. *El País Vasco. Pluralismo y nacionalidad.* Madrid: Alianza Editorial.

González Ceballos, S. 2003. "The Role of the Guggenheim Museum in the Development of Urban Entrepreneurial Practices in Bilbao." *International Journal of Iberian Studies* 16, no. 3: 177–186.

Gren, J. 1999. *The New Regionalism in the European Union.* London: SIR.

Guasch, A. M., and J. Zulaika, eds. 2005. *Learning from the Bilbao Guggenheim.* Reno: Center for Basque Studies, University of Nevada Press.

Harvie, C. 1994. *The Rise of Regional Europe.* London: Routledge.

Ibarra. 1987. *La Evolución estratégica de ETA.* Pamplona, Spain: Txalaparta.

Ibarretxe, J. J. 2002. Presentación en la London School of Economics and Political Science.

Ibelings, H. 1998. *Supermodernism: Architecture in the Age of Globalization.* Rotterdam: Netherlands Architecture Institute.

Jáuregui Bereciartu, G. 1999. "Basque Nationalism at a Crossroads." In *Basque Politics and Nationalism on the Eve of the Millennium,* ed. W. Douglass, C. Urza, L. White, and J. Zulaika, 44–54. Reno: University of Nevada Press.

————. 1981. *Ideología y estrategia política de ETA: Análisis de su evolución entre 1959 y 1968.* Madrid: Siglo Veintiuno.

Juaristi, J. 1997. "Bilbao: la metamorfosis de una ciudad." *El País Semanal* 1,079: 26–36.

————. 2006. Entrevista a ETA, GARA, April.

Keating, M. 1998. *The New Regionalism in Western Europe: Territorial Restructuring and Political Change.* London: Edward Elgar.

————. 2001. "Rethinking the Region: Culture, Institutions and Economic Development in Catalonia and Galicia." *European Urban and Regional Studies* 8, no. 3: 217–234.

Keating, M., and J. Hughes. 2003. *The Regional Challenge in Central and Eastern Europe: Territorial Restructuring and European Integration.* Brussels: College of Europe Publishers.

Keating, M., and J. Loughlin, eds. 1997. *The Political Economy of Regionalism.* London: Frank Cass.

King, A. D. 2004. *Spaces of Global Cultures: Architecture, Urbanism, Identity.* London: Routledge.

Knox, P. L., and P. J. Taylor. 2005. "Toward a Geography of the Globalization of Architecture Office Networks." *Journal of Architectural Education* 58, no. 3: 23–32.

Krause, L., and P. Petro, eds. 2003. *Global Cities: Cinema, Architecture, and Urbanism in a Digital Age.* Rutgers, N.J.: Rutgers University Press.

LeGales, P., and C. Lequesne, eds. 1998. *Regions in Europe.* London: Routledge.

Logan, J., and H. Molotch. 1987. *Urban Fortunes: The Political Economy of Place.* Berkeley: University of California Press.

MacLeod, G. 2001. "New Regionalism Reconsidered: Globalization and the Remaking of Political Economic Space." *International Journal of Urban and Regional Research* 25, no. 4: 804–829.

Maravall, J. M. 1982. *The Transition to Democracy in Spain.* London: Croom Helm.

Markusen, A. 1999. "Fuzzy Concepts, Scanty Evidence, Policy Distance: The Case for Rigor and Policy Relevance in Critical Regional Studies." *Regional Studies* 33, no. 9: 869–84.

Marston, S. A., P. L. Knox, and D. M. Liverman. 2002. *World Regions in Global Context: People, Places and Environments.* Saddle River, N.J.: Prentice Hall.

Martin, R. 2001. "EMU versus the Regions? Regional Convergence and Divergence in Euroland." *Journal of Economic Geography* 1: 51–80.

Martin, R., P. Sunley, and D. Turner. 2002. "Taking Risks in Regions: The Geographical Anatomy of Europe's Emerging Venture Capital Market." *Journal of Economic Geography* 2: 121–150.

McNeill, D. 1999. "Globalization and the European City." *Cities* 16, no. 3: 143–147.

———. 2005. "In Search of the Global Architect: The Case of Norman Foster (and Partners)." *International Journal of Urban and Regional Research* 29, no. 3: 501–15.

Mesa Nacional de Batasuna. 2005. Carta abierta a José Luis Rodríguez Zapatero (Open letter to José Luis Rodríguez Zapatero, President of the Spanish government). January 14.

Montero, M. 1996. La transición y la autonomía vasca. In *La transición en el País Vasco y España,* ed. J. Ugarte, 93–121. Bilbao, Spain: Universidad del País Vasco.

———. 1998. *Historia del País Vasco. De los orígenes a nuestros días.* San Sebastián, Spain: Txertoa

Moya, C. 1975. *El poder económico en España (1939–1970). Un análisis sociológico.* Madrid: Tucar.

Ohmae, K. 1995. *The End of the Nation-State: The Rise of Regional Economies.* London: Harper Collins.

O'Riain, S. 2004. *The Politics of High-Tech Growth: Developmental States in the Global Economy.* New York: Cambridge University Press.

Pérez-Agote, A. 1982. "Problemas de legitimación del Estado franquista en el País Vasco." In *Estudios de historia contemporánea del País Vasco,* ed. J. C. Jiménez de Aberasturi, 279–303. San Sebastián, Spain: Haranburu.

Pérez Pérez, J. A. 1999. "La transformación del mundo laboral en el área industrial del Gran Bilbao, 1958–1977. Trabajadores, convenios y conflictos." Ph.D. diss., Universidad del País Vasco.

Satler, G. 1999. "The Architecture of Frank Lloyd Wright: A Global View." *Journal of Architectural Education* 53, no. 1: 15–24.

Saunders, W. 2005. *Commodification and Spectacle in Architecture: A Harvard Design Magazine Reader.* Cambridge, Mass.: Harvard University Press.

Simmonds, R., and G. Hack. 2000. *Global City Regions: Their Emerging Forms.* London: Carfax.

Sklair, L. 2005. "The Transnational Capitalist Class and Contemporary Architecture in Globalizing Cities." *International Journal of Urban and Regional Research* 29, no. 3: 485–500.

———. 2006. "Iconic Architecture and Capitalist Globalization." *City: Analysis of Urban Trends, Culture, Theory, Policy, Action* 10, no. 1: 21–47.

Smith, M. P. 2001. *Transnational Urbanism: Locating Globalization.* Malden, Mass.: Blackwell.

Storper, M. 1997. *The Regional World: Territorial Development in a Global Economy.* New York: Guildford.

Tellitu, A., I. Esteban, and J. A. González Carrera. 1977. *El Milagro Guggenheim: Una ilusión de alto riesgo.* Bilbao, Spain: Diario El Correo.

Totoricaguena, G. P. 2004. *Identity, Culture, and Politics in the Basque Diaspora.* Reno: University of Nevada Press.

Tzonis, A., L. Lefraivre, and B. Stagno. 2001. *Tropical Architecture: Critical Regionalism in the Age of Globalization.* New York: Academy Press.

Ugalde, A. 1997. "La contribución del Gobierno Vasco a la acción de la República Española ante Naciones Unidas en 1945–46." In *La política exterior de España en el siglo XX,* ed. J. Tusell. Madrid: Universidad Nacional de Educación a Distancia (UNED).

———. 1999. "The International Relations of Basque Nationalism and the First Basque Autonomous Government (1890–1939)." In *Paradiplomacy in Action: The Foreign Relations of Subnational Governments,* ed. F. Aldecoa and M. Keating. London: Frank Cass.

Umbach, M., and B. R. Huppauf, eds. 2005. *Vernacular Modernism: Heimat, Globalization and the Built Environment.* Stanford, Calif.: Stanford University Press.

Ziakzadeh, C. E. 1991. *A Rebellious People: Basques, Protests, and Politics.* Reno: University of Nevada Press.

Zulaika, J. 1997. *Crónica de una seducción.* Madrid: Nerea.

5

Contesting the Legitimacy of Urban Restructuring and Highways in Beirut's Irregular Settlements

Agnès Deboulet and Mona Fawaz

The struggle between the state and particular social groups seeking recognition or independence is generally depicted in the context of direct and sometimes violent conflicts such as guerrilla warfare, terrorist attacks, or the coercive state occupation of strategic spatial locations. However, open conflicts are only a part of how politics of identity are manifested, and it is possible to investigate how these politics penetrate the context of everyday urban life, such as in processes of spatial or service acquisition. There, struggles are sometimes conducted in open confrontations that translate well defined and pre-established group strategies (Tarrow 1998; Touraine 1973), and are, at other times, fought indirectly through silent ruse and subterfuge, within quotidian practices of everyday life (Scott 1985; de Certeau 1990) or what Bayat (1997) called (in the case of Tehran) the "silent encroachment of the poor." Struggles between nation states and contestant communities are also conducted in the course of everyday urban governance, notably during the planning and execution of urban development projects. These projects are indeed often the physical embodiment of the visions that dominant groups seek to perpetuate about what the city should look like, who should be included among its dwellers, and who should be entitled to participate in its making (Holston 1999; Yiftachel 1998). Over the past decades, these dominant groups have been comforted in their positions by international practices that exacerbate exclusive urban policies (Onçu and Weyland 1997). Conversely, such urban development projects also create opportunities for dwellers to contest these dominant visions and carve out their own space in the city. Thus, they could be interpreted and explored as new modes of regulation or elementary forms of socialization (Simmel 1950), rather than simple manifestations of crisis.

In this paper, we investigate how local, national, and international claims over space are formulated in the context of urban development projects. We look at

how institutional actors, political parties, and various social groups read and position themselves vis-à-vis the execution of highway segments through dense
urban neighborhoods, and how they attempt to impose their view or negotiate
their place in a context where individuals are often subsumed to communal, religious, and sectarian identities. In addition, we explore how political parties and
central state agencies and actors oppose and redefine urban legitimacies through
planning interventions.

Two main directions guide our inquiry. The first seeks to investigate how identities and political expressions are rearticulated in the course of a major global/
local event such as the politics of reconstruction and highways, looking particularly at emerging forms of hegemony and contradictions between identity,
territory, and financial interests, while exploring the complex interplay between
local actors, such as sectarian political parties and low-income urban dwellers,
in preserving autonomy and control in the midst of theses changes. The second
looks at how the displacements triggered by these projects are translated into
major risks that threaten city dwellers with severe concerns (Cernea 1998; Navez-
Bouchanine 2004).

With this strategy, we will bridge some of the gaps between two approaches to
investigating the social impacts of highway developments. The first stems out of
traditional political-economy approaches that (at least since the 1970s) acknowledge that decisions about highway locations are made in the political arena, based
on the organizational capabilities of public and governmental groups who negotiate the additional value of transport service provided by the road in relation to
other externalities, such as the environmental effects of the highway, whether
local or regional (Wheeler 1976). In these investigations, the resistance launched
against highways in developed countries is depicted as the reflection of conflicting political agendas and value systems (Logan and Molotch 1987; Wheeler
1976); differing class practices and interests (highways going through low-income
neighborhoods); conflicting local community and government visions of the city
(McCreery 2000); or competing private benefits between, for example, different
transport sectors (such as the Roads Union in France, see Dunn 1995). The second
approach stems out of socioanthropological views of identity and cultural redefi-
nitions (Abrams and Waldren 1998) that see in development projects a moment
of important destabilization of the community and a reformulation of communal
identities (Gans 1962). Building on the contributions of these two approaches, we
also pay special attention to the capabilities of "ordinary" city dwellers (Giddens
1987) or their competences (Berry-Chikhaoui and A. Deboulet 2001) to perform,
act, and express themselves in the public sphere (Joseph 1998). This is especially
important when these practices are inscribed in the weak democratic structures

of lower-income countries, where channels of participation are frequently dysfunctional and independent signs of community participation are generally negatively perceived by political actors (whether public agencies or political parties).

Our hypothesis is that, by contesting technical or professional definitions of how territories should evolve, and through a sequence of multiple and not necessarily coordinated interventions on urban projects, city-dwellers contribute, in a nonlinear way, to redefining legitimacies and sometimes sovereignties. In the context of postwar Beirut, where our case studies were conducted, we argue that urban development projects, most notably highways designed to intersect low-income dense residential neighborhoods, generate a space in which sectarian religious identities and relative entitlements to the city are negotiated and strengthened. Such negotiations, we will show, are heavily influenced by identity politics because dwellers learn about, interpret, and position themselves vis-à-vis these projects on the basis of pre-established frameworks embedded in their social, religious, and political environment and histories. Furthermore, we argue that the community's identity and, more specifically, its sectarian (religious) allegiances are formed and changed during the interactions with the national state, as low-income urban dwellers seek to access urban services, face development projects, and secure their claims to dwelling in the city. Hence, ethnic or religious group identification doesn't necessarily precede the formation of the nation-state, nor do contestant groups oppose a priori the nationalist project. In these cases, the identifications and claims are *solidified* by public policy.

The rest of the chapter is divided into seven sections. After a brief methodological overview describing the research approach and a section placing the implementation of these projects in their regional context, the paper is divided into five sections that examine how dwellers learn about, interpret, and negotiate the highway; how public decisions are taken in this context; and how these decisions are consolidated from the perspective of dwellers. The paper concludes with a reflection on the intersections between, on the one hand, local and international claims on the city and, on the other, development projects and identity politics. These conclusions are then projected on a brief analysis of the post–July 2006 war reconstruction project in the southern suburbs of Beirut to show the continuity of these dynamics in other urban projects.

Methodology

Our investigation of the social context in highway developments within large Middle Eastern capital cities emerged from previous research conducted in Cairo, Beirut, Tehran, and Casablanca (Deboulet and Fawaz 2004). It was triggered by a recognition of the speed at which urban landscapes are being transformed by the continuous construction of highways, overpasses, bypasses, and other rapid throughways that strongly affect the ways in which the city is read, lived, and practiced. While our findings concurred with others that showed the highway as a tool to distort space in favor of higher-income social groups (Henderson 2006; Harvey 1975; Urry 2004), we also found it to be the instance of more complex social and spatial transformations. We saw in the conception and implementation of highways and, more generally, road systems, a permanent—and unrecognized—laboratory of social and spatial changes in developing cities, one that is poorly investigated although it transforms the social and built space faster than any other type of urban intervention or policy.

The paradoxical impact of these technical productions on the city is that while their development profoundly alters sociospatial equilibriums and local economies, it also generates the outside "community threat" which sociologists of social movements often identify as a trigger to the mobilization of threatened dwellers in the form of "defended neighborhoods" (Gans 1962). In Cairo, for example, dwellers in several low-income neighborhoods mobilized against the execution of overpasses near their homes in a form and on a scale unequaled by any other kind of social mobilization in this city. In Cairo, for example, dwellers in several low-income neighborhoods mobilized against the execution of overpasses near their homes, and did so in a form and at a scale unparalleled by any other kind of social mobilization in the city.[1] We observed that a social mobilization to resist the development of overpasses near low-income neighborhoods had a form and scale unequaled by any other kind of social mobilization in this city. In this process, the highway appears for those "affected individuals" (if we adopt the World Bank terminology) to release claims of citizenship.

In investigating these issues, the case of Lebanon is interesting in more than one way. First, Beirut is a metropolis that relies almost exclusively on roads for individual transportation since collective buses amount to only sixteen percent of daily commutes (Huybrechts and Verdeil 2000). As a result, an innumerable number of highway and high-speed roads have been built in and around the city since the end of the Lebanese civil war in 1990. Second, to our knowledge, Beirut is the only place in the Arab World where a highway project has been halted by popular mobilization (political parties, populations, and important figures). This provides an interesting case in this region where—and contrary to the appearance of pervasive authoritarian decision-making processes—negotiations occupy a central place in the execution of public projects and enable dwellers to activate their capacities and know-how in the making of the city. Third, there is the central role played by political parties during the execution of public projects: in articulating, acquiring, and diffusing information; in developing claims; and in negotiating on behalf of dwellers, as was particularly observed in the displacement of squatters to make way for development projects during the postwar era.[2] Finally, we should point out that the Lebanese political context creates an environment where mobilizations are necessarily channeled through sectarian lines, even if these do not automatically go through established political parties. This condition makes the investigation of identity (sectarian) issues particularly relevant. Indeed, Lebanon's political system is based on the religious sectarian notion of citizenship affiliation, whereby citizens are registered in one of seventeen acknowledged institutions of "personal affairs" (*al-ahwal al-shakhsiyya*) directly managed by the seventeen nationally recognized religious institutions. Thus, marriages, births, obituaries, and all other civil transactions are recorded in religious registries. Sectarian affiliations are also translated in political representation since a system of quotas defines public posts for specific sects. This system was already present in the 1943 National Pact established shortly after the Lebanese Independence and upheld with a different balance of power in the 1989 Taʾif Agreements that marked the end of the Lebanese civil war (1975–1990) (Bahout 1994). It is worth pointing out that this sectarian system has privileged certain sects over others, and that within these balances of power the Shiʿite communities were historically considered as underrepresented (Norton 1987; Fawaz and Harb 2001) even though today this balance has been corrected.

In order to examine the interplay of these forces, we selected three contrasting case studies that document the execution of highway segments intersecting densely inhabited low income neighborhoods located in Lebanon's capital city, Beirut, which is home to an estimated 1.3 million dwellers (UN-ESCWA 2000). The three cases are located in popular suburbs where they have either displaced or threatened to displace hundreds of households. All three neighborhoods emerged as small nuclei during the 1960s and rapidly grew during the civil war years (1975–1990) to their current scales: Hayy el Sellom is the largest informal settlement of Beirut and includes an estimated 100,000 inhabitants; Jnāh and Ouzāʿi are estimated to house respectively 16,000 and 20,000 inhabitants.[3] All three neighborhoods are in violation of one or several urban or property regulations: two (Jnāh and Ouzāʿi) are squatter settlements where access to property and constructions is illegal, while the third (Hayy el Sellom) was built following the rules of property rights, but in violation of urban and building regulations. The three cases also present different scenarios with respect to the execution of the highway: the first highway section (in Jnāh) was completed in the 1990s, the second one (in

Ouzāʿī) has been blocked by local mobilization since the mid 1990s, and the third section (Hayy el Sellom), the only highway segment seen in a positive light by the neighborhood population, remains at the stage of planning.

Data Collection

Our study is based on a long-term research project that was initiated in 2002.[4] Between 2002 and 2004, we conducted about 100 open-ended interviews with dwellers, local and national decision makers, and stakeholders such as members of political parties, private consulting offices entrusted with the design of highways, and public sector officials who commissioned or participated in the project (i.e. municipalities, Council for Development and Reconstruction, public planning agencies, ministries). A semi-structured questionnaire was prepared for public sector agents in order to understand how these actors formulated the highway plans, and then how they developed and altered them as pressures arose from within and outside the context of the neighborhoods we opted to investigate. This approach inscribed our findings in the wider context of urban policymaking in Beirut.

In our data collection, we relied on residents' responses on open-ended, semi-structured interviews that inquired into the ways they learn about, form opinions of, and negotiate highway trajectories in the absence of formal democratic structures of urban governance that could inform them of such developments or ensure the accountability of their public representatives. In the neighborhood context, where tenure is insecure and severely threatened by highway projects and real estate pressures, and given the presence and strong control of political parties, our ability to conduct fieldwork depended on building trust and familiarity with a number of dwellers who enabled us to play the "insiders' card." In Hayy el Sellom, where one of the authors had conducted her Ph.D. dissertation research, this was possible because of the familiarity of the researcher with the site. In Jnāh, this was made possible because the researchers established a good relationship with a limited number of families and actors who introduced them in the neighborhood and allowed them to partake in its daily activities (including visits, family reunions, and other events) over a period of two months. In Ouzāʿī, however, the presence of researchers was more occasional and discrete. In all three cases, the choice of interviewees among dwellers was made incrementally, as fieldwork progressed, with a mix of preselected and targeted respondents, successive corrections, and "swarming," a technique directed by our preference for a "natural" immersion and observations that can overcome the early mistrust demonstrated by various actors during the first stages of fieldwork.

Archival work (mostly using newspaper records) was also conducted in order to corroborate dates and verify information.[5] We were also able to consult a few public documents describing the execution of the projects, such as feasibility studies, but access to documentation was considered "sensitive" and generally restricted.

Relation between Projects and Territories in Metropolitan Beirut

Reconstruction, Urban Restructuring, and the Politics of Mobility

Since the end of the Lebanese civil war (1975–1990), Lebanon has engaged in a large scale postwar reconstruction process that seeks to reclaim the country's regional role as a service and tourist center and to position the Lebanese capital city on the chessboard of international cities (Kassab 1997). These visions have helped define a new body-politic for the city, one that favors interests aligned with global capital. Their physical materialization in Beirut has notably occurred with the implementation of a network of highways, expressways, and flyovers designed to facilitate high-speed circulation to and from the city and hence increase mobility for those who can use this network (Kaufmann 2005). Highways are perceived as complementary to other large-scale investments, such as the newly rebuilt international airport, the development of downtown Beirut into a high-end business center with leisure and residential facilities targeting rich expatriates and Arab tourists, as well as other exclusive resorts and commercial centers. In all these project choices, however, it is clear that the so-called national or public interests are subsumed to international ambitions and global pressures, as well as foreign expertise and sources of funding.[6]

But if the postwar reconstruction of the 1990s created the fertile ground for the implementation of these highways, the projects themselves are not new. In fact, highway infrastructure has historically benefited from a central position in Lebanese urban planning, where since independence (1943) it has constituted the most executed type of public project. This is clearly reflected in the successive master plans for the city of Beirut,[7] which systematically allocated a central position to highway networks designed to facilitate vehicular circulation by cutting through the city's busy neighborhoods. This is because professionals and lay people alike perceive the highway as the emblem of modernity and progress within a framework that conceptualizes the city in terms of networks where motorized connections are of paramount importance (Urry 2005). In doing so, they are not far from the normative aspirations of the planners of the early modern era such as Howard, Le Corbusier, or Wright—whose *Good Cities* inevitably included a central space for highways (Graham 2000; McCreery 1996). However, while this vision has been widely contested in the West, it continues to dominate the reflections of actors in Lebanon until today. Even those who condemn the social consequences of these roads, such as members of the Hezbollah political party and others, still see in them a modality of improving circulation in the city. Hence, highways are unquestioned as an engine of development while public transportation and other alternatives are rarely considered. Perhaps the most eloquent materialization of this ideology is the discourse that has surrounded the reconstruction of the neighborhoods of the southern suburbs of Beirut that were leveled to ground by the 2006 Israeli air strikes. In the eyes of most professionals, the demolition of the dense prewar urban fabric constitutes an opportunity to execute the modern circulation networks which would otherwise have been impossible to implement and which, they argue, will be the main component in the "improvement" of those neighborhoods.[8]

In terms of the modalities of execution, highways are selected and implemented through an extremely centralized system, orchestrated by the Council for Development and Reconstruction (CDR), an executive body that depends directly on the prime minister's office and bypasses all public planning agencies (such as the directorate general of urbanism) and local governments. Although Lebanon is nominally a democracy, there are no formal channels of public participation in the choice and implementation of these highways.

It is worth dwelling a little longer on the general design and significance of the highway network. Despite the major demographic and physical changes that have occurred in Beirut during and since the fifteen years of civil war, the transportation scheme implemented throughout the 1990s and up to today still replicates the 1963 road system that was approved in the master plan of that same year (with minor revisions). This scheme has led to large population displacements in neighborhoods that were almost empty four decades ago but have become, since then, dense urban neighborhoods. In this process, hundreds of dwellers are displaced or still threatened to be displaced, but no social or spatial impact studies are estimated or taken into account. Decision makers rarely assess the number of households to be displaced prior to deciding on a highway trajectory, and once they do, it is in strictly financial terms. There are no legal provisions to compensate illegal land occupants, but the political feasibility of project implementation has forced public authorities to allocate payments or compensations that are considered nonetheless illegal and disbursed through back-door processes to dwellers who are depicted as profiting unfairly from the construction of the highway.

More cynically, implementing highways can also be conceived by policymakers as a way of dealing with illegal neighborhoods located on extremely attractive sites. Highway execution is hence an indirect "cleaning" process that enables them to address the "challenge" of illegal settlements and territories out of their control.[9] One can also read symbolic significance into the highways in the context of a war-torn city where much of the urban development in the fifteen years of civil war occurred outside public jurisdiction. That is, the opportunity for the state to create a network of roads symbolizes its dominance over the contested territories of its suburbs, using the highway as a tool to expand its power in a place where other strategies have until now failed. This is what is commonly referred to by members of political parties and some of the interviewed residents in Beirut as the highways' *hidden agenda.*

The Southern Suburbs of Beirut

The sociogeographic context of the southern suburbs of Beirut in which these highways are implemented renders identity politics particularly relevant. Indeed, the southern suburbs of Beirut exhibit an identifiable social, political, and religious territorial identity in postwar Lebanon, one that is often interpreted in opposition to the national project of state building in Lebanon (Sharara 1997; Harb 2003). This suburb is generally considered the Shiʿite stronghold of Beirut because its population has been dominated by Muslim Shiʿite communities since the mid-1970s and heavily controlled by the two Shiʿite political parties, the Amal Movement and the Party of the Islamic Resistance in Lebanon, Hezbollah. These political parties play a central role in allowing or preventing the execution of public projects in or through the area and, as we will see below, have managed to prevent the extension of the large-scale development plans and networks of highways in the southern suburbs of Beirut, contrary to what happened in all other suburbs of the city (Harb 2000).[10] Furthermore, Hezbollah provides many services to the dwellers of these suburbs, such as drinking water, schooling, hospitalization, microcredit, and others, and has also established its political headquarters and the seats of all its social organizations within the area (Harb 1996; Fawaz 2004). It is this same area of Greater Beirut that was severely targeted by the July 2006 Israeli bombardments, under the claim that they were attacking Hezbollah's "stronghold," as described in more detail in this chapter's postscript.

Physically, the southern suburbs of Beirut include a number of villages that have been integrated into the realm of Greater Beirut since the 1960s (Khuri 1975; Harb 2003), as well as a number of informal settlements, including squats and illegal land subdivisions. Dwellers in this area differ considerably in terms of class, regional, and religious affinities.[11] These neighborhoods and the heterogeneous populations they house (old bourgeoisie of these suburbs, rural migrants,

war refugees) are nevertheless generally lumped together in the city's imagination and in public discourses and are condemned for their "unlawfulness" (Harb
2003). These representations have justified an aggressive history of public policies
toward the area, marked with several attempts to bulldoze neighborhoods (Fawaz
and Peillen 2002; Cobban 1985). As a result, many of the southern suburbs' dwellers openly display their distrust toward public agencies whose authority and control over the built environment is severely contested.[12]

Dwellers' attitudes are reinforced by political parties, who mobilize along lines
of religion and belonging and have managed to position themselves as the public
representatives or protectors of the communities in the face of what is widely condemned as threatening public policy. It is, in fact, through the mediation of these
two political parties that many of the negotiations are conducted between dwellers and the state, as we will see below. This is not to say that these parties adequately represent all the residents of these areas. For example, along with public
authorities, they disregard the large number of migrant workers (Syrian, Asian,
African, and others) who rent housing in various neighborhoods of the suburbs
and are neither represented in negotiations nor compensated when evictions happen, although they are often the first group coerced into leaving (Deboulet 2008).
Neither are all dwellers supportive of or supported by political parties: residents
are far from constituting a monolithic support group for the acts and rhetoric of
the political parties, even if openly contesting the sectarian line is not easy.

Uncertainty and Information Deficit

Dwellers in the investigated neighborhoods and millions of others throughout
the urban world (Du Plessis 2006; UN-Habitat 2003) have learned that "metropolitan expectations" (UN-Habitat 2004) challenge their chances for residential
and environmental stability. Indeed, living near a highway or on its projected
trajectory considerably modifies one's sense of security, experiences of urbanity,
and ability to plan and control life projects by generating a severe threat of residential destabilization, whether dwellers are to be displaced or not (Cernea 1998).
The urban dwellers of the investigated popular neighborhoods are exposed to two
levels of uncertainty: political and social, to which is added the threat of eviction
generated by the highway, another aspect of the contemporary "risk society" described by Beck (2001). They have to invest time and energy in gathering information, mobilizing energies, and negotiating the highway trajectory and/or their
displacement within this context of high uncertainty.

Well before its physical implementation, the highway project generates uncertainty and insecurity for low-income dwellers. First, information about the proj-

ect is unreliable. There are no formal participatory procedures, not even those that could inform them of the actual trajectory or temporality of the project, nor about the amount of compensations that might be disbursed to fund the relocation of displaced households. Moreover, highway trajectories are repeatedly altered; thus the list of affected households changes continuously. As a result, dwellers are left to rely on speculations and rumors about the actual risk of eviction. Second, there is no official warning of the coming of the project prior to the eviction notice that generally occurs once surveyors arrive to estimate the costs of compensations and delimit the houses on site, leaving little time for families to organize the displacement process. Third, there is no public relocation scheme, no formal social supports, and displaced households are left to their own devices, whatever their social and financial capital happens to be. They are forced to re-evaluate their living arrangements and decide whether they should negotiate their departure or attempt to stay, knowing that compensations are often insufficient for dwellers to purchase housing elsewhere in Beirut, except in other illegal settlements located further away from the city.

Since the request for information is the only means available to dwellers in order to address uncertainty, information emerges as a key resource. Dwellers generally first hear about the project when information leaks to the press, although information can also be made available through well-connected developers or other key figures in the neighborhood. At this stage, dwellers actively seek more information through the press, but also—and especially—through political parties, local neighborhood committees (made out of local residents, notables, and members who are considered close to the political parties), or well-placed members of their social circles. The latter navigate through social networks that connect dwellers to relatives or co-villagers who have better access to information, notably low-level public sector employees or officials. In this process, residents are far from equal: those who are embedded in a broader network of relations with public authorities, such as larger business owners, tend to have better capacities to gather information and filter unfounded rumors. Information then spreads to the populations through informal gatherings, for example in local grocery stores or bakeries, or in formal meetings, generally organized in the meeting hall of the mosque, the *husseniyahs,* and controlled by one of the two dominant political parties in the investigated neighborhoods.

The amount of rumors and disinformation in this context is abundant. An example taken from Hayy el Sellom is telling. When the municipality and the CDR undertook, in 2003, a project to upgrade some of the basic physical infrastructure in the neighborhood, the rumor rapidly circulated that the highway project that had loomed over the neighborhood since 1973 was finally being implemented.[13]

Residents had access to a copy of the official gazette but misinterpreted its text and concluded that the listed lots on which works were to be conducted were earmarked for demolition to make way for the highway. These rumors were rapidly followed by more dramatic ones linking these demolitions to a foreign real estate development that was to build hotels near the highway and displace thousands of households. As time passed, none of these rumors proved to have any foundations and dwellers went on with their lives until the next wave of information was announced. Rumors and conspiracy theories abound in Ouzāʿī and Jnāh, where everyone comments about high-end beaches for the rich replacing low-income houses, a theory that is credible, given the location of these neighborhoods on prime seafront land.[14]

In order to understand why and how these rumors and the attitudes that generate them are produced, it is important to place the highway project within the history of the interaction of these dwellers with the state and understand how dwellers read the projects in this context, as we will describe in the next section.

Reading Highway Projects

The collective experience of dwellers and their knowledge of power relations generate a number of filters or frames that inform their readings of a development project. Among these, we will analyze the most dominant filter, the sectarian religious readings of the project that are based on the history of the interaction of these dwellers with the state as Shiʿite Muslims, as a low-income group, and as dwellers in the southern suburbs of Beirut. In doing so, dwellers appeal to their familiar social, moral, and religious context in order to describe, analyze, and develop meaning for the events they live. In the face of contradictory situations, this context provides the interpretive basis on which schemes of explanation can be based (Snow 2001).

In this framework, residents and the political parties who represent them read, interpret, and denounce highway projects as part of the long lineage of their interaction with the nation-state, which, they argue, has refused to grant them formal recognition as urban dwellers and maintained discriminatory policies against their neighborhoods. Highway projects are described to be in continuity with the sectarian Lebanese public policy that has systematically marginalized members of this religious group in the public sphere, excluding or under-representing Shiʿites in public offices and employment. This reading is confounded with a class dimension, since this religious belonging is associated with the lower socioeconomic characteristics of the Shiʿite community, which is the poorest religious group in Lebanon, a social status that many members of this community blame

on discriminatory public policies that have not provided them with equal opportunities. It is hence impossible to dissociate between class and sectarian dimensions when analyzing the dwellers' claims and readings.

It is worth opening a short parenthesis to introduce, even if briefly, the history
of the Shiʿite community in Lebanon and its mobilization vis-à-vis the state (Nasr
1985; Norton 1987; Ajami 1987; Sharara 1997; Fawaz and Harb 2001). Shiʿites in
Lebanon are known to have historically suffered from discrimination that denied
them access to education, public employment opportunities, and adequate political representation. Since the 1960s, claims have been put forth in the political
arena by political movements who mobilized the members of this community,
seeking to adjust the public representation of Shiʿites (both political and administrative).[15] Denouncing discrimination against the Shiʿite community remains
to date a dominant organizational principle of Shiʿite political parties (Amal and
Hezbollah), who historically referred to their constituencies as "the deprived"
(al-mahroumeen) and "the oppressed" (al mazloumeen) in the 1960s. More recently, Hezbollah has used "taken for weak" (al mustadʿafeen). All these termi-
nologies are used to connote the oppressive policies waged against members of
these groups. Over the last decade, and given Hezbollah's dominant role in the
military resistance that ended the Israeli occupation of Lebanon (1978–2000), the
position of Hezbollah, and consequently that of the members of the community it
pretends to represent, have been considerably strengthened, and today it is arguable whether one can still talk of such systematic discrimination against Shiʿites.
This language nonetheless remains dominant in the discourse of political parties
and members of the community alike, and can be seen, in the case of political
parties, as a strategically adopted frame, one that enables them to strengthen
"community" organization and mobilization (Gotham 1999; Zald 1996).

Historically, and to date, public sectarian policies are also perceived to deny
low-income dwellers in general, and Shiʿites in particular, access and entitlement
to the city,[16] notably by refraining from providing their neighborhoods with proper
urban services.[17] In the southern suburbs of Beirut, an area that houses close to
half a million people, there are very few health clinics and public schools. The
situation is even worse in informal settlements where the label of illegality has
perpetuated a policy of no service provision (Fawaz and Peillen 2002). As a result, dwellers have had to fend for themselves and many of the urban services in
all three investigated neighborhoods were provided either through self-help or via
"grants" obtained through the sectarian channels of public representation, be it
political parties or political figures.[18] Furthermore, and since the 1970s, political
parties have maintained an alternative strategy of making up for the deficiency
of public services. This is notably the case of Hezbollah, which began providing

urban services such as water provision and garbage collection during the civil war years. Since the late 1980s Hezbollah has operated services in the southern suburbs of Beirut through a network of well-organized NGOs that provide healthcare, education, microcredit, and others (Harb 1996; Fawaz 2004). This presence as a service provider (funded by Shiʿite money, predominantly Iranian), and the flagrant deficiencies of the Lebanese public agencies in this same domain create one of the main bases of Hezbollah's claims to sovereignty over the territory of the southern suburbs. It also enables political parties to use the experience of public sector neglect and activate it as a frame through which highway displacements should be read, as we will see below.

In the neighborhoods, our interviews with dwellers were rich with references to the historical stigmatization of the southern suburbs of Beirut, and especially its Shiʿite dwellers, thus making the execution of these projects an occasion where state authority and legitimacy are severely challenged. Many did not hesitate to include these highways in the list of discriminatory policies against them, including the history of violent eviction attempts waged against informal settlements in the area. Some depicted the projects as only part of a trend to refuse Shiʿites, and/or the poor more generally, their right to the city and its services. Others interpreted the execution of these projects as offensive because the state's willingness to implement such budget-intensive infrastructure projects with an international dimension is seen as symbolic violence against those who have historically suffered from the dire absence of the state in local issues, especially in service provision. Distrust toward the state and its willingness to pay proper compensation were also frequently and openly expressed. For example, an old man in Hayy el Sellom insisted that he would never leave his house "even if they demolished it on my head since I know that the state will never pay adequate compensations."[19]

The most extreme of these versions go as far as connecting the highway to regional politics and historically national political divisions, like the state's decisions to normalize[20] relations with Israel, a proposition rejected within this community and in Lebanon more generally. Several interviewees in Hayy el Sellom explained that the highway going through their neighborhood is meant to connect Beirut to Naqoura (the last Lebanese village before the Israeli-held territory) and beyond (Tel Aviv) and is part of the normalization of the Lebanese-Israeli relations that they oppose. According to others, the highway was designed as part of a larger tourist and military base to which foreign tourists (especially "Americans")[21] will be invited and which will be funded by Arab Gulf money. Half bragging, a young man told us that if the highway were to be implemented, he would seek "martyrdom."[22] "It is a legitimate target," he added, "since the highway is meant to connect Beirut to Israel."[23] While such claims may be recognized as exaggerated, even among dwellers, they adequately illustrate the weight of dwellers' perceptions vis-à-vis the Lebanese state. They indicate the alienation that dwellers feel toward a postwar reconstruction project designed for *others* and funded by Arab money, which doesn't have room for their visions and experiences of the city. They also appeal to the organizational culture and political history of the Shi'ite community in Lebanon, which was developed around the revival of historic notions the concept of martyrdom and its yearly celebration are a central pillar (Mervin 2000).

In Jnāh and Ouzā'ī where the highway projects are integrated with a broader public project of neighborhood upgrading that entails the development of high-end resorts on the seafront areas[24] currently occupied by the dwellers we interviewed, the highway is read as an integral part of their perception of the historical social injustice that their communities have faced in attempting to claim their own spaces in the city. Residents in these neighborhoods recurrently described themselves as excluded from the benefits of urban living, including the highways that are directed to more mobile and richer population groups.[25] Furthermore, displacement in these two neighborhoods is interpreted as a project executed at the expense of popular (Shi'ite) classes and in favor of private interests, notably those of rich Arab investors and their partners in the Lebanese government.[26]

Such readings are strongly echoed by the two political parties, who promote a politicized reading of the projects and loudly denounce their discriminatory nature. Although highway planning is not contested as such, several Hezbollah officials who were interviewed in the course of this fieldwork, for example, used technical arguments, such as the abundance of highways planned for the volume of traffic and the size of the city, to express certainty that such highways are designed explicitly to displace "unwanted" populations, and not to serve traffic needs.[27]

That said, the way such sectarian politics translate judgment of the projects differs from one neighborhood to another, depending on the stage of execution of the highway, its estimated impact, living conditions in the neighborhood, and dwellers' perception of land prices and opportunities in the areas where they live. In Ouzā'ī and Jnāh, two neighborhoods occupying prime seafront land where real estate values are high and commercial activities conveniently located on busy arteries, residents associate their displacement as an attempt to deny Shi'ites the right to live in desirable locations in the city. The Association of Storeowners in Ouzā'ī also accuses public planners of denying their right to work in the city, describing the highway project which, in its last version, entailed a bridge bypassing the area entirely, as an attempt to "kill" their neighborhood by asphyxiating the stores that survive on through traffic. In Jnāh, where the highway was executed ten years ago, displacing an estimated 250 families and creating a permanent rupture within the neighborhood, dwellers described the highway as a destabilizing experience that they were poorly prepared for, with negative repercussions on their daily living conditions that are still felt. In Ouzāʿī, where the highway was to extend in order to connect Beirut to its international airport, dwellers perceive the highway as a major threat to their living conditions and have managed, at least partially through their active mobilization, to prevent its execution.

Conversely, in Hayy el Sellom, the highway is seen by many dwellers as an opportunity for the development of their living spaces and/or an occasion to leave the neighborhood. Here, many dwellers complained about the *slow* implementation of these projects rather than their execution at all, bringing a dimension of social injustice to an argument that decries the unequal development of the country. Many dwellers described the highway as a development opportunity and talked about the entitlement of the neighborhood to the attention of the state and its share of public projects. Here, the highway acquires unsuspected credentials, coming, in the eyes of some residents, to correct the history of injustice inflicted by public policies toward the neighborhood, notably by providing better access to and from an area suffering from the poor transportation networks connecting it to the city.[28]

Aside from such communal representations, the variety of project-related perceptions and decisions depends on a wide array of individual factors. People's positions are often ambiguous, as they want to stay, but simultaneously recognize the need to leave. Such positions contradict the homogenizing vision of sectarian behaviors and reactions by revealing the impact of individuation (Castel 1995) in societies described to be following a communitarian view. Individual factors include the duration of residency and hence participation in a shared history of neighborhood building (which is generally correlated with a strong preference for staying, especially among the elders). Dwellers' position about a possible displacement is also strongly influenced by a prospective resettlement in the absence of public housing projects and the knowledge that they have to rely on a housing market that lacks affordable options. This position is also influenced by the vulnerable conditions of their livelihoods, by earlier models of displacement trajectories they have observed in their context, and by their evaluation of the potential success of waging an opposition to the project. Finally, people's individual preference and choice to negotiate or not depends on their personal relations with powerful groups and political parties: those supported by the more powerful groups are naturally more inclined to invest in negotiations. At the end of the day, sociospatial inequalities are reinforced at the local level with the execution of the highway. Those who stayed suffer now from proximity to the executed highway, with all the nuisances that it can bring by way of noise and air pollution, but are not able to take advantage of this proximity (except, perhaps, in access to collective taxis) since they rarely possess a car. Furthermore, their property has become undesirable and hence almost impossible to trade. Conversely, it is possible to argue that those households who were able to secure good compensations (because they agreed to leave early on or were well backed when they negotiated their compensations) did not lose in the transaction. Once decisions affect the individual's residential trajectory, questions of identity are often relegated to a secondary level.

Negotiating Highway Projects in a Context of Land Rights Privation

Three groups of actors participate in negotiations: public actors, neighborhood dwellers (more or less mobilized and organized in neighborhood committees), and political parties. None of these groups forms a unified or coherent unity, but each seeks to negotiate the best possible outcome they can get to offset their losses, keeping in mind that even if political parties are included as representatives of the community, it is very much a three-party negotiation that is taking place—with the dwellers and political parties sometimes displaying opposing interests. Furthermore, as they interact and devise strategies in relation to each other, actors develop and modify their readings, positions, and identities in relation to the context and the urban intervention that they are negotiating. They do not, therefore, possess positive, durable, or fixed identities (Cefaï and Trom 2001).[29] Furthermore, the alignment of "opinions" between individuals, groups, committees, and political parties (Snow 2001) fluctuates considerably in the local arena.

It is interesting to point out that none of these groups puts forth a claim of "common good" or "public interest" in their position vis-à-vis the highway. In their critiques of the project, dwellers decry the unfairness of the negotiation process, mostly low indemnities or erratic processes of public decision, or a lack of a coherent transportation strategy (there are too many highways, etc). It is thus difficult to associate dwellers' claims and their mobilization (whether to deviate the highway trajectory or reclaim more equitable indemnities) with a social movement since their discourse doesn't carry a global critique of the highway projects or a claim for an alternative understanding of what the common good would entail for, in this context, all Lebanese. Similar observations can also be made about public initiatives that justify highway development with the need for economic growth, rather than describing a public interest, which have until now refrained from connecting these highway segments to a comprehensive network outside the city, prioritizing instead localized bypasses that facilitate their own plans for development, such as a connection between the business central district and the airport.

The relative power of each of the three coalitions of actors depends on their interaction with each other and the fact that there is much overlap between the three. Generally, dwellers' power is generated from the support they can gather from the political parties to their cause, knowing that both recognize in the integrated (religiously homogenous) character of this Shiʿite community (Oberschall 1973), which holds most of the property in the neighborhoods, a major asset in the negotiation process. This dependence on political parties—which function as conduits for the demands from the rest of the society (Oberschall 1973)—is exacerbated by the state's unwillingness to negotiate directly with dwellers, preferring to rely on political parties in these tasks and strengthening their role in the process. We should also remember that these negotiations are *granted* by public authorities to dwellers, political parties, or neighborhood associations in response to political mobilization and not recognized as an entitlement. This has important repercussions on the outcome of the negotiations, as we will see in the next section.

While dwellers and political parties sometimes attempt to negotiate the trajectory of a highway, the main object of these negotiations is the financial compensations to be paid to dwellers, especially because there are no relocation policies. These compensations have in fact become a central cost item on highway budgets and, as a result, largely determine the decision to execute a given project. As outlined above, however, compensations are illegal according to the strict words of the Lebanese law, since most of these dwellers have built their houses in violation of public regulations, including sometimes property rights. They are nominally paid in recognition of the hardship to be incurred by families, but they can only be *secured* through political mobilization and pressures supported by political parties. As a result, there is no transparent scale to evaluate these payments. The adopted criteria are based on quantitative (surface) and qualitative (design, interior finishes, whether engineers consider a space "nice," etc.) valuations, assessed during site visits by engineers. The informality of the qualitative criteria makes each item of the equation controversial and often critiqued, as compensations claims vary considerably from one case to another on the basis of, for example, dwellers' perception of the value of the land on which they are squatting.[30] Indemnities also vary with individual aspects of the negotiation process. During the execution of the Jnāh highway in 1993, payments varied considerably from one household to another, we were told, depending on the tenacity of the household, the resistance they waged, and the relative importance of their web of social relations.

Decisions without Deliberations: The Ambiguities of Public Strategies

The modality and outcome of these negotiations is heavily determined by the macro-political environment where, as outlined above, there are no formal channels of public participation, state–citizen relations are heavily mediated by political parties, and the legal system is inefficient and renders lawsuits unfeasible. The political reactions that emanate from these neighborhoods nonetheless include solid claims that are expressed in the form of public discontent, which is at least partially channeled and often manipulated by the political parties. Any attempt by the government to intervene without prior negotiations with these parties is likely to be considered an unacceptable interference with their authority which claims a form of autonomy in running the affairs of its territorialized religious community.

Our field findings indicate that final decisions are systematically taken behind closed doors, in highly confidential political meetings that include central public agents and high-ranking members of political parties (which doesn't necessarily imply that they won't be eventually recuperated and transformed at the local scale). Debate is hijacked by deliberative negotiations among influential political actors such as the prime minister, the head of the parliament, members of Hezbollah's political bureau, or delegates representing these actors. Neither the engineers of the CDR who execute these projects nor the neighborhood representatives of political parties are present in these meetings. Hence, the engineer entrusted at the CDR with the file of the Hayy el Sellom highway admitted that he was not included in the negotiations about the highway implementation, explaining that such decisions are taken by "high-ups" and that he doesn't always know when meetings are held. It is furthermore widely believed among technical actors that the decision making process is political (which, in Lebanon, translates essentially as sectarian or confessional) and that technical issues are only secondary. In the two interviews he gave us, the engineer at the CDR reiterated his certainty that the highways will never be executed, unless "one day a politician decides, for a reason that concerns him only, to make it his project and, as a result, the project is executed rapidly."[31] However, the decisions are highly influenced by what happens on the street and it is with this knowledge in mind that dwellers, public authorities, and political parties approach the negotiation process, both vis-à-vis the state and vis-à-vis each other.

The modes of mobilization reflect the history of the relation of one or several groups with existing, historically situated frames of power that form the structures of political opportunity—which is a function, as was shown by Tarrow (1998), of the level of openness of the regime and the configurations of political alliances. The forms that opposition to highways take borrow heavily from a historically situated "repertoires of collective action" (Tilly 1986) that fall within forms familiar to members of Amal or Hezbollah, including street action, occupation, or the threat of physical violence. Still, new forms of contention emerge, such as petitions, notably due to the interventions of nonaligned dwellers who sometimes seek to distance themselves from the political parties. This was the case, for example, for a committee of storeowners in Ouzāʿī who developed a petition to be put forth to all public representatives in protest of the looming threat of the highway on their businesses, and for a minority of non-Shiʿite residents in Hayy el Sellom who organized private delegations to visit the prime minister's office independently of the cover of the political parties.

Thus, the street where public protests are staged is an important space that complements closed-room negotiations by allowing actors to keep each other in check. Protests are most commonly orchestrated by political parties as a show of force vis-à-vis public authorities and coincide with deadlocks in the negotiation processes or when political parties feel coerced or weakened in negotiations. They can also be interpreted as a strategy of the political parties to strengthen local identities and the claims based on these identities by rendering inseparable the significance of identity as a collection of attributes and identity as a feeling of belonging (Neveu 2005).[32]

The street has, however, also been used by public authorities to test local power relations. The sudden announcement of the inauguration of work for the Ouzāʿī bridge in June 2002 and the unexpected on-site visit of the Prime Minister's delegate can indeed be read as an attempt by public officials to *test* community resistance and the power of political parties. Violent opposition that made the front pages of all the Lebanese papers for several days illustrated the scale of the local reaction and explains why the project execution was immediately halted.[33] The street can also be used by dwellers to protest the outcome of negotiations if the consensus reached is deemed unacceptable. The Ouzāʿī incident again illustrates this process since the political parties who had acquiesced to public plans were forced to back up and realign themselves with dwellers, even if they had already negotiated different positions behind closed doors.

Dwellers Caught between Two Claims of Sovereignty

Dwellers are clearly caught between public projects, on the one hand, and political parties who claim to represent them, on the other. The latter are central interlocutors in highway negotiations where their interests should not be confused with those of dwellers, even if these interests sometimes intersect and positions often appear to coincide. This is most evident in the opposition of political parties to population displacement, a position that was explained (by members of Hezbollah) on the basis of their need to retain territorial control over the areas where they claim to represent the population. Conversely, many interviewed dwellers admitted in private that even if they preferred to obtain financial compensations and move to less congested neighborhoods, they were forced to align themselves to the parties' claims.[34] Loyalty to the party stems from the sectarian feeling that is activated and reinforced by physical segregation, by the nature of the projects, which are perceived as outwardly hostile to the dwellers, and by the identity negotiations described above. This loyalty is, however, far from being uncontested, since many respondents seemed alarmed by the loss of autonomy of the neighborhood families and social institutions vis-à-vis the political parties or recognized having given in to conformism because of the fear of being perceived negatively by other members of their local communities. The outcome of negotiations is thus often a compromise that satisfies the political parties' territorial visions, even if this is achieved at the expense of dwellers' life projects.

There are many reasons for dwellers not to challenge political parties. First, dwellers recognize that the support of these political parties is their only guarantee of receiving displacement compensations since these compensations are obtained through the mobilization waged with the help of these parties and *not* as the outcome of a public recognition of their entitlement to displacement compensations. Dwellers recognized an additional incentive to openly support political parties: previous experiences in Jnāh and elsewhere, such as in Beirut downtown, showed that political parties tend to favor their own members and those who support them loudly by securing higher compensations, while the "very poor," to paraphrase an interviewee in Jnāh, "did not see their entitlement recognized . . . because they were not *protected*." That said, the distinction between political parties and communities is far from clear, especially since the former are part and parcel of the neighborhood and many of their members are active in the local committees that have historically organized service provision in these areas. In fact, the local committees that were historically constituted on the basis of family and geographic representation have shifted to mostly include party members and, as a result, dwellers' margin of maneuver vis-à-vis these political parties is considerably reduced. In Jnāh, the only neighborhood where indemnities have already been paid and the highway implemented, the Amal political party seized control of the neighborhood and substituted itself for the local committees and, more generally, represented itself as the community's voice. Amal thus mediated the negotiations and established itself as the distributor of public funds, once compensations were paid, in a manner that, if we believe neighborhood dwellers, clearly favored its supporters.

That said, dwellers retain some kind of autonomy in this arena, which helps them maintain a ceiling on the concessions that will be made in their name and/ or at their expense by political parties and members of public agencies. Indeed, once public agencies and political parties reach an agreement on the road trajectory and the amount of compensation to be paid, dissatisfied dwellers still possess recourse as individuals (physical resistance to displacement and manipulation of personal networks of social relations) and groups (protests). If the compromise reached by political parties and public officials is rejected locally by an organized community, dwellers can rely on (sometimes violent) protests to keep the political parties in check, forcing them to withdraw from any deal they had reached. This was the case in Ouzāʿī, where violent protests waged by the local committee of storeowners and a number of dwellers culminated in a fistfight, forcing the Prime Minister's representative, who arrived to inaugurate the works on a highway flyover, to go back, and thus put the project on hold. For dwellers, this highway was an unacceptable compromise since it threatened the viability of their businesses and harmed the quality of life in their neighborhoods. Yet, political parties and state representatives had reached what they thought was an agreeable outcome: eliminating displacements would reduce the project costs for public authorities by deferring the costs of indemnities and allow political parties to retain their constituencies on site. Popular resistance, however, forced political parties to reconsider their stands and realign themselves with the claims of neighborhood dwellers.

Interviews with dwellers in Hayy el Sellom indicate that they evaluate properly the effectiveness of protests in their neighborhoods on public decisions and social calm. Hence, they loudly threaten a "social revolution" if they are not properly compensated and, in order to strengthen their claims, refer to earlier incidents where they managed through such protests to change public policies—including events of the civil war. Carried away by the conversation, an interviewed middle-aged man reminded us that "we (members of the Shiʿite community) have already staged more than a revolution in the country."[35] He then explicitly referred to the events of 6 February 1984, during the Lebanese civil war, when a (Shiʿite) fac-

tion of the Lebanese army seceded from the state authority in protest of its sectarian and discriminatory policies, considerably changing the balance of power
and forcing the state to recognize the authority of militias, notably Amal, as partners in governance (Cobban 1985; Picard 1996). Protests have also been proven
effective in previous confrontations between dwellers and public authorities on
the highway issue. In the case, for example, of the highway planned inside Hayy
el Sellom, the trajectory was "temporarily modified" and executed to go through
the airport domain without displacing any of the neighborhood's population. The
project engineer in the CDR explained that the difficulties faced in displacing ten
households in another informal settlement of the southern suburb (Raml) for the
first section of the highway had convinced public authorities to deviate the road
trajectory and investigate ways of reducing its impact.[36]

This mobilization of collective resources, however, is limited to the dominant
factions of the local populations: building owners, males, and Lebanese. Women,
for instance, are de facto excluded from meetings, which we were told are *for men
only*. Active participation in political parties also generally depends on sectarian identities and is hence essentially open only to members of the same religious
groups. It also only includes Lebanese citizens, while many foreigners—men and
women coming from Sri Lanka, the Philippines, Ethiopia, Syria, Sudan, and other
locations—are deprived of any entitlement of right to resist.

Before closing this section, it is worth pointing out that one of the effects of
the centrality acquired by political parties in the negotiation process is that the
outcome of negotiations often depends on national or regional factors that affect the relative positions of the parties and the state, irrespective of local forces.
In the context of a dependent and fragile country such as Lebanon, factors external to the neighborhood, such as the international position of Hezbollah and
political circumstances like international debt, also bias or hijack the outcome of
particular negotiations against the interest of dwellers.

Highway Struggles and Sovereignty: Concluding Remarks

In this chapter, we have investigated, in the context of postwar Beirut, how
highway development projects generated a new space in which competing claims
of sovereignty representing opposing sectarian/religious identities were negotiated, as political actors and dwellers deployed "identity issues" as a way to learn
about, interpret, and negotiate the implementation of highways threatening neighborhoods. Thus, mobilization in the face of high-speed roads in the southern suburbs of Beirut was a factor in the formation of coalitions of actors and the crys-
tallizing of a relation between identities and territory. We also showed how such

mobilizations formed the occasion to question, realign, and regenerate identities in the process of negotiations between communities and the national state. It is thus possible to interpret conflicts about highways as the expression of severe contradictions in the political and territorial sovereignty in Lebanon whereby city dwellers are redefining in a nonlinear way legitimacies, and sometimes sovereignties in and over urban space, by contesting technical or professional definitions of how territories should evolve.

Our findings are in line with a growing body of literature documenting "community identity" as a process of social construction that occurs within the work of social movements (Castells 1983). We showed that sectarian (religious) allegiances and identities were developed, changed, and strengthened through an involvement in the negotiation of the development projects and through the interface of the investigated communities with the national state projects. Faced with the threat of highway construction, dwellers resorted to political parties and community organizations that have enabled them to resist displacement (so far) or at least to secure better compensations. Rather than perceiving ethnic or religious group identification as latent forms of socialization that existed before the formation of the nation state, or as set in opposition to a nationalist project, we showed that these forms of belonging and these expressions of identity are a complex interplay between the outcomes of public policy and the modalities of territorial control exercised by sectarian political parties, which also stem from the history of modern Lebanon, notably since World War II. In other words, conflicts over the resources allocated by the national state foster the adoption of these identities just as much as the identities themselves eventually stand in the way of executing the state's projects.

Yet, our findings also indicated that dwellers also attempt to distance themselves from political parties and preserve the autonomy of their "residential projects." In fact, our investigations showed that these populations (whether actively mobilized or not) are well aware of the stakes. If they choose to side with political parties, they nonetheless retain their reflexive practices and a critical conscience that is not often recognized by researchers and which creates an important correction to the undifferentiated and hegemonic vision of Shiʿite political parties in the southern suburbs of Beirut.

The form that opposition to the highway projects has taken in postwar Beirut evokes the resistance lodged against expressways in the United States during the 1960s by social movements who appropriated the "civil rights" frame and activated it in their framing of urban renewal projects, sometimes successfully halting the passage of expressways that would displace a large number of residents in communities of color (Gotham 1999). In both of these cases, it is possible to argue in line with Gotham (1999) that the resistance to the highway built on an existing community identity, whereby social movements deployed concepts of "communal identity" as a strategic organizational tool that rallied the community and, by doing so, contributed to strengthening its sense of identity. These mobilization movements differ from other documented mobilizations against highways because they do not denounce the highway on technical grounds, such as environmental concerns, efficiency, equitable indemnity, or the accessibility of this form of transportation across class (McCreery 2000; Urry 2000; Fuks 1998; Wheeler 1976), nor because of the equitable indemnity to those who are losing their property. Instead, the highway is framed as a threat to a particular community targeted with displacement because its identity renders it "undesirable" in the city.

However, highway negotiations in Lebanon differ considerably from those of the civil rights movement in the United States primarily because of the political context in which they are cast. Indeed, the "civil rights" frame of 1960s American discourse deployed a repertoire of action that enabled activists to rely on the formal legal system in order to contest highway developments through the courts on the basis of racial discrimination (Gotham 1999, 342). Similarly, in France, environmental externalities created a space in which participation in public projects became an entitlement, making it possible to contest through the legal framework the development of highways and fast trains (TGV), even if the most fragile populations were rarely able to defend themselves.[37] Such a scenario is impossible in Lebanon, where no channels of equitable representation exist and where the legal system doesn't provide an adequate space for contestation. Furthermore, the civil rights mobilization ultimately sought the recognition of affected communities as equal citizens in the city. To the contrary, in Lebanon, identity issues are deployed in the opposition to the highway by political parties who are ultimately positioning the community against the state with an alternative claim for sovereignty over space, one in which the authority and interests of political parties is paramount. The fact that these struggles occurred consistently in neighborhoods whose legal status (and hence public recognition) was dubious further reinforced issues of sovereignty since it inscribed the contestation of urban projects in a wider framework of contested legitimacies and entitlement to the city.

More broadly, and setting internal Lebanese politics aside, it is the presence of squatters on territories deemed important for alternative visions of what the city should be that transform what could have been conflicts over land uses into negotiations between conflicting sovereignties. This is why it is possible to argue that globalization, by creating additional supranational visions of what the city should be, reinforces conflicting claims over space and targets particular neighborhoods *such as* informal settlements whose presence in the city is somewhat precarious

(Berry-Chikhaoui, Deboulet, and Roulleau-Berger 2007). Urban infrastructure projects thus become the tools with which the struggle over contested sovereignties is actually conducted. This is also how identity questions re-emerge and are shaped along the stakes of localities and spatialities. This is why we argue that the execution of development projects, a process conceived as part and parcel of the establishment of the sovereignty of the modern nation state, has eventually consolidated in Lebanon alternative forms of contesting sovereignties.

To conclude, we can say that approaching this investigation from the framework of sovereignty places a new light on the relation between globalization and social changes. It shows that globalization draws upon the mobility paradigm without questioning socially related issues. Taking a positive stance, we could ask whether major global projects might contribute to the shaping of new forms of expression in developing countries. Does it affect forms of citizenship and how does it allow us to rethink autonomy in politics? Studying how sovereignties are recomposed in urban contexts cannot be done without investigating the modes of expression of public discourse and the forms of collective legitimacies expressed outside the framework of the state, political parties, and their clientelistic and sectarian logics. This is all the more the case because these forms of legitimacy are threatened and destabilized by the logic of international projects.

Postscript

The 2006 Israeli war on Lebanon escalated the tensions between the three actors investigated in this paper exponentially, with Hezbollah accusing the national government of aligning its policies with Israeli interests and consequently withdrawing its members from the national Cabinet. In this context, and given the massive scale of the demolitions generated by the Israeli assaults, the postwar reconstruction brought struggles over contested sovereignties and identity politics to the heart of the urban process in the form of negotiations over reconstruction projects. Hence, the reconstruction of the highways, bridges, and rural and urban neighborhoods that were demolished during the Israeli assaults was negotiated between members of the Islamic resistance in Lebanon (Hezbollah) and public sector actors, each seeking to assert its authority over a particular territory and to define the forms that this reconstruction can take and how fast it can move. It was however in the neighborhood of Haret Hreik (South Beirut), the area that housed in the prewar years the headquarters of Hezbollah and many of its service-providing NGOs, that Hezbollah played its central card, reclaiming full authority over the reconstruction process by securing full legal delegations from over ninety percent of households and taking charge of the collection of compensations, the commissioning of building designs and their actual building after it developed its own master plan for the area which, it must be said, is in violation of state sanctioned urban and building regulations. Interviews with Hezbollah actors furthermore indicated that the selection of planning options is based on a deliberate attempt to limit the role of the public sector as much as possible (basically regarding the payment of financial compensations) and on retaining the party's territorial human base in the area (Fawaz 2007).[38] This was only possible because the reconstruction was cast within the tense political context where dwellers, threatened to see their entitlement denied on the basis of what they read as a discriminatory state position against the community, felt the need to align along identity/religious lines and interpret the reconstruction choices according to a framework of contested entitlement over the space of the city which, as Shi'ites, they were denied. Needless to say, the formulation of the reconstruction process along these lines was powerfully mastered by the Party (Fawaz 2009). In other words, the reconstruction/recomposition of the built environment after the 2006 war generated an important opportunity to strengthen religious/sectarian identities and consolidate alternative sovereignties and territorialities. It also enabled Hezbollah to step up its role, moving from supporting the resistance of development projects to actually playing the role of public planner itself and implementing the reconstruction project of the neighborhood of Haret Hreik, on behalf of the community.

Notes

The authors dedicate this chapter to the memory of Francoise Navez-Bouchanine. Funding for the fieldwork was provided by the AUB University Research Board.

1. Most of this mobilization took place in parallel to the negotiations in the early 2000s, around the implementation of the latest sections of the ring road. They were documented through field research and quoted in Deboulet, 2004. More recent negotiations are also documented in several articles in *Cairo Contested* (D. Singerman 2009, Cairo: American University in Cairo), including "The Dictatorship of the Straight Line and the Myth of Social Disorder: Revisiting Informality in Cairo." Since 2008, mobilization against highways has also occurred in the popular neighborhood of Imbaba due to the planned extension of the ring road and a road-widening scheme that threatens some 30,000 dwellings with forced displacement (data gathered by Valentine Lecomte, a Masters student working with Agnès Deboulet).

2. The role of political parties is particularly clear in the displacement policies related to postwar development projects or highway constructions. In the southern suburbs of Beirut, and as of 1996, a public agency entrusted with the "redevelopment" of the southwest suburbs of the city, Elyssar, helped in the formation of new local committees that

often superseded original neighborhood groupings. The "Elyssar committees" include representatives of the political parties active in the area. While early on negotiations revolved around relocation and resettlement options, all parties have shifted to negotiations about the amount of financial compensations.

3. Estimates of population vary according to sources considerably. For this chapter, we have adopted the estimates developed by Fawaz and Peillen (2002). For more on the issue, please consult their paper, listed below.

4. This research was conducted under the joint program "Programme de Recherches Urbaines en Développement," financed by the French Ministry of Foreign Affairs. Our team submitted a comparative research proposal "L'Entre-deux des politiques institutionnelles et des dynamiques sociales" covering Lebanon, Morocco, Algeria, Mauritania, and Egypt and was coordinated by F. Navez-Bouchanine. The paper proceedings are due for publication in 2010.

5. We are grateful to Sandra Bsat, Rania Ghosn, Yasmine Machnouk, and especially Kristine Samra for their assistance in fieldwork. We are also thankful to all those who took the time to answer our queries.

6. This change in project justification creates an important difference between the organization of these projects and the community struggles lodged against highways that were documented in the Unites States and Europe during the 1970s (see, for example, Harvey 1992). The mobilization against urban renewal projects and urban motorways went in parallel in the United States, leading sometimes to the creation of stable grassroots organizations such as "community development corporations" (CDCs). This was the case in Boston where a CDC emerged in reaction to a highway project that was to lead to the demolition of 10,000 apartments, according to Donzelot et al. (2003).

7. The first master plan of the city of Beirut was prepared by the French urban planner Michel Ecochard in 1943 and revised with the *Schéma Directeur pour Beyrouth Métropolitain* in 1963. These were followed by several studies conducted by French consultants such as BCEOM (1983) and IAURIF (1986). For details on this highway planning, see Ghorayeb (1998).

8. These are the recommendations that we have heard since September 2006 from members of municipal councils as well as engineers and architects discussing the reconstruction of these neighborhoods.

9. This is clearly the example of the above-mentioned Elyssar Project (see fn. 2), as described by Harb (2000) and Clerc (2002). Fouad Awada, Eric Huybrechts and Jean-Louis Pagès also discuss this process in a special issue of Cahiers de l'IAURIF, on Lebanon, *Liban: retours sur experience,* March 2006. Mona Fawaz (2004) provides a historical dimension of this aspect of policy making in Lebanon.

10. The main reference here is the Elyssar Project that was designed as a large-scale restructuring project for the southwest suburbs of Beirut and included the implementation of a large network of highways, the development of leisure facilities along the coast, and rehousing thousands of households currently squatting public and private premises

in housing projects within the area. The Elyssar project never materialized. For more, see Harb 2000; Clerc 2002.

11. When referring to a Shiʿite community, it should be clear that many differences exist among community members, including in class and place of origin (e.g. Beirut, the Biqaʿ, South Lebanon). Other divisions occur along lines religious (e.g. tenants vs. opponents of particular religious authorities or *marjaʿiyya,* partisans of quiet vs. politicized religious commemorations), political (e.g. leftists, communists, nationalists vs. families and clans vs. new legislative elites from Amal and Hezbollah), and economic (e.g. immigrants vs. locals) (Fawaz and Harb 2001; Picard 1996).

12. The most recent of these confrontations occurred between the police force and the dwellers of one of these settlements (Raml) in October 2006 and led to the death of two community members resisting demolitions.

13. The Hayy el Sellom highway was first projected in 1973 and, since then, the trajectory has been modified several times without ever executing it (Fawaz 2004).

14. These theories were in fact confirmed in our interviews with a former high-ranking member of the Lebanese administration.

15. The Movement of the Deprived (*Harakat al Mahroumeen*) led by Imam Musa al-Sadr was to become a powerful movement denouncing the injustice deployed against the Shiʿite community. Through *Harakat al Mahroumeen,* al-Sadr demanded changes in the existing political system (notably through more public posts in the government allocated to Shiʿites) and in the distribution of resources among regions in view of providing a more equitable share to Shiʿite regions. Al-Sadr also strived for a better representation for the Shiʿites, notably through the institution of a public body representing the interests of members of this community in front of the state, similar to those representing all other sectarian groups in Lebanon. During the 1970s, and with the advent of the Lebanese civil war (1975–1999), the Movement of the Deprived was to develop into a militarized party (Amal) and then a militia. Later, in 1982, a new political and military movement that upheld military resistance to the Israeli occupation of Lebanon was founded: Hezbollah (Nasr 1985; Ajami 1987; Norton 1987).

16. The use of the expression "the right to the city" or "entitlement to the city" should be understood as both spatial (equal access to the infrastructure and other facilities that are provided in the rich neighborhoods of the city) and metaphorical, in line with the definition proposed by Henri Lefebvre in the well known essay "the right to the city," where the concept indicates also the right to access the city and its centrality, as described by the author, as an important component of citizenship (Lefebvre 2000).

17. For the relation between the Shiʿite mobilization movements before the war and city, see Nasr (1985).

18. Aside from Hezbollah and Amal, we should include here the services provided historically and to date by important Shiʿite feudal figures (Harb 2005).

19. Interview held in November 2003 with a dweller in Hayy el Sellom, on the street.

20. By normalization, we refer here to the establishment of "normal" relations with the

State of Israel in the absence of a just settlement on the historical question of Palestine, an issue which is anathema for almost all Lebanese citizens, but is particularly felt in this community.

21. The popular perception identifies the United States with a continued interventionist colonial project in the Middle East, be it in Israel, Iran, the Arab Gulf, or, more recently, Iraq. As a result, this identification of the tourists as "Americans" is here significant and symbolic of the association made among dwellers between development projects and "evil" outsider forces coming to evict them from their houses.

22. This is based on interviews conducted in November 2003. Note that such attitudes are likely to be considerably reinforced today with the events of the summer of 2006 that further glorified the resistance attitude of the Shiʿite community.

23. Interviews held between November 4 and 29, 2003, with a number of dwellers, together and separately, in Hayy el Sellom. The idea of the highway connecting Beirut to Tel-Aviv was mentioned by several respondents and commonly circulates in Hayy el Sellom.

24. This is the Elyssar project, see reference above.

25. About the dominant paradigm of mobility, see Urry (2005).

26. Reference is made here to the late Prime Minister, Rafiq Hariri, who was seen to carry a large-scale development vision of Lebanon as a service country to rich Arab Gulf capitals (Becherer 2005).

27. The positions of these political parties has in fact been described as deliberately seeking to challenge state authority because of a project of creating a counter-society, to use the terms put forth by Picard (2005) speaking of the communist party in France after World War II. This in fact has become a recurrent theme in the analysis of processes of reconstruction (most notably in France), where the struggle for independence during the war strengthens local communal identities and thus creates a severe impediment for the reimposition of national state authority, even when the populations who suffered under the militia occupation loudly reclaim the state authority (Picard 1994).

28. Dwellers are not aware that the original highway design didn't include an exit in the neighborhood.

29. Cefaï and Trom (2001) argue that: "the different groups of actors are not defined beforehand; they are formed in the process of public interventions. These actors do not possess positive and durable identities. The transformation of these identities goes in pair with the causes that they defend and depends on the context of interaction in which they are engaged" (Cefaï and Trom, 18).

30. In Ouzāʿi and Jnāh, where a development plan intends to transform squatted beaches into the extension of a desirable coast, dwellers know that they are "sitting on gold" and modify their claims in relation to what they perceive to be the real value of the prime land they occupy.

31. Interview held with an anonymous architect in the CDR.

32. "Identity is the result of a continuous work of negotiation between acts of *attribution*, principles of identification stemming from others, and acts of *belonging* that seek to

express identity for oneself, meaning the categories through which the individual intends to be perceived" (Neveu 2005, 77). (Translation by authors.)

33. This is clear in daily newspaper records of June 2002. See, for example, *An-Nahar* and *As-Safir* June 25–28, 2002.

34. A similar dynamic occurs today in the neighborhoods demolished by the 2006 Israeli assaults in Lebanon where Hezbollah insists on the necessity of all dwellers returning to their previous homes, as explained in more detail in the conclusion to the this chapter. Still, this dynamic is not unique to the southern suburbs of Beirut. Khayat has shown that manipulations were equally strong in the Armenian municipality of Borj Hammoud, in the northeast suburbs of Beirut (Khayat 2001).

35. Interview held in Hayy el Sellom.

36. Interview with an anonymous architect in the CDR in June 2003.

37. The right to participate in the elaboration of public decisions is bound in the French law to planning and environmental issues. In particular, participation is a right when public decisions have an "effect on the environment." It is supported by the Aarhus convention (25 June 1998) that recognizes a right of the public to participate in public decisions, but mainly for the sake of guaranteeing the protection of environment (Jegouzo 2006).

38. For example, despite the fact that the existing 1970s building guidelines are inadequate for the contemporary urbanization of this area, a decision was taken at the level of the political party to rebuild the neighborhood within this planning framework because the development of new urban regulations would require the approval of public planning agencies and consequently provide a larger window of intervention for the Lebanese state.

Works Cited

Abrams, S., and J. Waldren. 1998. *Anthropological Perspectives on Local Development Knowledge and Sentiments in Conflict.* London: Routledge.

Ajami, F. 1987. *The Vanished Imam: Musa al-Sadr and the Shia of Lebanon.* Ithaca, N.Y.: Cornell University Press.

Bahout, J. 1994. "Deux ans après les elections législatives de l'été 1992, où en est le parlementarisme libanais?" *Relations Internationales et Stratégiques* 16: 57–66.

Bayat, A. 1997. *Street Politics—Poor People's Movement in Iran.* Cairo: AUC Press.

Becherer, R. 2005. "A Matter of Life and Debt: The Untold Costs of Rafiq Hariri's New Beirut." *The Journal of Architecture* 10: 1–42.

Beck, U. 2001. *La société du risque sur la voie d'une autre modernité.* Paris: Champs-Flammarion.

Berry-Chikhaoui, I., and A. Deboulet. 2001. *Les compétences des citadins dans le monde arabe: penser, faire et transformer la ville.* Paris: Karthala.

Berry-Chikhaoui, I., A. Deboulet, and L. Roulleau-Berger. 2007. *Villes internationales: entre tensions et réactions des habitants.* Paris: La Découverte.

Berry-Chikhaoui, I., and F. Navez-Bouchanine. 2005. "L'entre-deux des politiques urbaines et des dynamiques sociales dans les villes marocaines: injonctions et résistances à l'éviction dans le contexte du renouvellement ou de l'aménagement urbains." In *Intégration à la ville et services urbains au Maroc*, ed. Claude de Miras, 43–96. Paris: Rabat. INAU PRUD, IRD.

Castel, R. 1995. *La métamorphose de la question sociale.* Paris: Fayard.

Castells, M. 1983. *The City and the Grassroots.* Berkeley: University of California Press.

Cefaï, D., and D. Trom, eds. 2001. *Les formes de l'action collective: mobilizations dans des arènes publiques.* Paris: Editions de l'Ecole des Hautes Etudes en Sciences Sociales.

Cernea, M. M. 1998. "Déplacement forcé et réinstallation de populations: recherche, politique d'intervention et planification." In *La dimension humaine dans les projets de développement—les variables sociologiques et culturelles*, ed. Michael M. Cernea, 207–235. Paris: Karthala.

de Certeau, M. 1990. "L'invention du quotidien." *Arts de Faire* 1. Paris: Folio.

Cobban, H. 1985. *The Making of Modern Lebanon.* London: Hutchison and Co. Publishers Ltd.

Deboulet, A. 2004. "Quand le global fait mal: le périphérique du Caire." *Urbanisme*, no. 336: 37–38.

———. 2008. "Ethiopiennes, Philippines et Soudanais: voisinages migrants et confrontation aux sociétés d'accueil à Beyrouth." *Studi Emigrazione* 172: 837–852.

Deboulet, A., and M. Fawaz. 2004. "Entre reconstruction et déconstruction, la négociation locale des projets à Beyrouth." *Urbanisme*, no. 336: 34–36.

Du Plessis, J. 2006. "Forced Evictions, Development and the Need for Community-Based Locally Appropriate Alternatives: Lessons and Challenges from South Africa, Ghana and Thailand." In *Informal Settlements: A Perpetual Challenge?*, ed. M. Huchzermeyer and A. Karam, 180–206. Cape Town, South Africa: University of Cape Town Press.

Donzelot, M. C., and A. Wyvekens. 2003. *Faire société-la politique de la ville aux Etats-Unis et en France.* Paris: Seuil.

Dunn, J. A. 1995. "The French Highway Lobby: A Case Study in State Society Relations and Policymaking." *Comparative Politics* 27: 275–295.

Fawaz, M. 1998. "Islam, Resistance, and Community Development: The Southern Suburbs of Beirut." Masters thesis, Massachusetts Institute of Technology.

———. 2004. "Strategizing for Housing: An Investigation of the Production and Regulation of Low-Income Housing in the Suburbs of Beirut." Ph.D. diss., Massachusetts Institute of Technology.

———. 2007. "Beirut: The City as Body-politic." *ISIM Review* 20 (Autumn): 22–23.

———. 2009. "Hezbollah as Urban Planner? Questions to and from Planning Theory." *Planning Theory* 20, no. 4: 323-334.

Fawaz, M., and M. Harb. 2001. "Mobilization Strategies of Shiʿa Groups in Lebanon (1970s–1990s)." Paper presented at SSRC/CERMOC workshop on Cities & Citizenship II: Questions of Comparison, Beirut, Lebanon.

Fawaz, M., and I. Peillen. 2002. "The Slums of Beirut: History and Development 1930–2002." Paper prepared for United Nations Center for Human Settlements.

Fuks, M. 1998. "Environment-Related Litigation in Rio de Janeiro: Shaping Frames for a New Social Problem." *International Journal of Urban and Regional Research* 22: 394–407.

Gans, H. J. 1962. *The Urban Villagers: Group and Class in the Life of Italian-Americans.* New York: Free Press.

Ghorayeb, M. 1998. "The Work and Influence of Michel Ecochard in Lebanon." In *Projecting Beirut: Episodes in the Construction and Reconstruction of a Modern City*, ed. Peter Rowe and Hashim Sarkis. Munich, Germany: Prestel Publishing.

Giddens, A. 1987. *La constitution de la société. Eléments de théorie de la structuration.* Paris: PUF.

Gotham, K. F. 1999. "Political Opportunity, Community Identity, and the Emergence of a Local Anti-expressway Movement." *Social Problems* 46: 332–354.

Graham, S. 2000. "Constructing Premium Network Spaces: Reflections on Infrastructure Networks and Contemporary Urban Development." *International Journal of Urban and Regional Research* 24: 183–200.

———. 2000. "Introduction: Cities and Infrastructure Networks." *International Journal of Urban and Regional Research* 24: 114–119.

Harb, M. 1996. *Politiques urbaines dans la Banlieue-Sud de Beyrouth.* Beirut: Centre d'Etudes et de Recherches sur le Moyen-Orient Contemporain.

———. 2000. "Post-War Beirut: Resources Negotiations, and Contestations in the Elyssar Project." *The Arab World Geographer* 3: 272–288.

———. 2003. "La dâhiye de Beyrouth: parcours d'une stigmatisation urbaine, consolidation d'un territoire politique." *Genèses* 51: 70–91.

———. 2005. "Action publique et système politique pluricommunautaire: les mouvements politiques chiites dans le Liban de l'après-guerre." Ph.D. diss.

Harvey, D. 1975. *Social Justice and the City.* Baltimore, Md.: Johns Hopkins University Press.

———. "Social Justice, Postmodernism, and the City." *International Journal of Urban and Regional Research* 16 (1992): 588–601.

Henderson, J. 2006. "Secessionist Automobility: Racism, Anti-urbanism, and the Politics of Automobility in Atlanta, Georgia." *International Journal of Urban and Regional Research* 30: 293–307.

Holston, J., ed. 1999. *Cities and Citizenship.* Durham, N.C.: Duke University Press.

Huybrechts, E., and E. Verdeil. 2000. "Beyrouth entre reconstruction et métropolisation." In "Gouverner les métropoles" in *Villes en parallèle*, no. 32–33, 63–87. Nanterre, France: Laboratoire de géographie urbaine, Université de Paris X-Nanterre.

Joseph, I. 1998. *La ville sans qualités.* Paris: L'aube.

Kassab, S. 1997. "On Two Conceptions of Globalization: The Debate around the Reconstruction of Beirut." In *Space, Culture and Power: New Identities in Globalizing Cities*, ed. A. Onçu and P. Weyland. London: Zed Books.

Kaufmann, V. 2005. "Mobilités et réversibilités, vers des sociétés plus fluides?" *Cahiers Internationaux de Sociologie* 17.

Khayat, T. 2001. "La route de la discorde: construction du territoire municipal et aménagement métropolitain à Dorj Hammoud." In *Municipalités et pouvoirs locaux au Liban,* ed. A. Favier, 201–225. Beirut: Les Cahiers du Cermoc.

Khuri, F. 1975. *From Village to Suburb: Order and Change in Greater Beirut.* Chicago: University of Chicago Press.

Lefebvre, H. 2000. *Espace et politique.* Paris: Editions Anthropos.

Logan, J., and H. Molotch. 1987. *Urban Fortunes.* Berkeley: University of California Press.

Mathieu, L. 2004. "Comment lutter? La sociologie des mouvements sociaux: un déplacement du regard." Paris: Textuel.

McCreery, S. 1996. "Westway, Caught in the Speed Trap." In *Strangely Familiar,* ed. Ian Borden et al. London: Routledge, 1996.

Mervin, S. 2000. *Un réformisme chiite: ulémas et lettrés du Gabal Amil (Actuel Liban-Sud) de la fin de l'Empire Ottoman à l'indépendance du Liban.* Paris: Karthala.

———. 2000. "The Claremont Road Situation." In *The Unknown City: Contesting Architecture and Social Space,* ed. Ian Borden et al. Cambridge, Mass.: MIT Press.

Mével, C., and A. Wyvekens. 2003. *Faire société—la politique de la ville aux Etats-Unis et en France,* trans. J. Donzelot. Paris: Seuil.

Nasr, S. 1985. "La transition des chiites vers Beyrouth: mutations sociales et mobilisation communautaire à la Veille de 1975." In *Mouvements communautaires et espaces urbains dans le mashreq* by CERMOC, 87–116. Beirut: Centre d'Etudes et de Recherches sur le Moyen Orient Contemporain.

Navez-Bouchanine, F. 2004. "L'entre-deux des politiques institutionnelles et des dynamiques sociales: Liban, Maroc, Algérie, Mauritanie." Rapport de synthèse, Programme Prud. Paris: Karthala.

Neveu, E. 2005. *Sociologie des mouvements sociaux.* Paris: La Découverte, collection Repères.

Norton, R. A. 1987. *Amal and the Shiʾa: Struggle for the Soul of Lebanon.* Austin: University of Texas Press.

Oberschall, A. 1973. *Social Conflicts and Social Movements.* Englewood Cliffs, N.J.: Prentice-Hall Publishing.

Onçu, A., and P. Weyland, eds. 1997. *Space, Culture and Power: New Identities in Globalizing Cities.* London: Zed Books.

Picard, E. 1994. "Les habits neufs du communautarisme Libanais." *Cultures et Conflits,* no. 15–16: 49–70.

———. 1996. *Lebanon, a Shattered Country: Myths and Realities of the Wars in Lebanon.* Translated by F. Philip. New York: Holmes & Meier.

———. "Retrait Syrien du Liban, que fera le Hezbollah?" www.alternatives.ca/article1771 .html (accessed 27 March 2009).

Scott, J. C. 1985. *Weapons of the Weak.* New Haven, Conn.: Yale University Press.

Shami, S. 1994. *Population, Displacement and Resettlement-Development and Conflict in the Middle East.* New York: Center for Migration Studies.

Sharara, W. 1997. *The HizbʾAllah Nation: Lebanon as an Islamic Society.* Beirut: Dar Al-Nahar.

Simmel, G. 1950. "The Metropolis and Mental Life." In *The Sociology of George Simmel.* ed. K. H. Wolff, 409–424. Glencoe, Ill.: Free Press.

Snow, D. 2001. "Analyse de cadres et mouvements sociaux." In *Les formes de l'action collective-mobilisation dans les arènes publiques,* ed. D. Cefaï and D. Trom, 27–51. Paris: Editions de l'EHESS.

Tarrow, S. 1998. *Power in Movement: Social Movements and Contentious Politics.* Cambridge: Cambridge University Press.

Tilly, C. 1986. *The Contentious French.* Cambridge: Belknap Press.

Touraine, A. 1973. *La Production de la société.* Paris: Seuil.

Urry, J. 2004. "The 'System' of Automobility." *Theory, Culture, and Society* 21: 25–39.

——. 2005. *Sociologie des mobilités.* Paris: Armand Colin.

——. 2007. *Mobilities.* New York: Polity Press.

UN-ESCWA. 2000. *Survey of Economic and Social Developments in the ESCWA Region.* New York: United Nations.

Wheeler, J. O. 1976. Locational Dimensions of Urban Highway Projects: An Empirical Analysis. *Geografiska Annaler, series B, Human Geography* 58: 67–78.

Yiftachel, O. 2000. "Social Control, Urban Planning and Ethno-class Relations: Mizrahi Jews in Israel's Development Towns." *International Journal of Urban and Regional Research* 24: 418–438.

Zald, M. N. 1996. "Culture, Ideology, and Strategic Framing." In *Comparative Perspectives on Social Movements: Political Opportunities, Mobilizing Structures, and Cultural Framings,* ed. Doug McAdam, John D. McCarthy, and Mayer N. Zald, 261–274. Cambridge: Cambridge University Press.

6

Urban Locational Policies and the Geographies of Post-Keynesian Statehood in Western Europe

Neil Brenner

In this chapter, I argue that urban governance restructuring provides an illuminating analytical window through which to explore some of the broader transformations of state space and state sovereignty that have been unfolding across western Europe during the last thirty years.[1] From this perspective, the entrepreneurial, growth-oriented approaches to urban governance that have proliferated since the 1980s (Harvey 1989) can be interpreted as expressions and catalysts of "urban locational policies" oriented toward a fundamental rescaling of national state space and, more generally, of national state sovereignty.[2] In contrast to the project of national territorial equalization and administrative standardization associated with Keynesian welfare national states, urban locational policies promote the formation of what I have elsewhere (Brenner 2004) termed Rescaled Competition State Regimes (RCSRs) in which (a) significant aspects of economic regulation are devolved to subnational institutional levels; (b) customized, place- and region-specific regulatory arrangements are constructed, particularly within strategic economic zones; and (c) political strategies are mobilized to concentrate major socioeconomic assets within the most globally competitive urban regions and industrial districts. This ongoing rescaling of statehood has, on the one hand, eroded the nationalized formations of urban governance and the standardizing, territorially redistributive forms of state spatial policy that prevailed during the Fordist-Keynesian period. Just as importantly, newly emergent RCSRs have also systematically enhanced fiscal constraints and competitive pressures on European cities and regions, impelling their national, regional, and local regulatory institutions to privilege the goals of local economic development and territorial competitiveness over traditional welfarist redistributive priorities.

As Ong (2004, 75) has noted in the East Asian context, such spatially selective locational policies (in her terms, "zoning technologies") have been tightly interlinked with broader transformations of state sovereignty: they "provide the mechanisms for creating or accommodating islands of distinct governing regimes within the broader landscape of normalized rule, thus generating a pattern of variegated but linked sovereignty." Analogously, through their promotion of highly customized, place- and region-specific models of economic regulation, western European RCSRs have likewise profoundly reorganized the geographies and "socially constructed practices of political authority" (Agnew 2005, 441) at a range of spatial scales. This still ongoing rearticulation of state sovereignty is embodied not only in the territorial transformations associated with the consolidation of European Union (EU) governance institutions (Ansell and di Palma 2004; Rumford 2006), but equally, in a wide-ranging recalibration of interscalar relations among inherited tiers of state power and in the associated "splintering" of regulatory arrangements among distinctive urban-regional institutional configurations (Graham and Marvin 2001; Swyngedouw 2000; Sassen 2005).

In order to develop this argument, the next section examines the role of urban governance in the production and transformation of state spatial configurations and sovereignty regimes. Subsequent sections explore the evolution of state spatiality and state sovereignty in relation to changing approaches to urban governance in western European cities and metropolitan regions since the early 1960s. Four phases of urban restructuring and state spatial reorganization are examined—Spatial Keynesianism (early 1960s–early 1970s); Fordism in Crisis (early 1970s–early 1980s); State Rescaling Strategies, Round One (1980s); and State Rescaling Strategies, Round Two (1990s). A concluding section summarizes the implications of newly emergent RCSRs for the political geographies of western European capitalism and associated patterns of state sovereignty. I interpret the rescaling of urban governance in western Europe as an important politico-institutional mechanism through which the "variegated" formation of sovereignty postulated by Ong (2006; 2004) in the East Asian context has been established in the E.U.

Urban Governance as an Arena and Medium of State Spatial Restructuring

The concept of urban governance refers to the broad constellation of social forces that mold the process of urbanization within modern capitalism. Urban governance occurs at a range of geographical scales insofar as capitalist urbanization encompasses individual cities, metropolitan regions, cross-border agglomerations, national city-systems, and supranational urban hierarchies (Lefebvre 1968). The state's impact on urban development processes has expanded considerably since the consolidation of organized capitalism during the early twentieth century. It was during this era, and particularly after the Second World War, that western European states began to invest extensively in the construction of large-scale infrastructures for capital circulation and social reproduction, to engage in long-term forms of spatial planning, and to intervene directly in the regulation of uneven geographical development (Lefebvre 2002 [1978]). Once the state began to operate as the "overall manager of the production and reproduction of social infrastructures" (Harvey 1982, 404) within each national territory, the politics of national economic development were interlinked ever more closely with a variety of state strategies to regulate urbanization. Consequently, urban governance must be viewed as a key institutional arena in which states attempt to influence the geographies of political-economic life within their territories.

Just as crucially, as the urbanization process unfolds, the institutional-territorial matrix for urban governance is itself continually restructured, generally bringing with it broader shifts in the geographies of state regulation and state sovereignty. Insofar as the state's own spatial configuration impacts its capacity to confront place-, scale-, and territory-specific regulatory problems, states are often pressured to reconfigure their internal territorial hierarchies and jurisdictional frameworks, not least within major urban regions. During periods of sustained economic crisis, extant frameworks of urban governance may be viewed as ineffectual, and diverse social forces may promote the reorganization of inherited local or regional state structures, leading eventually to the introduction of qualitatively new geographies of state intervention and political authority. Urban governance is thus an important politico-institutional forcefield in which the geographies of state activity and state sovereignty are themselves continually reworked.

In an important recent contribution, Agnew (2005) has introduced the concept of "sovereignty regimes" to characterize the divergent institutional and spatial forms in which legitimate political authority may be articulated. Rather than subsuming all modern forms of state sovereignty under the rubric of the "Westphalian" model of statehood (Ruggie 1993), with its emphasis on self-enclosed, mutually exclusive territories, Agnew argues that states may exercise de facto sovereignty through diverse systems of rule that differentially combine central state power with various types of scale-, place-, and territory-differentiated spatial strategies. In this way, Agnew aims to respatialize the notion of sovereignty by systematically uncoupling it from that of (national) territoriality as well as from various prevalent assumptions regarding its de jure features (for instance, its conception as absolute or indivisible). I shall not, in the present context, undertake a broader discussion of theories of state sovereignty and their associated geographical or juridical assumptions. For present purposes, the key point is that the definitional reorientation proposed by Agnew can help illuminate the changing roles of cities and urban regions within ongoing struggles over the nature of state sovereignty and political authority, both within and beyond western Europe (see also Holston and Appadurai 1999).

To this end, in subsequent sections, I explore some of the multiscalar transformations of urban governance, state spatiality and state sovereignty that have unfolded during the last four decades in western Europe. While the following stylized narrative focuses on state strategies to regulate the process of urbanization, it interprets such strategies as important political mechanisms through which historically and geographically specific formations of state sovereignty are produced, destabilized, and transformed. Specifically, I argue that since the era of high Fordism, four successive configurations of urban governance have crystallized, each of which has been closely intertwined with historically specific, scale-differentiated strategies of state spatial regulation and formations of political authority. Crucially, the transformations of urban governance described by this periodization do not represent simple, unilinear transitions from one stabilized regulatory framework to another. They entail, rather, a path-dependent layering process in which inherited and emergent projects of state spatial regulation interact conflictually at various spatial scales (Brenner 2004).

Urban Governance and the Geographies of Spatial Keynesianism

The economic geography of postwar Fordism was composed of a functional division of space at various geographical scales. Spatial divisions of labor emerged within each national territory in the form of hierarchical relationships between large-scale metropolitan regions, in which the lead firms within the major, propulsive Fordist industries were clustered; and smaller cities, towns and peripheral zones, in which branch plants, input and service providers, and other subordinate economic functions were located. In western Europe, the heartlands of the Fordist accumulation regime stretched from the Industrial Triangle of northern Italy through the German Ruhr district to northern France and the English Midlands. Each of these regional production complexes was embedded within a nationally specific system of production. Throughout the postwar period, most major European urban regions and their surrounding industrial satellites were characterized by consistent demographic growth and industrial expansion. As the Fordist accumulation regime reached maturity, a sustained decentralization of capital investment unfolded as large firms began to relocate branch plants from core regions into peripheral spaces (Rodriguez-Pose 1998; Dunford and Perrons 1994). Under these conditions, urban governance acquired a key role in a variety of nationalizing regulatory strategies. For present purposes, three key components of this nationalized framework of urban governance and state sovereignty deserve particular emphasis.

1. *Urban managerialism.* In order to standardize the provision of welfare services and to coordinate national economic policies, national states centralized the instruments for regulating urban development, thereby transforming local states into transmission belts for centrally determined policy regimes (Mayer 1994). Insofar as the national economy was viewed as the primary terrain for state action, local and regional economies were treated as mere subunits of national economic spaces. A range of national social and economic policy initiatives—including demand-management policies, nationalized ownership of key industries, the expansion of public sector employment, military spending and major expenditures on housing, transportation and public utilities—served to underwrite the growth of major urban and regional economies (Martin and Sunley 1997, 280).

2. *Compensatory spatial policies.* The national states of the Fordist-Keynesian era introduced a variety of spatial policies intended to alleviate intranational territorial inequalities. From the Italian Mezzogiorno and Spanish Andalusia to western and southern France; the agricultural peripheries and border zones of West Germany; the Limburg coal-mining district of northern Belgium; the Dutch northeastern peripheries; the northwestern regions and islands of Denmark; the Scandinavian north; western Ireland; and the declining industrial zones of the English north, south Wales, parts of Scotland, and much of Northern Ireland, each European country had its so-called "problem areas" or "lagging regions," generally composed of economic spaces that had been marginalized during previous rounds of industrial development or that were locked into obsolete technological-industrial infrastructures (OECD 1976). Such regions "were conceived as blank spaces on the national map of industry, to be filled by the same development strategies as such voids were to be filled in the Third World" (Sabel 1994, 126). Accordingly, throughout the postwar period until the late 1970s, a broad range of spatial policies were introduced that explicitly targeted such peripheralized spaces. Generally justified in the name of priorities such as balanced national development and spatial equalization, these redistributive regional policies entailed the introduction of various forms of finan-

cial aid, locational incentives, and transfer payments to promote industrial growth and economic regeneration outside the dominant city cores; and they often channeled major public infrastructural investments into such locations (Clout 1981).

3. *Metropolitan institutional reform.* Within this nationalized system of urban governance, metropolitan political institutions acquired an important mediating role between managerial local states and centrally organized, redistributive forms of spatial planning. During the Fordist-Keynesian period, diverse types of consolidated metropolitan institutions were established in a number of major city-regions—including the Greater London Council (1963); the *Rijnmond* in Rotterdam (1964); the *communautés urbaines* in Bordeaux, Lille, Lyon and Strasbourg (1966); the metropolitan counties in Manchester, Birmingham, Liverpool, Leeds, Sheffield and Newcastle; the Metropolitan Barcelona authority; the Greater Copenhagen Council; the Greater Frankfurt Association (1974); and the Ruhr Municipal Agency (1975) (Sharpe 1995). These administrative bodies served as a key, coordinating tier within the centralized intergovernmental hierarchies of the Keynesian welfare state. By the early 1970s, metropolitan authorities had also acquired important roles in guiding industrial expansion, infrastructural investment, and population settlement beyond traditional city cores into suburban fringes.

In sum, urban governance was an essential pillar within the nationalized system of spatial Keynesianism that prevailed in western Europe from the late 1950s until the early 1970s. Within that system, national states attempted to redistribute the surplus not only socially, through institutionalized collective bargaining arrangements and national social welfare policies, but also spatially, through a variety of political strategies intended to centralize, homogenize, standardize and equalize national political-economic space. In each case, the goal of such spatial strategies was to bring "regions and localities within the economy under much greater central state control and dependence" by subordinating them "to the macro-economic and macro-redistributive imperatives of the center" (Martin and Sunley 1997, 279, 280). At the same time, the system of spatial Keynesianism established certain minimum standards of social welfare and infrastructure provision across national intergovernmental systems, "thereby incorporating [regions and localities] into an increasingly *collective* or *public* space-economy, which in some countries extended to large-scale state ownership and management of key industries, in addition to utilities and other collective goods" (Martin and Sunley 1999, 280). Spatial Keynesianism is thus best understood as a constellation of national state strategies designed to promote capitalist industrial growth by alleviating uneven geographical development within each national economy. These state strategies attempted to secure a structured coherence for capitalist growth (a) by transforming cities and regions into the localized building blocks for national economic development and (b) by spreading urbanization as evenly as possible across the national territory, like butter on a piece of toast (see table 6.1).

Urban Governance and the Crisis of Fordism

A new configuration of urban governance, state spatial regulation and state sovereignty began to crystallize during the early 1970s, as the Fordist developmental regime entered a phase of systemic, crisis-induced restructuring on a world scale (Lipietz 1994). A number of geoeconomic shifts occurred during this era that decentered the predominant role of the national scale as a locus of political-economic coordination and led to the rescaling of state regulatory capacities and political authority both upwards to supranational institutional forms such as the EU and downwards to the regional and local levels. The uneven, incremental, and contested character of these rescaling processes is illustrated vividly in the realm of urban governance.

While intensive efforts were made during the first half of the 1970s to preserve the regulatory infrastructure of spatial Keynesianism, the tide began to change by the end of the decade. At this time, the national scale became an increasingly important institutional locus for restructuring-oriented political projects that aimed to dismantle many of the standardizing, redistributive policy relays associated with the Keynesian national welfare state. During the post-1970s recession, as national governments were pressured to rationalize government expenditures, national grants to subnational administrative levels were significantly reduced. These new forms of fiscal austerity caused local governments to become more dependent on locally collected taxes and non-tax revenues such as charges and user fees. In the wake of these shifts, local governments sought additional local revenues in economic development projects and inward investment strategies.

In contrast to their earlier focus on welfarist redistribution, local governments began to introduce a range of strategies to rejuvenate local economies, beginning with land-assembly programs and land-use planning schemes and subsequently expanding to diverse firm-based, area-based, sectoral, and job-creation measures (Eisenschitz and Gough 1993). Although this new politics of urban economic development would subsequently be diffused in diverse political forms, during the 1970s it remained most prevalent within manufacturing-based cities and regions in which industrial restructuring had generated major socioeconomic problems. Thus, even as most western European national governments continued to pro-

Table 6.1. Spatial Keynesianism and the Geographies of Urban Governance under European Fordism

Geoeconomic and geopolitical context:
- Early 1960s to early 1970s: high Fordism
- Differentiation of global economic activity among distinct national economic systems under Fordist accumulation regime

Privileged spatial target(s):
- National economy

Major goals:
- Deconcentration of population, industry, and infrastructure investment from major urban centers into rural peripheries and "underdeveloped" zones
- Replication of standardized economic assets, investments, and public goods across the entire surface of the national territory
- Establishment of a nationally standardized system of infrastructural facilities throughout the national economy
- Alleviation of uneven development within national economies: uneven spatial development is seen as a limit or barrier to stabilized industrial growth

Dominant policy mechanisms:
- Locational subsidies to large firms
- Local social welfare policies and collective consumption investments
- Redistributive regional policies
- National spatial planning systems and public infrastructural investments
- Construction of large-scale metropolitan institutions and regional planning agencies

Spatio-temporality of economic development and state sovereignty:
- "National developmentalism": development of the entire national economy as an integrated, self-enclosed territorial unit moving along a linear developmental trajectory
- Standardized sovereignty: generalization of governance systems and infrastructural conditions evenly across the national state space

mote territorial equalization at a national scale, neocorporatist alliances between state institutions, trade unions and other local organizations within rustbelt cities and regions, from the German Ruhr district to the English Midlands, elaborated regionally specific sectoral, technology, and employment policies in order to promote what was popularly labeled "endogenous growth" (Stöhr and Taylor 1981). The goal of these neocorporatist alliances was to establish negotiated strategies of industrial restructuring in which economic regeneration was linked directly to priorities such as intraregional redistribution, job creation, vocational retraining, and class compromise (Hahne 1985).

These initiatives were grounded upon a neo-Fordist political project to res-cale the institutional infrastructures of spatial Keynesianism from a national to a regional or local scale. Regional and local economies were now recognized to have their own specific developmental trajectories and structural problems rather than being mere subunits within a unitary national economic space. At the same time, however, the basic Fordist-Keynesian priorities of social redistribution, ter-ritorial equalization, administrative standardization, and class compromise were maintained, albeit within the more bounded parameters of regional and local economies, rather than as a project to be extended throughout the entire national territory. In contrast to the central state's policies of national territorial redistri-bution, the new politics of endogenous growth were oriented primarily toward place-specific regulatory problems. Many of these neocorporatist local economic initiatives would continue during the 1980s, albeit in a radically transformed geo-economic environment. The salient point here is that such strategies of endoge-nous growth first emerged during a period in which neo-Keynesian priorities continued to prevail at a national level. Under these conditions, due to their dif-ferentiating impacts upon local economies, the subnational neocorporatisms of the 1970s explicitly counteracted the projects of national spatial equalization that were then still being pursued by most western European national states.

The 1970s is thus best viewed as a transitional period characterized by intense interscalar struggles between political alliances concerned to preserve the nation-alized institutional infrastructures of spatial Keynesianism and newly formed political coalitions concerned to introduce more decentralized, localized frame-works of territorial development and urban governance. It was through the con-flictual interaction of this newly emergent, subnational layer of state spatial regu-lation and the inherited national geographies of spatial Keynesianism that the broad contours of a new, rescaled landscape of state spatiality and state sover-eignty began to emerge as of the early 1980s. Insofar as the projects of endoge-nous growth of the 1970s entailed a clear divergence from the nationally equal-izing, redistributive agendas of spatial Keynesianism, they established a significant politico-institutional opening for the more radical rescalings of urban governance, state spatiality and political authority that would subsequently unfold.

Urban Locational Policy and the Rescaling of State Space

During the 1980s, most European national governments abandoned traditional Keynesian macroeconomic policies. Neoliberal political agendas such as welfare state retrenchment, trade liberalization, privatization, and deregulation were adopted not only in the United Kingdom under Thatcher and in West Germany under Kohl, but also in many traditionally social democratic or social/Christian-democratic countries such as the Netherlands, Belgium, France, Spain, Denmark, and Sweden (Brenner and Theodore 2002). This geopolitical sea change resulted in the imposition of additional fiscal constraints upon most municipal and metropolitan governments and, in some cases (London, Manchester, Barcelona, Copenhagen, Rotterdam), to the abolition of metropolitan institutions. The national preconditions for municipal Keynesianism were being eroded as local and metropolitan governments were increasingly forced to fend for themselves in securing a fiscal base.

During the same period, a new mosaic of urban and regional development crystallized throughout the European city-system. Across western Europe, the crisis of North Atlantic Fordism triggered the tumultuous decline of many large-scale manufacturing regions. Meanwhile, established metropolitan cores such as London, Amsterdam, Paris, Frankfurt, Milan, and Zürich were being transformed into strategic nodal points within global and European financial networks. As Veltz (1993) explains, the post-1970s period has witnessed the consolidation of an "archipelago economy" in which major corporate decision-making centers and most high-value-added economic activities have been concentrated within the most powerful metropolitan nodes. In a now famous report prepared for the French spatial planning agency DATAR prior to the consolidation of the Single European Market, Brunet (1989) famously described the core urban zone of the European archipelago economy as a "blue banana" whose strategic importance would be further enhanced as geoeconomic and European economic integration proceeded. Notably, Brunet's map of Europe's urbanized boom zone envisioned a nearly exact inversion of the geography of development zones that had been established during the era of spatial Keynesianism. Earlier spatial and regional policies had been based upon notions of cumulative causation in which the spatial diffusion of growth potentials was seen to benefit both cores and peripheries. In stark contrast, Brunet's model implied that winning cities and regions would form a powerful, densely interlinked, and relatively autonomous urban network dominated by advanced infrastructural facilities and high-value-added activities, leaving other regions to fend for themselves or risk being marginalized further in the new geoeconomic context. As Brunet's model dramatically illustrated, the economic transformations of the 1980s were causing the geographies of spatial Keynesianism to be turned inside-out. As of this decade, growth was no longer being spread outwards from developed urban cores into the underdeveloped peripheries of each national economy, but was instead being systematically reconcentrated into the most powerful agglomerations situated within European and global spatial divisions of labor.

As urban economic restructuring intensified in conjunction with processes of global and European integration, western European central governments began more explicitly to target major cities and city-regions as the locational keys to national economic competitiveness. In the "Europe of regions"—a boosterist catchphrase that became increasingly important in national policy discussions as of the mid-1980s—cities were no longer seen merely as containers of declining industries and socioeconomic problems. Instead, they were now viewed as dynamic growth engines through which national prosperity could be secured. This view of the city as an essential national economic asset became widely prevalent in mainstream policy circles in the late 1980s, as national and local governments attempted to prepare for the introduction of the Single European Market.

As Mayer (1994) has shown, a number of fundamental realignments of urban governance subsequently ensued:

- local authorities were constrained to engage more extensively and proactively in local economic development projects;
- local welfarist and collective consumption policies were increasingly marginalized or subordinated to production-oriented policies; and
- new forms of local governance, such as public-private partnerships, became increasingly prevalent.

By the late 1980s, this new, entrepreneurial form of urban governance had been diffused throughout Europe as fiscally enfeebled local and regional governments mobilized a range of economic regeneration strategies to attract inward investment and to promote property redevelopment (Harding 1997). Although urban entrepreneurialism was articulated in diverse political forms during this period—including neoliberal, social democratic, and centrist variants (Eisenschitz and Gough 1993)—all contributed to a trans-European diffusion of "beggar-thy-neighbor" inter-locality competition, in which local and regional governments struggled aggressively against one another to lure a limited supply of investments and jobs into their territories (Cheshire and Gordon 1996).

I have characterized the diverse institutional realignments and regulatory transformations associated with urban entrepreneurialism as forms of *urban locational policy* (Brenner 2004): they are the outcome of state strategies that explicitly target cities and urban regions as sites for the enhancement of territorial competitiveness. As conceived here, the essential feature of locational policies is their overarching goal of enhancing the international economic competitiveness of particular places, territories, or scales in relation to broader, supranational circuits of capital accumulation (see also Fougner 2006). Locational policies may involve direct subsidies and other public schemes to lure the investments of specific firms, but they are best understood as being oriented toward the *general* conditions for capital accumulation within particular territorial jurisdictions, at whatever spatial scale at which they are deployed. However, while locational policies have a long history under modern capitalism, they have most frequently been mobilized at a national scale, in conjunction with national-developmentalist strategies of industrialization and nationalized approaches to territorial development and infrastructural investment (Graham and Marvin 2001). It is only since the 1980s that western European states have deployed locational policies extensively and systematically at an urban scale, in the field of urban governance. Since this period, urban locational policies have been mobilized aggressively by national, regional, and local state institutions in order to promote the territorialized competitive advantages of strategic cities and regions in relation to supranational (European or global) spaces of economic competition. In this transformed political-economic context, cities are no longer seen as containers of declining industries and intensifying socioeconomic problems, but are increasingly viewed as dynamic growth engines through which national territorial competitiveness may be promoted. In short, as Lipietz (1994, 37) notes, the locality is increasingly construed as a "breeding ground for new productive forces," which state institutions at various spatial scales (European, national and local) are now actively attempting to cultivate.

Aside from attempting to undercut traditional redistributive regional policy relays, national governments now mobilized a number of institutional restructuring initiatives that were intended to establish a new, competitive infrastructure for urban economic growth within their territories:

- Local governments were granted new revenue-raising powers and an increased level of authority in determining local tax rates and user fees, and national fiscal transfers to subnational levels were diminished (Fox Przeworski 1986).
- New responsibilities for planning, economic development, social services, and spatial planning were devolved downwards to subnational (regional and local) governments. Decentralization policies were seen as a means to "limit the considerable welfare demands of urban areas and to encourage lower-level authorities to assume responsibility for growth policies that might reduce welfare burdens" (Harding 1994, 370).
- National spatial planning systems were redefined. Economic priorities such as promoting structural competitiveness superseded traditional welfarist redistributive priorities such as territorial equity and spatial equalization. In many European countries, the most globally competitive urban regions and industrial districts replaced the national economy as the privileged target for major spatial planning initiatives and infrastructural investments.
- National, regional, and local governments introduced new, territory- and place-specific institutions and policies—from enterprise zones, urban devel-

opment corporations, and airport development agencies to training and enterprise councils, inward investment agencies, and development planning
boards—designed to reconcentrate or enhance socioeconomic assets within
cities.

- The forms and functions of local states were systematically redefined. Whereas
postwar western European local governments had been devoted primarily
to various forms of welfare service delivery, these institutions were transformed into entrepreneurial agencies oriented above all toward the promotion of economic development within their jurisdictions.

The consolidation and diffusion of urban locational policy was premised upon
the establishment of new subnational layers of state and parastate institutions
through which cities could be marketed as customized, specialized and maximally
competitive locations for strategic economic functions within global and European
spatial divisions of labor. At the same time, the devolutionary, decentralizing initiatives of the 1980s fundamentally reconfigured entrenched intergovernmental
hierarchies and scalar divisions of regulation, imposing new pressures on subnational administrative units to fend for themselves within an increasingly uncertain geoeconomic environment. These newly constituted, state-organized interscalar
rule-regimes were explicitly designed to facilitate urban locational policies by
channeling "the strategic options and tactical behavior of local actors" (Peck 2002,
338) toward developmentalist agendas driven by competitiveness. More generally,
such interscalar rule-regimes were designed to institutionalize entrepreneurial,
competitiveness-oriented and "growth first" approaches to urban governance (a)
by exposing cities and regions more directly to geoeconomic pressures and (b)
by subjecting them to competitive regimes of intergovernmental resource allo-
cation based on market position, performance, and efficiency rather than social
need (Peck and Tickell 1994). Consequently, in direct contrast to postwar strategies of spatial Keynesianism, which sought to *alleviate* uneven intranational development, newly emergent urban locational policies actively *intensified* the latter (a) by promoting a systematic reconcentration of industry and population
within each national territory's most competitive locations, (b) by permitting
and even encouraging divergent, place-specific forms of economic governance,
welfare provision and territorial administration within major local and regional
economies, and (c) by institutionalizing intensely competitive relations, whether
for public subsidies or for private investments, among major subnational administrative units.

In sum, in contrast to the relatively standardized geographies of state space
and state sovereignty under Fordism, in which national states attempted to main-

tain minimum levels of service provision throughout the national territory, the establishment of an entrepreneurial, competitiveness-oriented institutional infrastructure for urban governance during the 1980s appears to have entailed an increasing *splintering* of state regulatory activities and an intensified spatial *variegation* of state sovereignty at various spatial scales. From this point of view, the new interlocality competition of the post-1980s period cannot be understood simply as the aggregate expression of localized policy responses to global and European market integration. On the contrary, the grim, neoliberal requirement for cities to "compete or die" (Eisenschitz and Gough 1998, 762)—which aptly encapsulates the aggressively competitive spatial logic underlying urban locational policy—must be interpreted as a politically constructed imperative that was imposed upon local and regional economies in significant measure through the rescaling of national state spaces and the construction of an increasingly variegated formation of state sovereignty (see also Ong 2004). Meanwhile, national states should not be conceived as static territorial containers within which urban locational policies have been mobilized. Rather, national state institutions actively promoted such policies by recalibrating their internal intergovernmental hierarchies, modes of intervention, and policy repertoires in order to facilitate the strategic positioning of their major local and regional economies within Europe-wide and global circuits of capital. The interplay between urban locational policies and the rescaling of state space is summarized schematically in table 6.2.

I propose to characterize the rescaled formation of national state spatiality that crystallized through these transformations as a Rescaled Competition State Regime (RCSR)—*rescaled,* because it rests upon concerted political strategies to reorganize national institutional hierarchies so as to position diverse subnational spaces (localities, cities, regions, industrial districts) within supranational (European or global) circuits of capital accumulation; a *competition state,* because it privileges the goal of structural competitiveness over welfarist priorities such as equity and redistribution; and a *regime,* because it represents an unstable, continually evolving institutional mosaic rather than a fully consolidated state form (see also Jessop 2002). Whether forged predominantly from below, through the initiatives of local and regional coalitions to manage economic restructuring, or from above, through central state strategies to enhance local and regional competitiveness, the institutional infrastructures of urban entrepreneurialism soon came to occupy pivotal regulatory positions within the newly forged scalar architectures of RCSRs. It is in this sense that urban locational policies provided an important institutional mechanism for the rescaling of national state space and the reconstitution of state sovereignty during the course of the 1980s.

Table 6.2. Urban Locational Policies and the Splintering of State Space

Geoeconomic and geopolitical context:
- Late 1970s–present: ongoing processes of regulatory experimentation in the wake of the crisis of North Atlantic Fordism and the rise of a European "archipelago economy"
- New interscalar tensions: global and European economic integration proceeds in tandem with an increasing opening of national economies to foreign direct investment and an increasing dependence of large corporations on localized and regionalized agglomeration economies
- The search for a new institutional fix proceeds at all spatial scales in a geoeconomic context defined by U.S.-led neoliberal dominance

Privileged spatial target(s):
- Major urban and regional economies situated within supranational and/or global circuits of capital

Major goals:
- *Reconcentration* of population, industry, and infrastructure investment into strategic urban and regional economies
- *Differentiation* and *splintering* of national economic space into increasingly specialized urban and regional economies
- Promotion of *customized,* place-specific forms of territorial administration and infrastructural investment oriented toward global and European economic flows
- Intensification of interspatial competition at all scales: uneven development is now seen as a *basis* for economic growth rather than as a limit or barrier to it

Dominant policy mechanisms:
- Deregulation and welfare state retrenchment
- Decentralization or devolution of intergovernmental arrangements, socioeconomic policies, and fiscal responsibilities
- Spatially selective investments in advanced infrastructures, generally within strategic cities, regions, and industrial districts
- Construction of newly customized place- and region-specific modes of economic intervention and spatial planning
- Local economic initiatives; "place-marketing" programs

Spatio-temporality of economic development and state sovereignty:
- "Splintered developmentalism": fragmentation of national space into distinct urban/regional economies with their own place-specific locational features and developmental trajectories
- "Variegated" sovereignty: establishment of place-specific regional and local institutional arrangements, governance strategies, and policy regimes

Metropolitan Regionalism and the Reconstitution of Urban Locational Policies

A number of commentators have emphasized the chronically unstable character of entrepreneurial, growth-first approaches to urban governance (Leitner and Sheppard 1998; Peck and Tickell 1994). Because entrepreneurial urban strategies intensify social inequality, social exclusion, and uneven spatial development, they undermine the socioterritorial conditions for sustainable capitalist expansion. While entrepreneurial urban strategies may unleash short-term bursts of economic growth within circumscribed local and regional economies, they generally fail to sustain such economic upswings beyond the medium-term. These contradictions within entrepreneurial forms of urban governance have been exacerbated since the 1990s in conjunction with the diffusion of urban locational policies and the consolidation of RCSRs throughout western Europe. As indicated, one of the major effects of urban locational policies has been to enhance competitive pressures on subnational administrative units and thus to intensify uneven spatial development within each national territory. While these institutional realignments may initially benefit a select number of globally competitive urban regions, they inflict a logic of regulatory undercutting upon most local and regional economies, a trend that may seriously downgrade national economic performance. At the same time, the increasing geographical differentiation of state regulatory activities induced through urban locational policies is "as much a hindrance as a help to regulation" (Painter and Goodwin 1996, 646). For, in the absence of mechanisms of meta-governance capable of coordinating subnational development strategies, these ongoing rescaling processes may undermine the national state's organizational coherence and operational unity, leading in turn to serious governance failures, inter-territorial conflicts, and legitimation deficits (Jessop 1998).

The contradictions of first-wave state rescaling strategies and urban locational policies became widely apparent throughout western Europe starting in the 1980s; they have subsequently had important ramifications for the institutional and scalar architectures of RCSRs. During the 1990s, faced with the pervasive regulatory deficits of their own predominant strategies of economic intervention, many RCSRs have mobilized various forms of institutional restructuring and rescaling in order to manage the disruptive consequences of unfettered inter-locality competition. Thus, whereas the rescaling of urban governance during the 1970s and 1980s was catalyzed primarily through strategies to manage economic crisis and to promote industrial regeneration, the rescaling projects of the 1990s and early 2000s have been mediated increasingly through initiatives designed to contain the governance failures associated with previous rounds of state re-scaling.

The proliferation of regionally focused strategies of state rescaling during the last decade must be understood in this context. During the 1980s, the first wave of state rescaling strategies focused predominantly on the downscaling of formerly nationalized administrative capacities and regulatory arrangements toward local tiers of state power. It was under these conditions that many of the metropolitan institutional forms that had been inherited from the Fordist-Keynesian period were abolished or downgraded. During the 1990s and early 2000s, however, the regional or metropolitan scale became a strategically important site for major projects to modify the geography of state regulatory activities throughout western Europe. From experiments in metropolitan institutional reform and decentralized regional economic policy in Germany, Italy, France, and the Netherlands to the Blairite project of establishing a patchwork of Regional Development Agencies (RDAs) in the United Kingdom, these developments led many commentators to predict that a "new regionalism" was superseding both the geographies of spatial Keynesianism and the forms of urban entrepreneurialism that emerged following the initial crisis of North Atlantic Fordism (Keating 1997). Against such arguments, however, the preceding discussion points toward a crisis-theoretical interpretation of these rescaling initiatives as an important evolutionary modification of RCSRs in conjunction with their own immanent contradictions (Brenner 2004). Although the politico-institutional content of contemporary metropolitanization and regionalization strategies continues to be an object of intense contestation, they have been articulated thus far in two basic forms in most western European states.

On the one hand, regionally focused strategies of state rescaling have frequently attempted to transpose inherited approaches to urban locational policy upwards, onto a metropolitan or regional scale, generally leading to a further intensification of uneven spatial development throughout each national territory. In this scenario, the contradictions of urban locational policy are to be resolved through the integration of local economies into larger, regionally configured territorial units, which are in turn to be promoted as integrated, competitive locations for global and European capital investment. In this approach to state rescaling, the spatial selectivity of RCSRs is modified in order to emphasize metropolitan regions rather than localities; however, the basic agenda of spatial reconcentration, unfettered interspatial competition and intensified uneven development is maintained unchecked.

On the other hand, many contemporary strategies of metropolitanization and regionalization have attempted to countervail the dynamics of unfettered inter-locality competition by promoting selected forms of spatial equalization *within* strategic regional institutional spaces. Although such initiatives generally do not significantly undermine uneven spatial development between regions, they can nonetheless be viewed as efforts to modify some of the most disruptive aspects of first-wave strategies of state rescaling within major metropolitan zones. Indeed, this aspect of regional state rescaling may be viewed as an attempt to reintroduce a downscaled form of spatial Keynesianism *within* the splintered, variegated regulatory architectures of RCSRs. The priority of promoting equalized, balanced growth is thus reintroduced at a metropolitan or regional scale, within delimited subnational zones, rather than throughout the entire national territory.

Which mixture of these opposed approaches to state rescaling prevails within a given national, regional, or local institutional environment hinges upon political struggles in which diverse social forces strive to influence the geography of state regulatory activities toward particular political ends. Nonetheless, both of the rescaled forms of crisis management outlined above arguably represent significant scalar rearticulations within the RCSRs that were consolidated during the 1980s. In this newest approach to urban governance, the twin priorities of economic competitiveness and crisis-management are juxtaposed uneasily within an unstable, shifting institutional and scalar matrix. While there is little evidence at the present time that either of these regionalized regulatory configurations will engender sustainable forms of economic regeneration or territorial governance, it currently appears likely that they shall further intensify the geographical differentiation of state space and the uneven development of capital across western Europe. In this way, such rescaled regulatory configurations have also contributed to a further territorial and scalar differentiation of state sovereignty, which is now increasingly organized through variegated strategies, institutional conditions and forms of political authority across the E.U.

Cities, Locational Policies, and the New Landscape of Sovereignty

In the preceding analysis, I have argued that the proliferation of entrepreneurial approaches to urban governance in western European cities—analyzed here under the rubric of urban locational policy—has been closely intertwined with a broader redifferentiation, splintering, and rescaling of national state spaces and inherited, nationalized formations of state sovereignty. The four successive rounds of urban governance restructuring discussed above have, I have suggested, superimposed qualitatively new, increasingly variegated scalings and territorializations of political authority upon inherited formations of state space, and in this way, contributed to a significant reworking of state sovereignties. The proposed periodization of these transformations is summarized in table 6.3.

Table 6.3. State Spatial Strategies and the Geographies of Urban Governance: A Schematic Periodization of the Western European Case, 1960–2000

Historical Formation	Dominant Form of State Space	Dominant Form of Urban-regional Regulation	Major Conflicts and Contradictions
Spatial Keynesianism: early 1960s–early 1970s	National states promote economic development by spreading industry, population and infrastructural investment evenly across the national territory	Urban managerialism: local states operate as agents of welfare service provision and collective consumption	Urban cores and growth poles may overheat due to rapid growth and physical expansion
	Primacy of the national scale of statehood: national economies and national societies are viewed as pre-given territorial arenas	Metropolitan institutions coordinate the provision of welfare services and manage the physical expansion of Fordist urban agglomerations	Interterritorial and interscalar distributional struggles proliferate as peripheral regions intensify their demands for central state subsidies
Fordism in Crisis (transitional phase): early 1970s–early 1980s	Preservationist alliances within national states initially maintain their commitment to balanced national growth and the redistributive project of spatial Keynesianism	Gradually, national redistributive policy relays are retrenched, forcing regional and local states to fend for themselves under conditions of enhanced geoeconomic uncertainty	National and local fiscal crises ensue as struggles intensify over the appropriate balance of growth vs. redistribution
	The geographies of spatial Keynesianism are redifferentiated, as national urban policies are introduced to address the structural problems of declining industrial cities and regions	A new "bootstraps" politics of endogenous growth emerges in crisis-stricken industrial regions: goal is to mobilize customized policies to confront place-specific forms of economic decline	Political conflicts intensify between preservationist social forces concerned with protecting the institutional settlement of Fordism and "modernizing" alliances oriented toward a systemic reorganization of inherited regulatory arrangements
	The entrenched role of the national scale as a locus of political-economic coordination is destabilized		

Historical Formation	Dominant Form of State Space	Dominant Form of Urban-regional Regulation	Major Conflicts and Contradictions
State Rescaling Strategies, Round I: 1980s	The rise of first-wave strategies of urban locational policy: national states promote the reconcentration of economic capacities and advanced infrastructure into the most globally competitive cities and regions within their territories	Urban entrepreneurialism: local states acquire key roles in promoting local economic development and place-marketing strategies	Intensified uneven development and zero-sum forms of interlocality competition undermine national economic stability
	Place- and jurisdiction-specific forms of territorial administration are introduced in key sites within many strategic urban regions	Traditional managerial-welfarist forms of local socioeconomic policy are retrenched	Urban locational policies trigger systemic governance failures due to a lack of supralocal policy coordination
		Metropolitan institutions are abolished or downsized in conjunction with welfare state restructuring	National and local legitimation crises ensue as territorial inequality intensifies
State Rescaling Strategies, Round II: 1990s–present	The rescaling of urban locational policies: national states target large-scale metropolitan regions rather than cities or localities as the most appropriate scales for economic rejuvenation	Competitive regionalism: metropolitan institutions are rejuvenated in conjunction with projects to establish coordinated programs of regional economic development	Metropolitan institutional reforms trigger an upscaling of the problems of uneven development, intensified sociospatial inequality, inadequate policy coordination, and legitimation to major metropolitan regions
	New scalar layers of state space are established to address some of the major regulatory deficits and governance failures associated with first-wave urban locational policy	Metropolitan institutions acquire new roles in various aspects of crisis displacement, interscalar management, and meta-governance	The crisis tendencies and governance failures of first-wave urban locational policies are rescaled but remain chronically unresolved at a national scale
		New institutional forms and policy strategies are mobilized that attempt to balance the priorities of economic regeneration and crisis management	

This discussion of urban governance and state rescaling in western Europe provides ample support for Sassen's (2005, 535) contention that contemporary sovereignties are "far more complex than notions of mutually exclusive territories can capture." The preceding analysis has attempted to decipher some of that complexity on the basis of the concept of the Rescaled Competition State Regime (RCSR), which is intended to provide a theoretical basis on which to explore the tangled new layerings of state spatiality and the reworked formations of state sovereignty that have been produced through contemporary rescaling processes.

Within newly consolidated RCSRs, national governments have not simply downscaled or upscaled political authority, but have attempted to institutionalize competitive relations between major subnational administrative units as a means to position local and regional economies strategically within supranational (European and global) circuits of capital. In this sense, even in the midst of the wide-ranging rescaling processes that have unsettled traditional, nationally focused regulatory arrangements and institutional forms, national states have attempted to retain control over major subnational political-economic spaces by integrating them within operationally rescaled, but still nationally coordinated, accumulation strategies. Crucially, therefore, the processes of urban governance restructuring and state rescaling explored here do not entail the consolidation of a "denationalized" formation of state sovereignty or the purported "decentering" of national state power that has been postulated by many scholars of globalization. Rather, such rescaling processes have produced a new, pluralized and variegated formation of sovereignties in which national states actively create differential conditions for political-economic relations—"spaces of exception," in Ong's (2006) terms—among the various urban and regional zones within their jurisdictions. Sovereignty, as Sassen (2005, 535) explains, "remains as a systemic property," but its political, institutional, and spatial expressions are being significantly rewoven, not least within cities and city-regions, within the E.U. and beyond.

The rescaled configurations of state spatiality and state sovereignty that have been consolidated during the last two decades have systematically undermined the nationalized forms of sociospatial redistribution that had been established during the Fordist-Keynesian period in western Europe, while simultaneously recasting the institutional structure and operational functions of the national scale as a site for political authority and regulatory strategies. This rescaled landscape of market-oriented political regulation has generated new forms of sociospatial inequality and political conflict that limit the choices available to progressive forces throughout Europe. In the current geoeconomic climate, the project of promoting territorial equalization within national or subnational political units is generally seen as a luxury of a bygone era that can no longer be afforded in an age of globalized capital, lean management and fiscal austerity. Yet, even as these rescaling processes appear to close off some avenues of political regulation and democratic control, they may also establish new possibilities for sociospatial redistribution and progressive, radical-democratic political mobilization at other spatial scales. To date, the processes of European integration and eastward enlargement have been dominated by orthodox neoliberal agendas that reinforce and even intensify the entrepreneurial politics of interspatial competition. Nonetheless, the supranational institutional arenas associated with the E.U. may provide a powerful political mechanism through which progressive forces might once again mobilize social and spatial programs designed to alleviate inequality, uneven development, and unfettered market competition, this time at a still broader spatial scale than was considered possible during the era of high Fordism (Dunford and Perrons 1994).

It remains to be seen whether the contemporary dynamics of state rescaling will continue to be steered toward the perpetuation of neoliberal geographies of uneven spatial development based upon chronic macroeconomic instability, intensifying inequality and social exclusion, or whether—perhaps through the very contradictions and conflicts they continue to unleash—they might be rechanneled to forge a negotiated settlement at a European scale based upon substantive political priorities and new interscalar compromises. At the present time, it appears unlikely that RCSRs will successfully establish a new structured coherence for capitalist growth, for they have yet to establish a stabilized framework for territorial governance or interscalar management in any national context, much less at the E.U. scale. Yet, because the institutional and scalar framework of European state space is in a period of profound flux, its future can be forged only through ongoing political struggles, at once on local, national, and supranational scales, to rework the geographies of sovereignty, economic regulation, and sociopolitical mobilization.

Notes

1. This chapter draws on parts of an earlier article, "Urban Governance and the Production of New State Spaces in Western Europe, 1960–2000," *Review of International Political Economy* 11, no. 3 (2004): 447–488. The arguments developed here are elaborated at greater length and more concretely in my book *New State Spaces: Urban Governance and the Rescaling of Statehood* (Brenner 2004).

2. The notion of "locational policy" is derived from the German notion of *Standortpolitik,* which has gained currency in post-unification Germany through ongoing political debates on *Standort Deutschland* (Germany as an investment location). However, as elaborated below, the term locational policy is used here a more specific, social-scientific sense.

For more detailed discussions of the ideology and practice of locational policy in post-unification Germany, see Brenner (2000).

Works Cited

Agnew, J. 2005. "Sovereignty Regimes: Territoriality and State Authority in Contemporary World Politics." *Annals of the Association of American Geographers* 95, no. 2: 437–461.

Ansell, C., and G. di Palma, eds. 2004. *Restructuring Territoriality: Europe and the United States Compared.* New York: Cambridge University Press.

Brenner, N. 2000. "Building 'Euro-regions': Locational Politics and the Political Geography of Neoliberalism in Post-unification Germany." *European Urban and Regional Studies* 7, no. 4: 317–343.

———. 2004. *New State Spaces: Urban Governance and the Rescaling of Statehood.* London: Oxford University Press.

Brenner, N., and N. Theodore, eds. 2002. *Spaces of Neoliberalism: Urban Restructuring in North America and Western Europe.* Oxford: Blackwell.

Brunet, R. 1989. *Les villes 'europeennes'.* Paris: DATAR.

Cheshire, P., and I. Gordon. 1996. "Territorial Competition and the Predictability of Collective (in)action." *International Journal of Urban and Regional Research* 20, no. 3: 383–399.

Clout, H., ed. 1981. *Regional Development in Western Europe,* 2nd edition. New York: John Wiley & Sons.

Dunford, M., and D. Perrons. 1994. "Regional Inequality, Regimes of Accumulation and Economic Development in Contemporary Europe." *Transactions of the Institute of British Geographers* 19: 163–182.

Eisenschitz, A., and J. Gough. 1993. *The Politics of Local Economic Development.* New York: Macmillan.

Fougner, T. 2006. "The State, International Competitiveness and Neoliberal Globalisation: Is There a Future beyond 'the Competition State'?" *Review of International Studies* 32: 165–185.

Fox Przeworski, J. 1986. "Changing Intergovernmental Relations and Urban Economic Development." *Environment and Planning C: Government and Policy* 4, no. 4: 423–439.

Graham, S., and S. Marvin. 2001. *Splintering Urbanism.* New York: Routledge.

Hahne, U. 1985. *Regionalentwicklung durch Aktivierung intraregionaler Potentiale. Schriften des Instituts für Regionalforschung der Universität Kiel.* Band 8. Munich: Florenz.

Harding, A. 1997. "Urban Regimes in a Europe of the Cities?" *European Urban and Regional Studies* 4, no. 4: 291–314.

Harvey, D. 1989. "From Managerialism to Entrepreneurialism: The Transformation in Urban Governance in Late Capitalism." *Geografiska Annaler* B, no. 71: 1, 3–18.

Holston, J., and A. Appadurai. 1999. "Introduction." In *Cities and Citizenship,* ed. J. Holston, 1–17. Durham, N.C.: Duke University Press.

Jessop, B. 2002. *The Future of the Capitalist State*. Cambridge: Polity.

———. 1998b. "The Rise of Governance and the Risks of Failure: The Case of Economic Development." *International Social Science Journal* 155: 29–46.

Keating, M. 1997. "The Invention of Regions." *Environment and Planning C: Government and Policy* 15: 383–398.

Krätke, S. 1993. "Stadtsystem im internationalen Kontext und Vergleich." In *Kommunal-politik,* ed. R. Roth and H. Wollmann, 176–193. Opladen, Germany: Leske Verlag.

Lefebvre, H. 1968. *Le droit à la ville.* Paris: Anthropos.

———. 2002 [1978]. "Space and the State." In *State/Space: A Reader,* by N. Brenner, B. Jessop, M. Jones, and G. MacLeod.. Boston, Mass.: Blackwell, 84–100.

Lipietz, A. 1994. "The National and the Regional: Their Autonomy vis-à-vis the Capitalist World Crisis." In *Transcending the State-Global Divide,* ed. R. Palan and B. Gills, 23–44. Boulder, Colo.: Lynne Rienner.

Martin, R., and P. Sunley. 1997. "The Post-Keynesian State and the Space Economy." In *Geographies of Economies,* ed. R. Lee and J. Wills, 278–289. London: Arnold.

Mayer, M. 1994. "Post-Fordist city politics." In *Post-Fordism: A Reader,* ed. A. Amin, 316–337. Cambridge, Mass.: Blackwell.

OECD. 1976. *Regional Problems and Policies in OECD Countries.* Paris: OECD.

Ong, A. 2006. *Neoliberalism as Exception: Mutations in Citizenship and Sovereignty.* Durham, N.C.: Duke University Press.

———. 2004. "The Chinese Axis: Zoning Technologies and Variegated Sovereignty." *Journal of East Asian Studies* 4: 69–96.

Painter, J., and M. Goodwin. 1995. "Local Governance and Concrete Research." *Economy and Society* 24, no. 3: 334–356.

Peck, J. 2002. "Political Economies of Scale." *Economic Geography* 78, no. 3 (July): 332–360.

Peck, J., and A. Tickell. 1994. "Searching for a New Institutional Fix." In *Post-Fordism: A Reader,* ed. A. Amin, 280–315. Cambridge, Mass.: Blackwell.

Rodriguez-Pose, A. 1998. *The Dynamics of Regional Growth in Europe.* Oxford: Clarendon Press.

Ruggie, J. 1993. "Territoriality and Beyond: Problematizing Modernity in International Relations." *International Organization* 47, no. 1: 139–174.

Rumford, C. 2006. "Rethinking European Spaces: Territory, Borders, Governance." *Comparative European Studies* 4, no. 2–3: 127–140.

Sabel, C. 1994. "Flexible Specialisation and the Re-emergence of Regional Economies." In *Post-Fordism: A Reader,* ed. A. Amin, 101–156. Cambridge: Blackwell,.

Sassen, S. 2005. "When National Territory Is Home to the Global: Old Borders to Novel Borderings." *New Political Economy* 10, no. 4: 532–541.

Sharpe, L. J., ed. 1995. *The Government of World Cities.* New York: John Wiley & Sons.

Stöhr, W., and D. R. Taylor. 1981. *Development from Above or Below?* New York: Wiley.

Swyngedouw, E. 2000. "Authoritarian Governance, Power and the Politics of Rescaling." *Environment and Planning D: Society and Space* 18: 63–76.

Veltz, P. 1993. *Mondialisation, villes et territoires: l'économie d'archipel.* Paris: Presses Universitaires de France.

PART 3
SOVEREIGNTY, REPRESENTATION, AND THE URBAN BUILT ENVIRONMENT

7

Iconic Architecture and Urban, National, and Global Identities

Leslie Sklair

The material, ideological, and symbolic roles of architecture in the formation and/ or the expression of identities is a fairly well established, even if under-researched, motif in the histories of both architecture and politics. My argument is that buildings and spaces that become acknowledged expressions of local/urban, national, or global identities overlap in interesting ways with what has come to be known as iconic architecture.

The historical context of this argument is the hypothesis that the production and representation of architectural icons in the preglobal era (roughly before the 1950s) were mainly driven by those who controlled the state and/or religion, whereas the dominant forms of architectural iconicity for the era of capitalist globalization are increasingly driven by those who own and control the corporate sector. This implies that state- and/or religion-driven icons help form and express certain types of identities, while corporate-driven icons form and express other types of identities.[1] Iconicity in architecture is conceptualized as a resource in struggles for meaning and, by implication, for power. Therefore, to explain how iconic architecture works for the creation and sustaining of identities under the conditions of capitalist globalization we must ask questions about meaning and power.[2]

Iconic architecture works at several levels; here the focus is on the local/urban, the national and the global. My central question seeks to explain how buildings and spaces become iconic and to suggest some ways in which architectural iconicity may throw light on urban and other conflicts and, by implication, may play a part in resolving them. First, it is necessary to explain briefly how the idea of iconicity has been used with respect to architecture and how it is used here.

Iconicity: A Concept Ripe for Deconstruction

Over the last few decades the term "iconic" has entered common usage for those in and around architecture with a considerable overlap into the mass media.[3] My working definition of iconic for purposes of research has two central characteristics. First, it clearly means famous, at least for some constituencies; and second, it also involves a symbolic/aesthetic judgment. By this I mean that an architectural icon is imbued with a special meaning that is symbolic for a culture and/or a time, and that this special meaning has an aesthetic component in that it is a worthy and/or beautiful way to represent what is being represented. It is this unique combination of fame, symbolism and aesthetic quality that creates the icon.

Iconicity, while it is not entirely a matter of image, clearly connects with the production and dissemination of images. The importance of drawings and photography in establishing the iconic status of buildings or spaces is obvious in the history of architecture (see Rattenbury 2002). While in no way minimizing the centrality of the image in the production and iteration of iconicity, it is vital that what the image is an image of is properly acknowledged. A useful analogy is with advertising. Images in advertising may have symbolic qualities whether or not they persuade people to buy the products they represent, but from the point of view of the client the point of advertising is to sell products. "Symbolism"—for example, figurative or cubist or surrealist or abstract expressionist images—may help to sell products at one time or another, and when used this way the image serves the circuit of capital. With a few exceptions, an advertising image has little independent existence outside of the circuit of capital, and certainly does not displace or replace this circuit. Similarly, the point of the images of iconic architecture in the global era is generally to persuade people to buy (both in the specific sense of consume and in the more general sense of give credence to) the buildings and spaces and lifestyles and, in some cases, the architects they represent. Thus, while the images of iconic architecture can be great art, they are not the things they are images of. Iconicity is not simply a question of image or, by implication, fashion. Iconicity works because the buildings and spaces in which it inheres are built by architects and teams of others to symbolize something (possibly several things) apart from the program (functions) of the building itself. Under the new conditions of capitalist globalization, corporate interests, in a historically unprecedented way, have transformed the nature and scale of the fame of icons and what they symbolize.

The relation between image and reality is often complex. Those in and around architecture frequently report that the images they have seen of iconic buildings and spaces have totally unprepared them for the emotional (in some cases the spiritual) experience of actually seeing and being in a building and its spaces. (A notable example is the Pilgrimage Church of Notre-Dame-du-Haut at Ronchamp, built by Le Corbusier and a frequent object of architectural pilgrimages.) And this can work in the opposite direction where actual experiences of buildings and spaces do not match their iconic images.

Icons originally were representations—images, figures, portraits, illustrations, or, in the solid, statues. The Eastern Church turned icons into representations of sacred personages, objects of veneration, also regarded as sacred. The term "iconic" in the history of art was applied to the ancient portrait statues of victorious athletes, and hence to memorial statues and busts (so the labeling of sports celebrities as icons in the contemporary media does have classical origins). Iconography and iconology became branches of knowledge dealing with representative art. So the history of the icon is bound up with representation, symbolism and expression. Gombrich (1972, 124) explains: "These three ordinary functions of images may be present in one concrete image—a motif in a painting by Hieronymous Bosch may *represent* a broken vessel, *symbolize* the sin of gluttony and *express* an unconscious sexual fantasy" (italics in original). Then he proceeds to deconstruct these functions.

The icon as representation (let us call this Iconic I) does have some pedigree in architectural theory. Broadbent (1973), for example, distinguishes four approaches to design: pragmatic (using available materials and methods), iconic (copying), canonical (rule-bound), and analogical (from other fields or contexts). This meaning of iconic (not very different from his canonical) is still current in some architecture schools. In an internet debate in 2003 iconic design in architecture was defined as follows: "a culture has a fixed image of what an object should be like and . . . subsequent generations of that culture keep on building that object in the same way and with the same shape" (www.archnet.org/forum).[4]

ArchNet is a forum at MIT focusing on Islamic architecture and the debate reflected this. One respondent identified the icon as a stereotype, as when the word "mosque" brings up the image of the dome and the minar and all domes and minars look more or less alike (Iconic I). This respondent argued that architecture itself could provide an icon for a culture, as the Statue of Liberty has become for the U.S., Sydney Opera House for Australia, and Mies's Barcelona Pavilion for the new postwar Germany. There are two issues here. First, if an icon is a type then it cannot also be something unique. This sense of iconic recaptures the original meaning of the iconic mosque or Gothic cathedral or even office block that is simply a copy of some archetype of the mosque or cathedral or office block, because it looks like what it is supposed to be.

However, I would argue that, in the global age, iconic is more often used in an

entirely opposite sense. Responding to the rejection of a scheme for a major project in Liverpool, a spokesman for Alsop Architects commented: "if you propose
any icon the instant response is negative because it challenges perception: it is the
nature of an icon. None of the other schemes were icons. They were landmarks."[5]
This repetitive representational sense recalls the more mundane, even if loved,
landmark, the way in which Lynch (1960) appears to use it. For Alsop and his supporters, the iconic means a building or a space (and perhaps even an architect)
that is different and unique, intended to be famous and to have special symbolic/
aesthetic qualities. Let us call this Iconic II, with the added feature that such icons
can be proclaimed iconic before they are built and some are never built at all.

Works of art are routinely said to represent, symbolize, or express things or
feelings. This is relatively understandable in terms of the visual arts, or even
music or dance, in the way that a painting or a sculpture or a symphony or a bal-
let can represent, symbolize, or express a landscape or a family group or, more
abstractly, longing or love. But how can a building or a space be said to represent,
symbolize, or express anything? Clearly, some buildings actually do look like objects. Frank Lloyd Wright's Guggenheim Museum in New York is commonly said
to represent the spiral form in nature; Jorn Utzon's Sydney Opera House the sails
of a boat or the segments of an orange; Frank Gehry's Guggenheim in Bilbao fish
scales; Norman Foster's Swiss Re tower in London (the Erotic Gherkin) is one of
the latest phallic representations in a long line of tall buildings, and so on. This
is because, in some sense, all these buildings actually do look like real or stylized
versions of what they are said to look like.[6] Taking a lead from Gombrich (1972,
21), who argues that "Iconology must start with a study of institutions rather
than with a study of symbols," we can begin to connect iconic architecture and
the economic, political, and culture-ideology institutions of capitalist globalization. Whereas Iconic I icons, like landmarks, do not necessarily raise questions
about symbolism and expression, Iconic II icons always do and it is precisely in
the ways in which they do that we can find the different, special and unique qualities of Iconic II buildings, spaces, and architects.

From now on, I want to file away the representational, mimetic meaning (Iconic
I) and restrict the term to what is its much more common use in discussions of
architecture today, reference to the symbolism and expression of difference, the
special and the unique, as in the "iconic status" of notable buildings and spaces,
and of their sites and architects (Iconic II). While both forms of iconic status may
have symbolic significance, it is the institutional structures that dominate the
times and places and audiences of buildings, spaces, and architects that makes
them famous, and that provide the explanations for their iconicity that symbolic/
aesthetic qualities on their own cannot furnish. However, under conditions of

capitalist globalization, unless these qualities are acceptable to significant elites within the transnational capitalist class, it is unlikely—though not impossible—that large scale architectural icons could be built, given the financial risks involved (see Sklair 2005).

The case of the iconic architect further complicates the issue. When an architect becomes iconic for a particular building and then makes more buildings that resemble the original icon (Frank Gehry's Guggenheim Bilbao is an obvious example, but it is not the only one), this may well be considered repetitive in the representation sense, and so confuse Iconic I and Iconic II. On these grounds, iconic buildings and their signature architects (namely architects whose unique signatures, in the sense of recognizable features, are on their buildings) have been attacked. For example Farshid Moussavi and Alejandro Zaera-Polo of Foreign Office Architects (FOA), a booming young London-based transnational architectural practice (the principals are from Iran and Spain respectively), have argued that with "iconic architecture" now cropping up in every city these buildings are starting to cancel each other out: "Gehry is peppering the world with Bilbao Guggenheim lookalikes and if you've seen one building by Calatrava or Meier, you've seen them all" (quoted in *The Guardian* [London], 17 November 2003).[7] This discursive strategy of applying the law of diminishing returns to iconic architects begs the question of what it means to say that an architect is iconic. Certainly a select group of architects throughout history have been described in this way. When iconicity is ascribed to one or two buildings of some architects, iconicity starts to spread to all their buildings, past, present and future. This is certainly the case for the buildings of Frank Lloyd Wright and Le Corbusier, including those that exist only on paper. As the blurb on a recent book tells us: "This volume explores an unbuilt yet iconic project by Le Corbusier [the Venice Hospital]" (Sarkis 2001).

Now that the competing conceptions of iconicity that prevail in discussions of architecture today have been set out, we can proceed to deconstruct Iconic II icons in terms of three basic questions: Iconic for whom? Iconic for when? Iconic for where?[8]

Iconic for Whom?

The obvious way to approach this question is to distinguish between structures with meaning for those in and around architecture (professional icons) and those with meaning for the public at large (public icons). In what sense can a building be said to be iconic for architecture but not for the public? And conversely, in what sense can a building be said to be iconic for the public but not for architecture?

The easy answer, the one that bolsters professional confidence and even encourages professional snobbery, is that iconicity is simply a matter of publicity, fashion, self-promotion by the client or the developer, aided and abetted by the architect and by those who produce the images. This connects with the idea discussed above that there are no iconic buildings or architects, only iconic images. The focus here is on icons that are recognized to a greater or lesser extent by those in and around architecture and the general public alike. When we raise questions about iconicity and identities, these gross categories of professional and public icons will need to be broken down, at the very least to distinguish class, gender, and ethnic differences.

Iconic for When?

For my purposes it is useful to draw a line between icons of the preglobal era (before the 1950s) and the global era. This chronology relates to the research hypothesis raised above: to what extent is it the case that before the advent of capitalist globalization most iconic architecture was a product of the state and/or religion, whereas since the 1950s the dominant driver of iconic architecture has been the corporate sector? And, if this is true, how can we explain it? Why the 1950s? The answer lies in what is commonly agreed to be a necessary if not a sufficient condition for globalization in any of its forms, namely the electronic revolution. As it restructures economic, social and cultural life rapidly in the West, and more slowly but surely all over the world, varying forms of postcolonialisms, the creation of transnational social spaces, and new forms of cosmopolitanism—what can be conceptualized as *generic globalization*—open up some forms of architectural expression and production (for example, through the use of new technologies and new materials) and close down others (for example, the widespread and rapid dissemination of images puts a greater premium on visual originality in architecture).[9]

Iconic for Where?

In most cases iconic buildings and spaces have to be located in fixed places, the geographical scale of their iconicity is not fixed. Architectural icons can have local (mostly urban), national, or global significance and recognition, or any mixture of these three. This applies equally to professional icons, public icons, and those that have achieved iconic status in both respects. However, under conditions of capitalist globalization and the demands of the culture-ideology of consumerism, the social relations of production of icons will be similar whatever the intended or eventual scale of their iconicity. I suspect that this may not be the case for state and/or religious icons of the precapitalist globalization era.

Local icons are buildings and spaces that are well known though not necessarily well loved within circumscribed areas, usually in cities and neighborhoods, with definite symbolic significance for these places. They might be known to outsiders interested in these cities, and local icons in London or New York or Paris or Shanghai or Tokyo will certainly be better known than local icons in Leeds (England), Rochester (New York state), Nancy (France) and so on. This is largely due to what has become known as urban boosterism, the most common rationale for deliberately created iconic architecture. Those who drive this process, the urban affiliates of the transnational capitalist class—those who own and control cities—increasingly want their cities to be easily recognizable for purposes of commerce as well as civic pride. For many there is little difference, as Dovey (1999, chapter 11) illustrates for the case of Melbourne. The urban boosters deliberately attempt to create architectural icons in order to draw tourists, convention and mega-event attendees with money to spend, and the images they project are directed to this end. This is a truly globalizing business (see Jonas and Wilson 1999), and what Zukin (1996) has theorized as the cultures of cities plays an increasingly vital part in the marketing of cities within capitalist globalization. It is not surprising, therefore, that virtually all major museums around the world have become much more commercialized in recent decades.

The commodification of architecture, like urban boosterism, did not spring newborn into the late twentieth century; nevertheless, there is a general consensus that as capitalist globalization began to be the dominant mode of production, distribution, and exchange from about the 1950s, architectural practice also began to change. In his paper on "The architecture of plenty," Kieren expresses this succinctly: "The emerging model of the client is that of a buyer of architectural services in a free market. . . . When a tangible image is felt to be lacking, architecture is often turned to today for an associative icon" (1987, 28). This sentiment was reinforced by the deputy chair of CABE (the U.K. government-sponsored Commission for Architecture and the Built Environment) who doubted whether any firm that rejects "iconic commercial buildings" could survive in the current climate (reported in *Building Design* 22, March 2002, 20).

Documentary and interview evidence suggests that every place has its local iconic buildings and spaces and that these contribute strongly to place identity and the differentiation of one place from another. While it might sound faintly ridiculous to call Place Ville Marie in Montreal or the new Erasmus Bridge in Rotterdam or the Rotunda Tower in Birmingham iconic, in the sense that few outside these cities would ever have heard of them or seen images of them, these buildings and spaces are iconic for their localities, for the people who see them and use them on a regular basis; in short, these icons have a role in the formation of urban identities. When asked, most respondents in and around architecture could name such local icons, buildings, and spaces that everyone in their neighborhood or even city would almost certainly have heard of, for example places where young adults would congregate, and notably places where people would go on special occasions. When it was built in the 1960s, Place Ville Marie was seen as the first really "cool, hip symbol" of Montreal as a world-class city, known by the locals as "our Rockefeller Center." This was the period of Expo '67, but now it seems banal and lost among the skyscrapers of the city—a lost icon. The Erasmus Bridge in Rotterdam, on the other hand, is what we might call a replacement local icon, a stage in iconic succession at the local level. From the 1960s onward, the city's most prominent local icon had been the Euro Space Tower, a symbol of the new Rotterdam rising from the ashes of World War II, a "modernist" symbol that was reproduced incessantly in the marketing of the city. The new bridge has replaced the spire as both the physical icon for the city and as the symbolic/aesthetic icon for representing and marketing the city, for example on the front of the city map that greets you when you land at the airport and on the laundry bags in city hotels. The image of the Erasmus Bridge is a sleek high-tech structure of the type generally associated with Santiago Calatrava. The Rotunda, built in the 1960s, was the first prominent round tower in Birmingham (U.K.) and for no apparent reason apart from its shape (an example of what may be termed the "peculiar aesthetics" of icons) it has survived as a local icon while the Bullring that dominates the center of the city has been demolished and redeveloped. But it may be the very roundness of the tower in contrast to the New Brutalist architecture of the Bullring that accounts for its local iconic status.[10]

Can we generalize about what distinguishes local icons from all the other buildings and spaces in a neighborhood or a city? The idea of the landmark is fairly well developed in urban theory, especially in the work of Kevin Lynch. But landmarks in general stand out (usually up as well) and the designation of landmark has no particular symbolic/aesthetic significance, whereas icons need not necessarily stand out or up (in the Rotterdam example a tall spire was replaced by a relatively low-lying bridge) but they must have some institutionally sanctioned symbolic/ aesthetic significance to be iconic at any level. This is what makes sense of their perceived qualities, what makes them iconic and thus "famous" in the local context. In the global era these processes tend to be driven by the corporate sector, whether or not specific buildings and spaces are sponsored by the state, or the private sector, or both. It is obvious that the business of business is business, less obvious that the business of the state is, increasingly, business too (Sklair 2002).

National icons historically have tended to be buildings and spaces constructed by the state and/or religious bodies, and traditional national icons have invariably been characterized by great legibility in terms of their monumentality and, often, representational sculptural features. There is now a considerable literature on "architecture and power" that investigates how buildings and spaces, especially monumental buildings and spaces, express power relations and how the ordinary citizen and/or believer can read off political and religious values from these icons.[11] The iconic architecture of powerful states, including states that have once been powerful but are no longer, frequently crosses borders and the theme of "architecture and imperialism" has also attracted a good deal of scholarly attention.[12] Buildings and spaces created by states and religious institutions continue to be built, of course, and the study of iconic architecture and capitalist globalization raises questions about whether the processes of iconicity that predated the global era (in my terms starting from around the 1950s) carried over into the global era and persist today.

Historically, national icons start their careers as local icons in cities where holders of economic or political or culture-ideology power are or were based. This is clearly the case for the major imperialist powers of the past and the present. In the U.S., national icons are found in Washington D.C. (the Capitol, Lincoln Memorial) and in New York (certainly the Statue of Liberty and the Brooklyn Bridge, and many of my respondents made the case that the Twin Towers of the World Trade Center became national icons after 9/11). In Britain, they are in London—Buckingham Palace, Westminster, and Big Ben are the most commonly cited national icons; in France—the Eiffel Tower and Notre Dame in Paris; in Italy—the Coliseum and the Pantheon in Rome; in China—Tiananmen Square and the Forbidden City in Beijing; and so on. It is interesting to observe that most of these national icons predate the twentieth century and that many attempts to build new national icons in the twentieth century appear to have failed, for example, the belated World War II memorial in Washington (though a case could be made for Maya Lin's Vietnam Memorial Wall) and the ill-fated Millennium Dome in London.[13] The truly iconic buildings of the twentieth century in these countries in terms of fame and symbolic/aesthetic appeal to architects and public alike are more likely to be corporate, for example the Empire State and Chrysler Buildings in New York, Canary Wharf and Lloyd's in London, the HSBC building in Hong Kong, and Jin Mao Tower in Shanghai. The highly controversial new National Theatre in Beijing is said to be iconic, though its fame and its symbolism/aesthetics appear more corporate (certainly "foreign") than national.

Are there any genuinely global icons? In the aftermath of 9/11 there was a good deal of commentary on what the loss of the Twin Towers meant that is relevant to the question. David Dillon summed up the issues well in an article in the *Dallas Morning News* (18 September 2001) under the title "Attack on iconic buildings robs us of emotional compasses": "Iconic buildings tell us where we are, at a glance. The Eiffel Tower, Sydney Opera House, the Gateway Arch [St. Louis, U.S.], the Pentagon and the World Trade Center. Typically, they are large and exhibitionistic so that even a partial glimpse is enough to fix our visual and emotional compass. And when they disappear, a psychological gap appears, as if our memories have suddenly failed and we've become disoriented." The idea that global icons must be large is a very common one and connects the discussion of iconicity with that of monumentality,[14] skylines, and what van Leeuwen (1988) terms "the skyward trend of thought" (see also King 2004, chapter 1; Sudjic 2005).

Buildings and spaces that have been used in establishing shots and/or foregrounded in globally successful movies and TV shows are almost guaranteed a type of public iconic status today, though this does not mean that members of the public who recognize buildings can either name them or their architects. How many people outside Miami who have seen "Miami Vice" know the name of the Atlantis Building or have heard of the architects Arquitectonica; how many outside Los Angeles who have seen "Blade Runner" know the name of the Bradbury Building or George Wyman; even outside New York, how many who have seen "Men in Black" know the name of the Guggenheim or Frank Lloyd Wright (and he is certainly the most famous architect who ever lived, so far)? So, what turns local and national icons into global icons is a mixture of publicity and the peculiar symbolism/aesthetics of iconicity. There is no doubt that the electronic revolution that has transformed the mass media facilitates this process to a historically unprecedented extent. This works for both architecture of the past and architecture of the present, but not necessarily in the same way.

Iconicity and Identities

In many parts of the world, what I have termed architectural icons have been frequently connected with the formation, expression, and marketing of urban, national and global identities. This is clearly the case for the most spectacular remains of classical antiquity (notably the Acropolis/Parthenon, the pyramids and the Sphinx of Egypt, and the sites of Rome) and other civilizations (popular examples are the Taj Mahal, Machu Pichu, Gothic cathedrals, Barabadur, and the Statue of Liberty as portrayed at the end of the film "Planet of the Apes"). In each case political and/or religious elites have, as it were, attempted to make their special places iconic, sometimes in ways that strikingly resemble what happens in our times.[15] These have become national and, in some cases, global icons through the dissemination of their images for centuries, accelerated in the era of capitalist globalization as quantitative increases due to electronic media of communication lead to qualitative changes in global imaginations. It is unlikely that global icons expressing global identities spring up spontaneously, with the possible exception of planet earth itself, an argument that was made by Lasswell more than twenty-five years ago.[16] It is important to distinguish the role of architectural icons in the deliberate creation of new identities from attempts to represent old and, invariably, contested identities (see also, Vale 1999, on "mediated monuments").

How do urban (local) and national icons become global icons? The key may lie in the processes that transform urban identities into global identities in a dialectic that works against and is itself opposed by the processes involved in the creation of national(ist) icons. In his book on skylines Attoe suggests some valuable clues for understanding this phenomenon. He argues: "In view of the value attached to and found in skylines—their role as cultural indexes and collective symbols; their association with social rituals; their occasional unearthly beauty—it is not surprising to find that they sometimes are transformed into icon-like objects, idealized objects which are venerated and which are imbued with the power to intervene in men's [sic] lives" (Attoe 1981, 97). Tellingly, he gives as a historical exemplar, New Jerusalem, with the "vision of domes and glittering spires, and the countless representations of skylines in paintings, on postcards, and in corporate logos, advertisements, and civic emblems" (ibid., 98). Another ideal skyline serves "to fulfill the metaphor of Oxford as the city of dreaming spires" (ibid., 101), but it is purified by getting rid of the smoking chimneys of the real industrial Oxford, distilled into the icon of dreaming spires alone. So skylines become transportable on postcards and prints and electronic images, as do icons. Similarly, Attoe argues, newspaper columns use skyline icons as emblems, whether showing the generic big city skyline as does the *Auckland Sunday News* (his local/urban icon), or a specific one, the most famous example being the Manhattan skyline as used in Lewis Mumford's *New Yorker* column. In London, as in other globalizing cities, it is remarkable how quickly what I have termed "manufactured icons" of recent origin (see Sklair 2006) have been incorporated into promotional images of the skyline alongside the much older, well-established icons of the city.[17]

The iconic city skyline has a double function. First, it serves to forge a sense of urban identity and pride, often irrespective of the merits or the popularity of the individual elements that make it up, for those who want to identify with the city, and second, it serves as a marker, negative or positive, of the city for outsiders. Iconic skylines, thus, help both to identify and to identify with specific cities.[18] Class, gender, and ethnic dimensions of identity may well cloud this picture. It is quite possible that different class, gender, and ethnic factions in the city see the skyline and its individual elements quite differently, or that some see them and others fail to see them at all. The occupational groups differentially connected with these identities are also relevant. Drivers, those driven, and pedestrians may see their cities differently; those who clean and maintain iconic buildings may also see them differently to those who have highly paid jobs in them, for example.

These differences are multiplied at the national level and strictures on easy connections between architectural iconicity and national identity formation and expression are, if anything, more significant than at the urban level. Nevertheless, there are many clear examples of how those in control of the state have explicitly used iconic buildings, often in tandem with the capital cities in which they are located, to symbolize national identity (see Vale 1992). This, from a study of the return of the capital of reunified Germany to Berlin, states the case well: "Like stories written in stone, capitals across the globe embody national identity and historical consciousness. Be it the Mall in Washington, D.C., the Kremlin in Moscow, or the forbidden City in Beijing, capital city buildings and urban planning have the power to awe, to alienate, to inspire, and to intimidate" (Wise 1998, 11).

A much-researched case is the Eiffel Tower, the ultimate urban icon much disliked when it was first constructed, and its seminal role in identity formation for Paris and France. It has recently been claimed that: "No city in the world has been deployed as a symbol of national identity to the same degree as Paris" (Fierro 2003, 10). Be that as it may, what Fierro argues for late-twentieth-century Paris and France rings true for many other major cities and nation-states today all round the world: "Intrinsic to the emergence of Mitterand's glass buildings in Paris is a political concept: that physical construction might be endowed with the potential, through the medium of transparent skins, simultaneously to heighten, transcend, and make literal a politically construed metaphor of accessibility. . . . For Mitterand, primary elemental forms lined in refined details of glass and steel symbolized the most grandiose aspects of the French leftist [and not exclusively leftist] state" (Fierro 2003, xii).

That this is not exclusively a European phenomenon is illustrated by a study of Barragan's El Pedregal housing development in Mexico City. Eggener sees: "a major revision of the International Style, an icon of Mexican cultural identity, yet still intensely personal, poetic, and mysterious" (1999, 179) and points out that the real estate images for Pedregal houses showed a drawing very much like Frank Lloyd Wright's Fallingwater![19] Notable recent studies of the uses of architecture in the creation or invention of national identities, some very successful and others not so successful, include those on Turkey (Bozdogan 2001), Indonesia (Kusno 2000), Malaysia (Marshall 2003, chapter 10), and a more general one by King (2004).

While this process often takes place with the conscious participation of the architect—a good example is the patriotic strategy adopted by Daniel Libeskind in his struggle to win the WTC replacement competition (Sudjic 2005, chapter 13)—often it does not. Curtis, in his subtle analysis of what he labels "authentic regionalism" comments on how the work of Hassan Fathy has been put to ideological uses in terms that also apply to many other cases: "Through no fault of Fathy's own, his ideas—or rather his images—have been appropriated as a sort of instant Islamic identity kit" (Curtis 1986, 27). Indeed, the debate on critical regionalism has revolved around questions of identity and the challenge of modernism and its offspring to local and national traditions in architecture. In a book, significantly titled *Architecture and Identity in a Globalized World,* Lefaivre and Tzonis (2003) abandon the term "critical regionalism" and replace it with "critical realism," suggesting that the geographical reference is no longer the key point, and perhaps it never was. Lefaivre (ibid., 22–55) pointedly asks if critical realism can have its own icons, in my terms these would be urban/local and national icons in contrast to global icons whose symbolism and aesthetics are seen to be universal, allowing for the possibility that some so-called local or national symbols and aesthetics can also be made universal.

Though it is at least arguable that there are global icons in the sense of buildings or spaces that are recognizable all over the world and that express some global symbolic/aesthetic meaning, perhaps it is premature to speak of icons that express one global identity. Such buildings and spaces may already exist but we may not yet be aware of their global iconicity, just as, at the time when the Eiffel Tower was being built, the people of Paris and France were unaware that one day it would be iconic for them and help to forge their common identity.

Conclusion

The transnational capitalist class facilitates the production of iconic architecture in the same way and for the same purposes as it does all cultural icons, by incorporating creative artists, to a greater or lesser degree, to construct meanings and effectively represent its power in order to maximize commercial benefits for the capitalist class. The nature of the built environment powerfully reinforces systems of values and the choice of what buildings and spaces become iconic is never arbitrary, as the story of icons of resistance confirms. This is similar in some respects and in contrast in other respects to the ways in which state and/or religious elites before the global era facilitated the production of iconic architecture. Further study of iconic architecture in the global and preglobal eras—for example, how iconicity can be lost as well as gained and why most manufactured "icons" are unsuccessful and the implications for local/urban, national, and global identity formation—will expand our knowledge and understanding not only of buildings, spaces and architects but of the wider role of representation and symbolism/ aesthetics in making and remaking our world.

Notes

1. The comment that "'Commerce' rather than 'civitas' is now the inspiration drawn from the Los Angeles skyline" (Attoe 1981, 35) is equally true for the buildings that make up skylines in cities all over the world today.

2. The connection between my theory of capitalist globalization and iconic architecture underlying this discussion of urban, national, and global identities, is elaborated in Sklair (2005), where the focus is on the role of the transnational capitalist class, and Sklair (2006), where the focus is on iconicity. This chapter borrows from these two papers.

3. See Jencks (2005). My discussion is partly based on a series of interviews with people in and around architecture carried out in the U.S. and Europe in 2004 (ongoing) and searches of the general and specialist mass media. By "in and around architecture" is meant architects and the developers, urban planners, teachers, critics, and others who come into direct contact with them in an architectural context.

4. This topic produced six pages of discussion. A subsequent debate on "Why are famous architects famous?" produced ninety-eight pages, suggesting that architecture students are more interested in how architects become famous (and thus iconic) than how buildings become iconic.

5. This quotation is from the report in *Building Design* (13 December 2002). In summer 2004 funding was cancelled for several "iconic" projects in the U.K., leading *Building Design* (23 July 2004) to ask on its front page: "End of the iconic age?"

6. In my 2006 paper I develop this argument in terms of the "ducks and decorated sheds" of Venturi et al. (1997).

7. This would carry more conviction if FOA had not won some prestigious projects and competed unsuccessfully for other major iconic projects, including the World Trade Center site.

8. The first two questions are discussed in more detail in Sklair (2006), along with the very contentious issue of the canon.

9. See also the distinction between "age-value" and "newness-value" (Riegl 1998) in his discussion of what he called in 1928 the "modern cult of monuments." Sudjic (2005) calls this the edifice complex.

10. In 2005, it was announced that the Rotunda was being reinvented as a luxury apart-

ment block by the fashionable developers Urban Splash, whose spokesman enthused: "It's amazing. We've been inundated before we've even done any marketing. Everyone wants to live in an icon" (*Birmingham Post,* 5 September 2005). This raises issues of the class basis of some architectural iconicity, a topic that would repay further research.

11. Particularly useful for my own thinking on these issues have been Lehmann-Haupt (1954), Holston (1989), Vale (1992), Wharton (2001), and Fierro (2003).

12. For quite different approaches, compare Crinson (1996) and Cody (2003). Crinson's sympathetic critique of the application of "Orientalism" (Said 1978) to architecture is of particular interest.

13. The Dome cost £45 million to build and won prizes; the Millennium Experience with which it was temporarily filled cost about one billion and was roundly condemned. If the history of other icons (e.g. the Eiffel Tower, Sydney Opera House) is a guide, the Dome might one day receive the public acclaim it deserves. It is now one of the leading global entertainment venues.

14. For the debates around the issue of "monumentality" in the twentieth century, see Collins and Collins (1984) and the reprint of Giedion's paper of 1944, "The Need for a New Monumentality," in this same issue of the *Harvard Architecture Review.* Giedion (1984) argued that monumentality needed to be recovered from its totalitarian distortions and recreated in an emotionally literate and democratic form. Restrictions of space prevent me from exploring the relations between monumentality and iconicity here—suffice it to say that members of the transnational capitalist class appear to prefer their iconicity in skyscraper form, but not entirely to the exclusion of other innovative forms (Frank Gehry, for example, has not built any skyscrapers, yet!).

15. This is, of course, a complex historical process. "At what point, one may ask, did the pyramid become an Egyptian form? At first those sentinels at Giza must have seemed far more alien intrusions than anything Louis Kahn has conjured for Bangladesh. Yet today they remain the unchallenged architectural symbols of Egypt. And, like the Pyramids of Egypt or the Eiffel Tower, the Citadel of Assembly [in Dhaka] may someday be seen as being quintessentially of its country as well" (Vale 1992, 283–84).

16. "The iconic transformation of the Earth is already underway" through the UN Building in NYC, ICJ in the Hague, etc. According to Lasswell and Fox (1979, 68) "The iconic function of the Earth is to provide an image of identity and security."

17. Notably, the Millennium Wheel (the London Eye) and Foster's Erotic Gherkin (Swiss Re building) alongside St Paul's Cathedral, the Palace of Westminster (with Big Ben), and Tower Bridge in advertisements and promotional materials.

18. The controversy around the spread of "identikit International Style" skylines defined by glass and steel skyscrapers, for which Mies van der Rohe is held to be the chief culprit, is an extreme form of this argument.

19. The elitist Barragan did not share the leftist Juan O'Gorman's social agenda. O'Gorman, who had also been influenced by Wright, argued in an article in 1953: "This architecture that is called Modern . . . is the denial of what is Mexican, and its domineering charac-

teristic lies in its imitative condition of what is foreign. . . . It is only possible to understand this architecture as a reflection of the interests of a National Class for whom the industrialization of Mexico means the alliance with the International Capitalistic Class" (quoted in Eggener 1999, 256, n.55). See also Fraser (2000).

Works Cited

Attoe, W. 1981. *Skylines: Understanding and Moulding Urban Silhouettes*. Chichester, U.K.: Wiley.

Bozdogan, S. 2001. *Modernism and Nation Building: Turkish Architectural Culture in the Early Republic*. Seattle: University of Washington Press.

Broadbent, G. 1973. *Design in Architecture: Architecture and Human Sciences*. London: Wiley.

Cody, J. 2003. *Exporting American Architecture: 1870–2000*. London: Routledge.

Collins, C., and G. Collins. 1984. "Monumentality: A Critical Matter in Modern Architecture." *Harvard Architecture Review IV* (Spring): 15–35.

Crinson, M. 1996. *Empire Building: Orientalism and Victorian Architecture*. London: Routledge.

Curtis, W. 1986. "Towards an Authentic Regionalism." *MIMAR* 19 (January): 24–31.

Dovey, K. 1999. *Framing places: Mediating Power in Built Form*. London: Routledge.

Eggener, K. 1999. "Towards an Organic Architecture in Mexico." In *Frank Lloyd Wright: Europe and Beyond*, ed. A. Alofsin, 166–83. Berkeley: University of California Press.

Fierro, A. 2003. *The Glass State: The Technology of the Spectacle, Paris, 1981–1998*. Cambridge, Mass.: MIT Press.

Fraser, V. 2000. *Building the New World: Studies in the Modern Architecture of Latin America, 1930–1960*. London: Verso.

Giedion, S. 1984. "The Need for a New Monumentality [1944]." *Harvard Architectural Review* 4: 53–61.

Gombrich, E. H. 1972. *Symbolic Images: Studies in the Art of the Renaissance*. London: Phaidon.

Holston, J. 1989. *The Modernist City: An Anthropological Critique of Brasilia*. Chicago: University of Chicago Press.

Jencks, C. 1985. *Modern Movements in Architecture*. London: Penguin.

Jonas, A., and D. Wilson, eds. 1999. *The Urban Growth Machine: Critical Perspectives, Two Decades Later*. Albany: State University of New York Press.

Kieran, S. 1987. "The Architecture of Plenty: Theory and Design in the Marketing Age." *Harvard Architecture Review* 6: 103–13.

King, A. 1996. "Worlds in the City: Manhattan Transfer and the Ascendance of Spectacular Space." *Planning Perspectives* 11: 97–114.

———. 2004. *Spaces of Global Culture*. London: Routledge.

Kusno, A. 2000. *Behind the Postcolonial: Architecture, Urban Space, and Political Cultures in Indonesia*. New York: Routledge.

Lasswell, H., and M. Fox. 1979. *Signature of Power: Building, Communication, and Policy.* New Brunswick, New Zealand: Transaction Books.

Lefaivre, L., and A. Tzonis. 2003. *Critical Realism: Architecture and Identity in a Globalized World.* Munich, Germany: Prestel.

Lehmann-Haupt, H. 1954. *Art under a Dictatorship.* New York: Oxford University Press.

Lynch, K. 1960. *The Image of the City.* Cambridge, Mass.: MIT Press.

Marshall, R. 2003. *Emerging Urbanity: Global Urban Projects in the Asia Pacific Rim.* London: Spon Press.

Rattenbury, K., ed. 2002. *This Is Not Architecture.* London: Routledge.

Riegl, A. 1998. "The Modern Cult of Monuments: Its Character and Its Origins." In *Oppositions: Selected Readings from a Journal for Ideas and Criticism in Architecture 1973– 1984,* ed. K. M. Hays, 621–51. New York: Princeton Architectural Press.

Said, E. 1978. *Orientalism.* New York: Pantheon Books.

Sarkis, H. 2001. *Le Corbusier's Venice Hospital.* Berlin: Prestel Verlag.

Sklair, L. 2002. *Globalization: Capitalism and Its Alternatives.* Oxford: Oxford University Press.

———. 2005. "The Transnational Capitalist Class and Contemporary Architecture in Globalizing Cities." *International Journal of Urban and Regional Research* 29, no. 3 (September): 485–500.

———. 2006. "Iconic Architecture and Capitalist Globalization." *City* 10, no. 1 (April): 21–47.

Sudjic, D. 2005. *The Edifice Complex.* London: Allen Lane.

Vale, L. 1992. *Architecture, Power, and National Identity.* New Haven, Conn.: Yale University Press.

———. 1999. "Mediated Monuments and National Identity." *Journal of Architecture* 4: 391–408.

van Leeuwen, T. 1988. *The Skyward Trend of Thought: The Metaphysics of the American Skyscraper.* Cambridge, Mass.: MIT Press.

Venturi, R., D. S. Brown, et al. 1977. *Learning from Las Vegas: The Forgotten Symbolism of Architectural Form.* Cambridge, Mass.: MIT Press.

Wharton, A. J. 2001. *Building the Cold War: Hilton International Hotels and Modern Architecture.* Chicago: University of Chicago Press.

Wise, M. 1998. *Capital Dilemma: Germany's Search for a New Architecture of Democracy.* New York: Princeton Architectural Press.

Zukin, S. 1996. *The Cultures of Cities.* Oxford: Blackwell.

8

The Temptations of Nationalism in Modern Capital Cities

Lawrence J. Vale

Nationalism by Design

In a world riven by ethnic, racial, and nationalist conflicts, there is much appeal to the idea that cities might be able to transcend the pressures of their embeddedness in nation-states, and that an urban-centered identity could rally less destructive sorts of allegiances. One promising venue for testing such claims is the *capital city,* since—by definition—such places need to represent the seat of government and other "national" institutions. At the same time, capital cities are not equivalent to nation-states; they are still separately identifiable as cities, even though they are certainly cities of a very specialized kind. The act of designing a new capital city—or building significant new "national" institutions in an existing capital city—forces an engagement with questions of national representation.[1] Specifically, how are multiple social identities constructed through architecture and urban design? And, if such constructed identities matter, which groups in a plural society see themselves as represented in what gets built to represent supposedly *national* institutions? Does a capital city represent an opportunity to provide an alternative to nationalist discourse and subnational divisions, or does it serve to reinforce the sense that some people are included in the conception of the nation-state much more so than others?

In this chapter, I attempt to argue three things:

1. A wide variety of regimes have used urban design and architecture to advance a nationalist agenda, and this "design politics" operates at all visible scales.

2. When such regimes give in to the temptations of nationalism, the results are usually very divisive.

3. Conversely, it is possible to imagine ways that architecture and urban design can be used to heal political rifts.

Ernest Gellner, in his book *Nations and Nationalism,* defines nationalism as "a theory of political legitimacy" which holds that "the political and the national unit should be congruent" (Gellner 1983, 1). In other words, the political unit—what we generally call the nation-state, or more informally the "country"—and the national unit should coincide exactly if they are superimposed.

The problem is that the world is not organized this way, largely due to a long history of empires and colonialism, not to mention a variety of supranational political and economic alliances. If, as one extreme example demonstrates, one compares a map of Africa subdivided according to the borders of nation-states with a map showing the far more fine-grained subdivisions of ethnic groups that fall both within and across the boundaries of many nation-states, the two bear little resemblance and help explain major internal and international tensions. It is true that the system of African nation-states is far more equitable than the coarse grain of the imperially divided spoils that characterized the map of the earlier colonized continent, but the legacy of a continent fragmented by the wills of European colonists still suffers from the legacy of irrationally imposed borders. The modern system of nation-states—built mostly in the last two centuries (and especially during the last sixty years, a time when the number of nation-states has more than tripled) has not been easily superimposed on the system of ethnically defined nations or would-be nations, many of which find themselves to be subdivisions (or minority groups within) a nation-state that they do not recognize as legitimate. In short, the maps that depict peoples do not correspond very well with the maps that depict places.

If one turns to a reputable source like the newest *American Heritage Dictionary,* which is often serviceable for most purposes (though even that book's name seems to raise additional questions about this very topic), the proffered definitions of *nationalism* seem at least as evasive or incomplete as Gellner's. In the first instance, according to the *American Heritage, nationalism* denotes "devotion to the interest or culture of one's nation." What is not said, of course, is that "nation" in this sense may not exactly coincide with one's *nation-state.* In other words, nationalism can often be about devotion to some *subnational* portion of a pluralist nation-state that is attempting to harness and discipline many constituent nations within it. *Nationalism* can also be counter-posed to *internationalism,* as when the dictionary defines it as "the belief that nations will benefit from acting independently rather than collectively, emphasizing national rather than international goals." Finally, *nationalism* may denote "aspirations for national independence in a country under foreign domination."

This latter aspect seems particularly important, since it implies that nationalism is not necessarily tied to some fixed moment in political history. There is a *nationalism of aspiration*—embraced by those who do not yet control a nation-state but think that they should—as well as a *nationalism of consolidation*—championed by those who *do* control a nation-state but are struggling to make sure that the aspiring nations within its borders do not succeed in undermining the state's sovereign legitimacy. What I refer to as the "temptation of nationalism" in the title of this chapter is largely focused on the latter kind of nationalism. For those that are still aspiring to become nation-states, "the temptation of nationalism" is no more than an obvious tautology. For nation-states struggling to maintain their political hold on their constituent peoples (or to extend their hold onto adjacent territory), however, this *nationalism of consolidation* is both urgent and difficult to construct.

Nationalism in this sense is a two-stage proposition: the first stage—the *nationalism of aspiration*—supports a drive for independence in the name of freedom and self-determination, and the second stage—the *nationalism of consolidation*—is what is needed to define the self that has been freed. As political scientist Crawford Young puts it, the state which, before independence, had been the "foil against which unity was forged" is, after independence, "itself the main vehicle in the hands of the nationalist elite for the fulfillment of the mission" (Young 1978, 71). In other words, nationalist movements begin as struggles *against* the state but, if they succeed, they suddenly have to *become* the state, themselves. Because the hold on power is uncertain, the leaders of a nation-state are tempted to take nationalistic positions that endeavor to suppress or supersede pre-independence subnational identities that are not useful to the dominant group in power. The temptation of nationalism is the promise of unity and legitimacy, the dream of a consolidated nation-state unchallenged by those who would unravel it or secede.

The Links between City Building and Nation Building

Usually, those who study politics study the institutions of governance and the texts that set out policies, programs, and aspirations. It is an intellectual landscape of constitutions, parties, congresses, and speeches. Even if the focus widens to include countervailing social movements, it remains on the social structure and agency of groups and individuals. The built environment, if it is considered at all, is reduced to mere backdrop. It is regarded as a passive setting, thought to play little role in the action of politics. Yet, as I have argued extensively elsewhere, urban design, like war, can be seen as an extension of politics by other means. City building and nation building are linked, especially when the city is a modern capital.

Capital city design enters into the relationship between cities and nationalism at multiple scales. Most broadly, design matters at the international scale of nation-state relations. Many capital cities are where they are because of who else is nearby and how close. For example, in the 1950s the leaders of the newly founded state of Pakistan chose to locate its new capital, Islamabad, where it could be close to the contested border with India, yet set adjacent to the existing city of Rawalpindi, a military stronghold. A different kind of international political dimension occurred during the *apartheid* years in South Africa. In this case, the regime engaged in a bizarre attempt to create an international system within its own sovereign territory—by granting so-called "independence" to a series of benighted territories it called homelands. The homeland system served as a selective and effective means to export rural blacks and keep them from moving full-time to South Africa's cities, where they were not wanted. This now vilified South African method for achieving "homeland security" depended on elaborate constructions of "capital cities" for each of the several major tribal groups, a system that enabled the regime to buy off compliance from ethnic leaders by providing them with the lavishly produced illusion that they were in charge of their own independent countries, replete with parliament buildings and postage stamps. In this way, through sham capitals such as Bisho in the "Republic of Ciskei," the South African apartheid state provided the homeland leaders with a carefully bounded urban opportunity for nationalism, one exercised safely distant from real cities such as Soweto-Johannesburg. Spatially detached and amply policed, these nationalist temptations posed no threat to the sovereignty of the nation-state.

City building and nation building are also connected at the national scale. Capital cities, especially those designed to serve newly independent countries that are composed of many smaller units, often must serve as fulcrums that balance contending subnational forces based in diverse regional centers. It is not a coincidence that Canberra is between Sydney and Melbourne, or that Ottawa is between Toronto and Montreal, or that Washington, D.C. is between Philadelphia and Charleston. Sometimes governance is actually divided to accommodate branches of national government in multiple cities, as is the Netherlands and South Africa (quite apart from the matter of separate homelands). Or, in a variant of this, there is the highly complex sociopolitical proposition of Pakistan after the partition of British India—divided into the two wings of West Pakistan and East Pakistan separated by a thousand miles of India. East Pakistan eventually became Bangladesh, following a civil war, but before this post-Partition partition into separate nation-states, the Pakistani leadership faced intractable problems about how and where to site its capital, a struggle that both mirrored and prefigured the larger political battle over national identity for the Muslim state.

Often, a newly designed capital is marketed as a neutral center, even when it is no such thing. Brasília, for instance, could be seen as relatively equidistant from many of Brazil's larger existing cities, but its location was spurred by a desire to develop the nation-state's vast and underpopulated interior. It mattered less that the travel time from other cities were equivalent than it did that the other cities were just *distant*. In this case, sovereign control of the nation-state depended on staking a new spatial and political claim to the interior, and treating this as an opportunity to assert and symbolize the country's modernity to the world (Vale 2008, 132–145; Holston 1989). In Nigeria, by contrast, the decision taken in the 1970s to site Abuja—the country's new Federal Capital Territory—near the geographic center of the nation-state was not a move toward some neutral centrality. Rather, it could be seen as a politically motivated shift of the power center toward the Islamic north, and away from the non-Islamic affinities of the south coast, and safely removed from the corruptions and confusions of Lagos (Moore 1984, 175).

At the scale of the city, too, decisions about how to locate national institutions within it carry information about the meaning of capital cities, and convey information about how secure the sponsoring regime feels about the stability of its sovereignty. Frequently, especially in recent decades, regimes have sponsored construction of new capitol complexes—the seats for key "national" institutions—but have stopped short of the expense and audacity of building an entirely new capital city. Such capitol complexes, however, serve as condensed reminders about the power of urban design to convey the intended hierarchy of a city. It matters how and where within the city the government chooses to site the chief institutions that both house and symbolize its power. For some older capitals, located in mature democracies that are secure in their sovereignty, the national institutions are scattered across different parts of the city, with little effort to bequeath them an urbanistic pride of place. In Paris, for instance, the Louvre—erstwhile home to kings—appears central, but the more contemporary sites of French democracy, such as the Elysée palace, do not stand out. By contrast, designers and planners of new capital cities almost in variably seek to impose separate districts for government buildings.

At the still smaller scale of the capitol complex precinct, the true power of design politics often becomes especially powerful. In Sri Lanka, for instance, just as Tamil unrest simmered over into protracted civil war during the early 1980s, the Sinhalese-led government moved the national parliament out of Colombo and onto a man-made island in the suburbs, site of the 15th century capital of Sri Jayawardhanapura Kotte—the last place from which the Sinhalese successfully ruled the entire island. To make clear the subnational thrust of this "national" space, the urban design plan called for a "cultural grove" replete with Buddhist stupas, hardly a welcoming place for the island's Hindu and other minority populations (New Capital Project Division, 45). A parallel sort of urbanistic nationalism prevails at the parliament building in Australia's Canberra. Here, the chief evidence of aboriginal presence is relegated to a mosaic forecourt, leaving the trabeated portico of the building itself to represent "the advent of European civilization," at least according to a book sponsored by the Royal Australian Institute of Architects (Beck 1988, 20–25).

Subnational pressures also operate within buildings themselves. In the national parliament building for Papua New Guinea (PNG), for instance, the designers faced an immense challenge of representation. In an archipelagic nation-state composed of multiple cultures speaking hundreds of languages, deciding which piece of the richly diverse architectural legacy should symbolize the "national" proved exceptionally difficult. Rather than seek a neutral modernist way to avoid the issue, the architect instead chose to design the main structure of the capitol to resemble an abstracted spirit house (*haus tambaran*) specific to villages in the island's East Sepik province. Not surprisingly, this same province was home to Michael Somare, PNG's first prime minister, who championed the design (White 1972; *Sepik-Ramu* 1988; Vale 2008, chapter 6). Meanwhile, the round house form common to villages in the PNG highlands was relegated to the capitol's recreation block. In this way, even a single building exposes the tensions inherent in crafting a single national language for a pluralist nation-state. In such a charged symbolic climate, even choices about furniture and art objects can carry a poisonous design politics.

Four Temptations of Nationalism

The politicized design histories of capitol complexes in Sri Lanka and PNG illustrate the first of many temptations of nationalism: the temptation of subnationalism. In these pluralist nation-states, the built environment becomes a symbolic battleground for contending conceptions of "the national." Or, more precisely, buildings and their urban design settings become mechanisms for asserting the supremacy of the dominant culture in places where this dominance is challenged by other contending groups within a tenuous nation-state. Nationalism, in this sense, is no more (and no less) than the search for legitimacy by the largest subnational group. Architecture and urban design are essential tools in this constant quest for legitimacy and self-assurance.

This search for nationalist legitimacy is often carried backwards into the past, in what can be termed the temptation of invented history. Historian Eric Hobsbawm has observed that nation-states generally claim to be "rooted in the remotest antiquity" and be "human communities so 'natural' as to require no justification other than self-assertion," yet neither of these holds true. Instead, such nation-states are both "novel" and "constructed," forged by what Hobsbawm famously called "the invention of tradition" (Hobsbawm 1983, 13–14). It is this willingness to leap back across chasms of time, politics, and development that allows today's Iraqis to consider themselves direct descendents of Nebuchadnezzar and led Saddam Hussein to reconstruct the ruins of Babylon with scant archeological evidence in order to proclaim a continuity of culture and power. Similarly, the founders of Zimbabwe marked their independence from the colonial regime of Rhodesia by naming the new nation-state after the Shona phrase *dzimba dza mabwe,* meaning "Houses of Stone." Most directly, this referred to the remarkable stone complex of Great Zimbabwe, home to an estimated 10,000 people in the fourteenth century. It is wholly understandable that Zimbabwean leaders would seek to root their fledgling nation-state in such a dramatic example of precolonial culture. Prime Minister Robert Mugabe extended this use of history into less reputable nationalist ends, however, by claiming direct lineage to another "Mugabe" who once ruled the area of Great Zimbabwe, but conveniently ignored the fact that his own ancestors first came to the area a full two hundred years after the city's fifteenth-century collapse (Vale 1999).

In addition to the temptations of subnationalism and invented history, nationalism asserts itself through the built environment even more commonly through the mechanisms of display. Capital cities are particularly prone to the use of long axial vistas leading to privileged points, and these vistas are often used as ritual stages to demonstrate the power and achievements of the regime. Perhaps the most dramatic evidence of the temptation of display is the north–south axis for Berlin planned by Albert Speer in conjunction with his patron, Adolf Hitler. Although the advent of World War II kept nearly all of the project from being carried out, for sheer audacity it has remained unrivaled. The broad avenue, to be flanked not only by government buildings but also by outposts of major German industries, was to culminate in a Great Hall, scaled to hold between 150,000 and

180,000 persons standing, and deliberately envisioned to far outdo its domed predecessors from Rome—both the ancient Pantheon and the baroque grandeur of St. Peter's. Hitler and Speer intended the new city of Germania to be a global assertion of dominance, a signal to the rest of the world and to the German people themselves, that theirs was the greatest of all empires (Speer 1970; Helmer 1985; Ladd 1997). Not all nationalisms of display carry the fascist overtones of Nazi Berlin, of course, but the temptation to orchestrate the built environment for didactic purposes seems to extend across many types of regimes.

Capital cities always do more than house the institutions of sovereignty; they must also *display* them. The rulers of modern democratic India, for instance, artfully appropriated the central display zone of the British Raj in New Delhi. Whatever the intended political break achieved by Indian independence, no Indian leader wished to abandon the symbolic legacy bequeathed to the new regime by the broad axial upward sweep of the "King's Way." For Nehru and his followers, it was enough to rename the avenues and the buildings, and to reprogram the ceremonial uses of the parade routes to be in greater accord with the new nation. Modern India invented its own traditions for a space that was too tempting to relinquish, yielding a Republic Day display that remains a bizarre hybrid of lingering colonialist imagery and nationalist fervor (Irving 1991; Vale 2008, 104–113).

Other regimes have used urban design to inscribe a politics of nationalist display even more egregiously. The most famous examples in the twentieth century were the grand constructed squares of Moscow and Beijing. Once Moscow was reclaimed as the seat of government for the USSR, the Soviet leadership found ways to display the power of the regime by using Red Square with the walls of the Kremlin rising implacably above and behind it. Even before the construction of the Lenin Mausoleum provided it with a new focal point, the Kremlin side of the square became a vast stage set, designed to be viewed by the assembled masses (Berton 1977). Nationalist displays took two forms—the periodic celebratory parades of banners and military equipment that moved across the square, and the static tableau of assembled dignitaries posing for pictures against a backdrop of crenellated brick, challenging Western pundits to analyze who was in or out of favor based on their position. In this way, the "Kremlin" was transmuted from a mere location into a highly charged metonym for the regime itself.

Not to be outdone, in 1987 the North Koreans expanded Pyongyang's Kim Il Sung Square to the point where it would be larger than Red Square (Springer 2003). Pride of place for nationalist zones of display, however, must still go to Beijing. Following the People's Revolution of 1949, Mao demonstrated his consolidated power by turning the south-facing wall of the Forbidden City into a city-scaled gallery housing a single portrait—the iconic image of himself, scaled even larger than the massive archway beneath it. Mao also dramatically reconfigured Tiananmen Square itself, turning what had long been a more modest T-shaped palace approach into a vast masonry expanse intended to be able to assemble one million Party faithful (Hung 1991). And, as in Red Square, the quintessential political space of Beijing became a plane beneath a wall used to display the symbolic trappings of nationalism.

Urbanistic and architectural expressions of nationalism also give in to a fourth mode of representation—the temptation of isolation. In contrast to the gregarious ideological presence of parades and other displays, nationalist impulses can also appear in a more inward-looking guise. Especially for nation-states where the hold on power remains uncertain and contested, part of the regime's challenge is to maintain and enhance its own security. Sri Lanka's island parliament typifies this phenomenon; the isolation is politically justified by formalist "contextual" explanations that link the capitol to past examples of indigenous temple compounds aesthetically set off by water, but the security impulse remains undeniable (and wholly understandable). Similarly, the imposing formality of Louis Kahn's capitol complex constructed in Bangladesh uses water to separate the buildings from the citizenry, creating the appearance of a moated citadel arising from a vast green plain of grass (Vale 2008, chapters 7 and 9). This temptation of isolation is not limited to capitol complex precincts. Rather it seems to be nearly ubiquitous in postcolonial capital city urbanism.

Like many other instances of single-use zoning that have infected the planet since 1945, designed capital cities have assumed the need for a separate zone for government. All of the most famous designed capitals—from Chandigarh to Brasília to Islamabad to Abuja—have treated the seat of government as an object to be isolated in space. For Chandigarh, created as a state capital for the Punjab following the partition of India, Le Corbusier explicitly treated the main institutions of government as a distinct and privileged realm, a head ("la tête") atop the city's body. Lest this isolation be apparent only to those looking at a map, Le Corbusier introduced an enormous constructed embankment to block the view of the rest of the city from the capitol's plinth. In a sketchbook annotation, he made clear that these artificial hills constituted protection from "l'ennemi" of the city (Le Corbusier 1982 [1954]). Similarly, Islamabad has a very separate government zone at the summit of its central avenue, the designers of Brasília constructed a deliberately isolated "Plaza of the Three Powers" to separate the three branches of government, and Nigeria's Abuja features a similarly named—and equally detached—"Three Arms Zone." Often, the rhetoric here is about a democratic-sounding "separation of powers" but the reality entails the separation of all power from the rest of the urban context. The symbols of sovereignty, thus constructed, appear as separate and above the city.

These four temptations of nationalism—the temptations of subnationalism, invented history, display, and isolation—are not the only spatial manifestations of political machinations, but they do seem to appear with particular frequency in the constructed landscapes of postcolonial governance. Despite the number and power of the ways that regimes give in to the temptations of nationalism in the efforts to represent the nation-state as more stable and secure than it is, it is worth asking whether the techniques of design can be used to repair, rather than just to divide.

Can Design Work against Nationalism?

So far, the prevailing observation here is that pluralist nation-states share territory uneasily, and that the built environment provides many temptations to exercise nationalist impulses. Clearly, design helps to clarify the struggles over identity. Is there also hope for design to transcend difference, bypass nationalist conflict, or even to heal it?

At the architectural level, several nation-states have grappled with this challenge. The parliament building in Sri Lanka, designed by the late Geoffrey Bawa, marks a sophisticated effort to harness and blend diverse architectural traditions into a single building that is not immediately identifiable as narrowly Sinhalese, Tamil, or anything else (Bawa 1986, 16). It is a true Sri Lankan hybrid, just as those who seek peace would desire. That said, its political neutrality as a building is dramatically undercut by its partisan Buddhist/Sinhalese site plan. Even in PNG, where the awkward juxtaposition of a dominant Sepik province *haus tambaran* main block with a subservient Highlands roundhouse recreation wing threatens to exacerbate local tensions, there was nonetheless a demonstrable effort to include multiple cultures in the central symbolic structure of the nation-state.

Other architects have attempted to transcend subnational factions by relying more on the powers of abstraction. Rather than deliberate efforts to permit local people to see their own group represented in the "national," designers have sought to introduce new forms with less obvious iconographic reference to any single group. The goal here is to create a new form that can be accepted as part of a more inclusive embrace of a nation-state. Louis Kahn's celebrated "Citadel of Assembly," constructed as the parliament for Bangladesh, stands as perhaps the most dramatic architectural effort to advance the goals of democracy in a newly independent nation-state. At the very least, the striking presence of this utopian spatial manifestation of the centrality of parliamentary rule served as a persistent implied rebuke to the military rule that dominated the early decades of sovereignty in Bangladesh (Vale 2008, chapter 9).

An even more explicit attempt to use urban design as a healing force in nation building has taken form in Canada. Canada's national capital, Ottawa, was constructed on the political fault line between Ontario and Québec. Geopolitically, however, the capital gave the appearance of a domineering English sovereignty that sat separate and superior in its neo-gothic splendor on a riverside bluff above and opposite the small lowland city of Hull on the francophone side of the water. In recent years, even as Hull was renamed Gatineau to sound more French, the urban designers of the National Capital Commission worked to implement the capital's Confederation Boulevard (Le boulevard de la Conféderation) to provide symbolic linkage between the two sides. The boulevard—identified by things such as signage, flags, and special lighting—attempts to market Ottawa as a more inclusive capital region, a zone more fully representative of Canada as a whole. By connecting key institutions on the Ottawa side of the river (including Parliament Hill, the National Library, the National Archives, and the Supreme Court) with other "national" institutions on the Gatineau side (most prominently the Canadian Museum of Civilization, which emphasizes the contributions of First Nations), Canada's planners are seeking a more inclusive mode of representation to guard against narrower subnationalisms.[2]

Cities and Sovereignty by Design

Nationalism takes many forms, and most of those forms are visible if we look for them. Sociologists often talk in terms of social movements, but such processes of political assertion also take spatial forms. Regimes need to build strong institutions and construct popular trust. But, more simply, regimes need to build. What the build and where they build it is immensely revealing about who they think they are and who they think they represent. In this sense, government buildings are about building governments, and this is especially true in the case of capital cities.

It is no coincidence that the term *representation* is both a term of aesthetics and also a term of governance and politics. We often judge a work of architecture or an act of urban design primarily in aesthetic terms—indeed, the design professions depend on us to do this—but doing so misses the embedded ways that designed pieces of the city are experienced on the ground. The urban design of a capital city (and especially its capitol complex—the precinct that has been deliberately designed to represent "the national") is a product of the power balance (or imbalance) in the nation-state that makes the commission. As such, for better or worse, it is often a kind of microcosm of the place. Wherever sovereignty is contested, the societal fissures are made visible by the ways that sovereign leaders attempt to define and construct "national" places. Historically, the urban world has been filled with efforts to manipulate citizens through provocative acts of narrow subnational nationalism. The challenge now—for designers, politicians, and citizens alike—is to overcome the temptations of nationalism. We should recognize the power of design to signal and instigate intense attachments to particular places, but must nurture new ways to harness this power to support more inclusive forms of pluralist governance.

Notes

1. For a book-length treatment of these issues, see Vale 2008.
2. For a more skeptical account, see Taylor 1989.

Works Cited

Bawa, G. 1986. "Statement by the Architect." In *Geoffrey Bawa*, ed. B. B. Taylor, 14–18. Singapore: MIMAR.

Beck, H., ed. 1988. *Parliament House Canberra: A Building for the Nation.* Sydney: Collins.

Berton, K. 1977. *Moscow: An Architectural History.* New York: St. Martin's Press.

Gellner, E. 1983. *Nations and Nationalism.* Ithaca, N.Y.: Cornell University Press.

Helmer, S. 1985. *Hitler's Berlin: The Speer Plans for Reshaping the Central City.* Ann Arbor, Mich.: University of Michigan Research Press.

Hobsbawm, E. 1983. "Introduction: Inventing Tradition." In *The Invention of Tradition,* eds. E. Hobsbawm and T. Ranger, 1–14. Cambridge: Cambridge University Press.

Holston, J. 1989. *The Modernist City: An Anthropological Critique of Brasília.* Chicago: University of Chicago Press.

Hung, W. 1991. "Tiananmen Square: A Political History of Monuments." *Representations* 35, no. 1: 85–117.

Irving, R. G. 1981. *Indian Summer: Lutyens, Baker and Imperial Delhi.* New Haven, Conn.: Yale University Press.

Ladd, B. 1997. *The Ghosts of Berlin: Confronting German History in the Urban Landscape.* Chicago: University of Chicago Press.

Le Corbusier. 1982. *Le Corbusier Sketchbooks, Volume 3* (1954–1957), ed. Françoise de Franclieu. Cambridge, Mass.: MIT Press. (Sketchbook H31, no.23, 14 February 1954.)

Moore, J. 1984. "The Political History of Nigeria's New Capital." *Journal of Modern African Studies* 22: 167–175.

New Capital Project Division, Urban Development Authority [Sri Lanka]. N.d. *Master Plan for Sri Jayawardhanapura.*

The Sepik-Ramu: An Introduction. 1988. Boroko: Papua New Guinea National Museum.

Speer, A. 1970. *Inside the Third Reich.* New York: Macmillan.

Springer, C. 2003. *Pyongyang: The Hidden History of the North Korean Capital.* Budapest: Entente Bt.

Taylor, J. H. 1989. "City Form and Capital Culture: Remaking Ottawa." *Planning Perspectives* 4, no. 1: 71–105.

Vale, L. 2008. *Architecture, Power, and National Identity,* 2nd edition. New York: Routledge.

———. 1999. "Mediated Monuments and National Identity." *Journal of Architecture* 4, no. 4: 391–408.

White, O. 1972. *Parliament of a Thousand Tribes: Papua New Guinea: The Story of an Emerging Nation.* Melbourne, Australia: Wren Books.

Young, C. 1978. *The Politics of Cultural Pluralism.* Madison: University of Wisconsin Press.

Hurvat haMidrash—The Ruin of the Oracle

LOUIS KAHN'S INFLUENCE ON THE RECONSTRUCTION OF THE JEWISH QUARTER IN JERUSALEM

Eric Orozco

The most significant event to transform the Old City of Jerusalem in recent history was a presentation given at the Israel Museum in Jerusalem on 28 July 1968. On that day, an architectural model showing a reconstructed Jewish Quarter was unveiled by Louis Kahn before the Israeli public and the ministerial committee responsible for the restoration of the Jewish Quarter. The Jewish American architect had been flown in by his Israeli sponsors (among whom was included Jerusalem's mayor, Teddy Kollek) to present his proposal for the reconstruction of the Hurvah Synagogue, the most important edifice in the Quarter to have been destroyed by the Jordanians in 1948. The synagogue presented on Kahn's site model was a monumental edifice that would have visually matched the Dome of the Rock and the Holy Sepulchre as a signature monument of Jerusalem's skyline. The massive and striking form of the proposed synagogue was such that, undeniably, the structure could have stood in time to rival the Western Wall itself as Judaism's most visually recognized national monument. Kahn managed to transcend the pragmatic and tempered nationalisms of 1920s–1960s Israeli architecture to reclaim in his proposal a more Herodian way of building. The design that he presented that day provided a startlingly chauvinistic vision that appealed to a resurgent global Jewish nationalism in the wake of the Six Day War. While the Hurvah Synagogue structure itself was ultimately not realized, in many significant ways Kahn's proposal was to help shape the Jewish Quarter we know today.

At the time of the Jewish Quarter reconstruction effort, Israel was aggressively pursuing its first settlements in the territories formerly held by Jordan. The reconstruction of the Quarter therefore presented the state with a political liability.

Due to the potential impact of Kahn's Hurvah on the symbolically laden skyline of the Old City, the stodgily secular state had to suddenly evaluate the feasibility of a rather significant intervention within the sacred topography of the Old City. Louis Kahn appears not to have been sensitized to the background issues influencing Israeli concerns over their maneuvers of sovereignty in Jerusalem. In any case, he showed no interest in opposing such maneuvers, and his unhindered vision proved successful in winning support for a bolder conception for the reconstruction than his hosts could have conceived without his involvement. Despite the fact that his Israeli sponsors kept him largely removed from the decision making process, they would continue to credit him as the visionary eye behind the high-profile, politically sensitive projects they involved him in.

At the same time, Kahn was no mere figurehead in the effort to reconstruct the Jewish Quarter (albeit hints of frustration do so surface in his correspondence), and is arguably the most important visionary of recent history to have an impact on the planning of Jerusalem's historic district and surroundings. Kahn did engage the endeavor of reconstituting Judaism's presence in Jerusalem with near Solomonic ambition. He did not underplay the religious significance of his architectural charge, both in context of the Old City and in his personal critique of the convenient (and secular) pragmatism he encountered among Israelis in general.

An article written by the Israeli journalist Dan Mirkin, who had accompanied Kahn in a tour of Israel, appeared at the conclusion of Kahn's visit in the 29 July 1968 edition of the Israeli newspaper *Ma'ariv*. The article, titled "Louis Kahn versus Architects 'whose Religion is Solel Boneh',"[1] described anecdotes from Kahn's interactions with Israeli architects and recorded some of Kahn's most spirited thoughts about spirituality and architecture. During his tour, Kahn had provided an unblushing critique of the dehumanized, slipshod, and mechanistic attitudes of construction in Israel. Beholding the rapid absorption housing blocks erected by Solel Boneh, the construction company of the Histadrut union, Kahn wryly labeled the results as the products of a soulless "religion of Solel Boneh." He bemoaned the continuing truncated spirit of new building practices in Israel, which, among other things, flung up stone as mere veneer on buildings. "You must ask the brick, 'What do you want?' And you must ask the stone its will," Kahn explained to Mirkin. Noticing Kahn's loving inspection of the older Arab villages on the Beit Horon ridge, Mirkin would note, "he looked at the buildings like a believer who watches the prophet's tomb." The Israeli architect Ada Karmi-Melamede would reminisce later that Kahn had appeared "Biblical" in the Judean wilderness (Solomon 1997, fn. 83, 424).[2]

Louis Kahn's biblical stature was of such a kind that the Israeli architect Ram Karmi deferred the Hurvah project (which was arguably the greatest architectural commission of the Jewish world in recent times) to him a year before. Karmi had advised Yaacov Salomon, the Israeli lawyer who had initiated the Hurvah reconstruction effort, to approach Kahn with the project, purportedly considering him the only luminary at the time worthy of the charge. Knowing the climate of political expediency in Jerusalem, however, Karmi and other Israeli architects had hoped that Kahn's Synagogue would set a lofty enough design standard for the restoration of the Quarter, says Susan G. Solomon (1997, 445). At the time, the Minister of Religion, Zerach Warhaftig, had wanted to expedite the repopulation of the Quarter at the expense of the archeological investigations, careful planning, and restoration efforts of the Old City Restoration Team, headed by Yehuda Tamir. Karmi had apparently also acted shrewdly, sensing that the project's symbolic scale in such a culturally sensitive environment would require a headstrong "outsider," both to circumvent further internal controversies and to help gain approval for the overall restoration effort in the international community (ibid., 405).

Before its destruction during the 1948 war, the Hurvah had been one of the two primary Synagogues in the Jewish Quarter, the most important Ashkenazi Synagogue in Jerusalem. The first Synagogue erected on the site of the Hurvah had been built in 1701 by an immigrant group of Polish Hassidim. This building was destroyed not long afterwards when the group failed to pay back their Arab lenders. For over a century, the building remained in a state of ruins, receiving thus the name "Hurvah," Hebrew for "ruin."

In the early nineteenth century another Ashkenazi Orthodox group arrived in the Holy Land under the leadership of Rabbi Avraham Shlomo Zalman Zoref, an ancestor of Kahn's client Yaacov Salomon (who headed the effort to restore the Hurvah). Rabbi Shlomo Zalman Zoref's entreaties to Egyptian and then Ottoman rulers to reclaim the Hurvah's site proved successful. The original debt was cancelled and the community managed to erect a modest building. Through the aegis of the Rothschilds, the Austrian Emperor, and some engagement by the British, the community was later able to secure a permit from the Ottoman Sultan to construct a more stately edifice. In what may be seen as one diplomatic gesture of thanks to the British for their intervention in the Crimean War, the Ottoman Emperor graciously offered the services of his own royal court architect Assad Efindi, who was then working on the restoration of the Dome of the Rock. Efindi designed the Synagogue in the domed "Sinan style" of Ottoman mosques of the same (relatively small) size, and the building was completed in 1864 with funds provided from sources throughout the Diaspora.[3]

The Hurvah Synagogue was reduced to ruins by the Jordanians once again during the 1948 War. Not only does the history of this poignantly named Hurvah

Synagogue represent the travails of newly arrived Jewish immigrants to Jerusalem (and the devotion of the Diaspora toward the memory of Jerusalem's Jewish
heritage), its history makes readily apparent the idiosyncratic and often burdened
relationships in Jerusalem between international powers and the city's religious
institutions.

After 1948, the fledgling state of Israel for a time relinquished the Old City
both geographically and as a symbolic cultural monument, a situation that contributed to the increased recourse to "*Mamlakhtiut*," the statist project. In architectural expression, *Mamlakhtiut* (the "Zionist Statist Style") selectively appropriated cultural symbols for statist representation, implicitly secularizing their
historic and religious associations. The Israeli Knesset Building, whose stone
walls purposely appropriate the likeness of the Western Wall in order to recreate
the religious precedent as a secular symbol, is the most noteworthy example of
Mamlakhtiut—an act of willful displacement that stirred up some controversy in
its time. *Mamlakhtiut*, however, introduced an overt nationalistic expression in
architecture, replacing the more semantically neutral International Style adopted
by Zionism in the 1930s. Although modernism had provided a convenient departure from the "debilitating" vernaculars of Diaspora architecture, it had become
regarded as too aloof for self-representation.

Mamlakhtiut in Israeli culture emphasized the State above individual aspirations and traditionalist culture. In 1950s urbanism, *Mamlakhtiut* was simply a
willful continuation of the secular building project of Zionism, which had always
ignored the Old City and devoted its energy to establishing the Jewish center of
the city in West Jerusalem. As reflected in the thoughts of David Ben-Gurion, the
loss of the Old City in 1948 had conveniently advanced the Statist cause. The need
of the state to represent itself as the protectorate of world Jewry, however, eventually cultivated a return to traditional forms and preservationist attitudes. A "New
Zionist Style" in architecture and urbanism began to surface after 1956, which
openly reclaimed Diaspora symbols and Mediterranean vernacular architecture
and town planning (examples, says Yasir Sakr, include the restoration of Old Jaffa,
the Yad Vashem Holocaust Memorial Museum, and the Israel Museum). The state
also became far less reserved with the use of religious symbols in order to promote immigration.

Zionism in the early 1960s, however, began looking back with the preeminent
archeologist Yigal Yadin toward a more ancient heritage it could claim its own,
an attitude reinforced by the miraculous victory of the 1967 Six Day War. With
the heroic recapture of the Old City, even secular Israelis adopted the Western
Wall of Herod's temple mount, the most lasting achievement of Jewish construction in history, as a de facto symbol of national solidarity. At a time when overt

memorialization of the Holocaust was still very difficult among Jews (following the concerns of Theodor Adorno, for one), the rebuilding of the Jewish Quarter and reclamation of its monuments provided a convenient way to indirectly refer to the nation's redemptive mandate in contemporary history. The sight of the Hurvah's ruins provided the concrete directive to rebuild the Jewish Quarter. For those with a historical consciousness, the Hurvah reconstruction must have represented a chance to redeem nineteen hundred years of Diaspora experience and Jewish obscurity in Jerusalem.

The opportunity was not lost on Kahn. At the beginning of July 1968, Louis Kahn finally received the topographic drawings of the Hurvah site, which he had been waiting expectantly for from Ram Karmi. Karmi had experienced difficulty executing them due to the excavations still being undertaken in the Quarter and the general ruinous condition it was still in. Although Kahn had already put two of his assistants to work on two clay site models, he had not yet seriously undertaken the design work and site planning, waiting on the drawings. Yasir Sakr believes that Kahn had probably executed the design within the space of the two weeks leading up to his visit. He had initially planned to present his "first studies" in Jerusalem the month previous, coordinating with his visit to the Venice Biennale, but had canceled due to the fact that he had not yet readied a "presentation."

Evidence confirms that at the beginning of that July Kahn was still searching for an inspired thought for the design of the building, for on 2 July he had sent a letter (correspondence, Louis Kahn to Mrs. Serata, 2 July 1968) to the librarian at the Jewish Theological Seminary in New York requesting a copy of Louis Finkelstein's 1928 article "The Origins of the Synagogue." Kahn, having probably seen the title in a list of sources or known of it from his brief acquaintance with Finkelstein himself, had been hankering to read it, due to what certainly was to him a most provocative title. Indeed, not desiring to await its arrival by mail, he dispatched two (yes, not one but two) of his assistants to retrieve it from New York.

Kahn was so interested in "the Origin" that he confessed having rarely ever read a volume of history beyond its first or second chapter; he would simply continue to linger in the first chapter, longing to view "Volume Zero." If indeed he had read Finkelstein's article in its entirety, Kahn would not have needed to read much beyond the article's opening sentences to receive an inspiration critical to his approach to the Hurvah project:

The beginnings of the synagogue are hidden from us by the mists that gather about the horizon of Jewish history, no matter in which direction we look. When the synagogue rises into view during the Second Commonwealth it is already a well-established institution, and strangely the first mention of it is in a record of persecution, burning and destruction *(fn. Psalm 74:8).* (Finkelstein 1928, 49)

However thickly the mists gathered around Volume Zero here, I grant you that Finkelstein had captured Kahn's rapt attention with the allusion to the psalm. Finkelstein, indeed, continues on to eruditely infer Volume Zero amidst a time of great distress. He attributes the origins of the synagogue to a time of persecution during the reign of the evil king Manasheh, who raised an image of a pagan goddess in the temple and persecuted the prophetic party. Since Manasheh killed freely those who opposed him, the prophetic party developed a practice of gathering together for prayer in secret places. The place where they convened was called a *midrash,* theorizes Finkelstein, which in its primitive meaning had a locative sense and meant literally "the place of Divine communion" (Finkelstein 1928, 55). It was a place were one could "inquire" or "seek out" (*lidrosh*) an oracle from God. When the persecution ended, however, the practice still continued, Finkelstein argues, just as . . .

Maranos in Portugal are said to believe that true prayer can be offered only in secret synagogues. Having never worshipped in a synagogue openly and publicly recognized, they have come to regard what was forced by cruel circumstance on their fathers as normal religious life. (Finkelstein 1928, 54)

Thus, the pious continued gathering together in intimate places. Later in the second temple period, the word *midrash* lost its locative meaning, theorizes Finkelstein, as prophetic inquiry gave way to scriptural study as the basis for spiritual understanding. (*Midrash* today refers mainly to the traditional stories and the commentary of the Rabbinic sages that explicate the details of the biblical narrative.) The primitive institution of the *midrash* would, in time, bifurcate into places of communal prayer, the Synagogue of today, and places devoted to learning, the institution of the *beit hamidrash* (house of study), first mentioned by Ben Sirah in the early second century BCE. Finkelstein's linguistic association of the origin of a Jewish educational institution, the *beit hamidrash,* with the primitive synagogue, the *midrash* of the prophets, would probably have appealed to Kahn, who indeed tended to identify educational and spiritual programs as variations of the same "Quest."

In Kahn's mind, every composition was always in a searching analysis of its Origin. He would often assign motives to the various elements of his creations, which interacted with one another in cosmogonic dramas. A building's ruination was similarly significant to Kahn, who regarded ruins as structures returning to the struggle of their creation:

A building being built is not yet in servitude. It is so anxious to be that no grass can grow under its feet, so high is the spirit of wanting to be. When it is in service and finished, the building wants to say, "Look, I want to tell you about the way I was made." Nobody listens. Everybody is busy going from room to room. But when the building is a ruin and free of servitude, the spirit emerges telling of the marvel that a building was made. (Kahn 1973, 20)

The thought that the Hurvah had been named for its state of ruination probably expressed to Kahn the communal awareness of the building's anxious "wanting to be." While Kahn would have regarded the details in Finkelstein's article as more or less arcane (especially the linguistic areas of it), the example of the Portuguese Maranos makes Finkelstein's greater discussion sufficiently concrete: the Synagogue is an institutionalized continuity of piety born in travail. A ruinous synagogue returning to the struggle of its becoming expresses something not unlike the Quest that created the primitive *midrash:* the desire for the prophetic community to seek the oracle in the midst of cruel circumstances. To Kahn, the Hurvah's two destructions in history would have veritably stood as an eloquent expression of the Synagogue's "desire to be." Not only do we have here a possible motivation for Kahn's decision to incorporate the ruins of the original Hurvah into his proposal, but also his inspiration to conceive the new enveloping structure as an open-air "ruin" itself.[4] Kahn (often noted for his inclination to "wrap the building in ruins" in his later works) conceived of the building as an assembly space defined by concentric envelopes of concrete walls and volumes holding up four immense, inverted pyramidal concrete canopies that only incompletely sheltered the interior from the elements. Surrounding these central forms would be a screen of gigantic standalone stone pylons that tapered to the sky like relics of a more ancient (or numinous) structure.

We can here begin to understand something of what Kahn had meant when he related to Yehuda Tamir that his spontaneous conception for the new Hurvah structure came from "inspiration never before felt" (correspondence, Louis Kahn to Yehuda Tamir, 28 March 1969). That Kahn had read and appreciated Finkelstein's article is not only strongly suggested by his desire to preserve the ruins of the old Hurvah but also by his desire to associate the processional walkway between the Hurvah complex and the Western Wall with the prophets. The meandering spine, the key organizational element his master plan, was imagined as a succession of courts named after the prophets, tying together the educational centers of the Quarter. Kahn had desired to name the processional route "the Schools of the Prophets" or "the Street of the Prophets" (Solomon 1997, 427).

Serendipitously, in the first week of July 1968, a bulldozer exposed a stone ossuary in the clearing of an Israeli settlement site. It bore the name of one of the

Herodian temple's builders, "Shimon the builder of the temple." Louis Kahn had cut out the *New York Times* article describing the discovery at the very time he was just over one week into the site planning of his Hurvah proposal. The article, preserved in his Hurvah project files (Terence Smith, "Traces of Second Temple Found," *New York Times,* 12 July 1968, C18; in LIK 39, Kahn Collection) might have appeared as an uncanny sign of divine approval to him, but we do not know how the archeological finding inspired his vision. We may safely posit that it had some influence on the comprehensive reach of his master plan. The opportunity to spark the national imagination was something he must have sensed. Near the end of that July, he flew to Israel to present his vision for the entire Jewish Quarter.

True to form, as Mirkin would recount, Kahn had ignored the word "reconstruct" in his original charge, proposing instead to leave the Hurvah in its present ruined state. The Hurvah's ruins, Kahn explained, were to forever memorialize the Quarter's recapture in 1967, a bald nationalistic representation of his more probable motive to monumentalize the Synagogue's "desire to be." Kahn's new structure, which was four times the size of the original Hurvah, was to preserve the ruins of the old Hurvah as a ruinous memorial garden or "forecourt" partly incorporated into his entirely new structure. The new edifice, a concrete sanctuary square in plan, would rise just east of the original Hurvah. The four immense stone pylons on either side of the sanctuary resembled the pylons of the Temple of Amun in Karnak, and made the composite, half-cube mass of the building resemble a gigantic stone altar. Kahn's clay site model of the Quarter and Temple Mount showed that the New Hurvah Synagogue would not only dramatically overshadow the other buildings of the Quarter but would indeed visually match the lower massing of the Dome of the Rock. The Synagogue, along with its garden courts, was purportedly to serve as a harmonious complement to the plaza he proposed before the Wall. The Hurvah complex would thus serve as an assembly center in the Quarter to gather pilgrims together before undergoing their descent to the Western Wall along the Luxor-like spine of his proposed processional route.

Of course, the scale of Kahn's Hurvah drew a collective gasp at the moment of its public unveiling in the Israel Museum on 28 July 1968, and despite the immediate positive reception among the general public, the authorities were only slow to entertain its feasibility. The Prime Minister, Levi Eshkol, at least thrice postponed meeting (purportedly for health reasons) with Yaacov Salomon, the Hurvah Foundation's leader and Louis Kahn's chief advocate in Israel. In early August, several intellectuals would publicly criticize the apparent pretension of Kahn's Hurvah to consciously match the visual presence of the Dome of the

Rock.[5] A ministerial committee was put together to study the project, but, as the Israeli settlements in East Jerusalem (in Ramot Eshkol and the Mount Scopus area) increasingly drew global attention, the Prime Minister's office intuitively sensed the international provocation the project might stir. The Prime Minister wrote to Salomon:

> The matter has been put before me, and plans are to me, indeed, tremendous and beautiful. However, it seems to me that the carrying out of such a great project in the Old City should be put off for several years, as we have to worry first about the settlement of the Jews in East Jerusalem. Regarding money, as it is known, there is a limit. (Correspondence, Levi Eshkol to Yaacov Salomon, 19 September 1968)

He then brought up the reservations being voiced in the ministerial planning committee and wondered why "a more modest building" should not be considered. Jerusalem's mayor, Teddy Kollek, wrote directly to Kahn about the impasse:

> The decision concerning your plans is essentially a political one. Should we in the Jewish Quarter have a building of major importance which "competes" with the Mosque and the Holy Sepulchre, and should we in general have any building which would compete in importance with the Western Wall of the Temple? (Correspondence, Teddy Kollek to Louis Kahn, 29 August 1968)

It was not until almost half a year after the unveiling, on New Year's Day of 1969, that Salomon finally met with the Prime Minister and the ministerial committee headed by Yehuda Tamir that was overseeing the planning of the Jewish Quarter. The meeting's purpose was to discuss with the Prime Minister the feasibility of the scale of the project. Strangely, the project's symbolic and political drawbacks appear to no have become less salient, since the discussion, following Salomon's introduction to the symbolic intentions of the project, mainly settled on the rather more mundane matter of integrating the New Hurvah with the overall planning of the Quarter.

By that time, however, the symbolic issues had, in fact, already been deliberated at length on the national stage. In the previous month, a symposium had assembled to discuss Kahn's proposal. Various religious leaders, politicians, noted academics, heads of industry and other important personalities had attended the gathering. Yasir Sakr may be right in declaring that the symposium had offered the nation its first occasion of critical self-reflection regarding religious identity and national representation. The symposium had divided quickly into two opposing camps—as Sakr (1996, 72) labels them: "the religious and largely Jerusalemite-Diaspora culture" and another that "expressed a modernist, secular, and largely

Tel-Aviv cosmopolitan outlook." The former contingent, represented best by Rabbi Shar-Yeshuv Cohen, a war hero who had defended the Jewish Quarter during the 1948 war, was resentfully unimpressed with the unorthodox qualities of Kahn's design. Some of the critics attacked Kahn's blatant disregard of even the loose parameters established for synagogues in Halakhic literature, such as the need to provide for twelve "beautiful windows" (indeed, Kahn seems to have ignored the need for any glazing). But the most pointed remarks, which appear to unmask a conspiratorial negation of religious symbols in Kahn's design, were reserved against the proposal's perceived pretensions to not only supplant the Old Hurvah but the image of the Dome of the Rock and indeed all Jerusalem. The Dome of the Rock, explained Rabbi Cohen, looked back to Solomon's Temple in the minds of the Diaspora, and it stood over Judaism's holiest place. No one was fooled, he claimed, that the New Hurvah was not symbolically conspiring to supplant the Dome of the Rock through its imposing size and its visually higher footing on the adjacent hill, heretically striving thus to supplant the historical importance of the Temple by inference. Worse, he said, "I am not willing to see that the proposed new Khurvah [Hurvah] becomes with the passing of time a tradition and the final word: the alternative to the Temple" (Sakr 1996, 75).

That the once religiously aloof, modernist, "Tel-Aviv" nationalists successfully represented the greater national mood to recover and strengthen Jewish identity in the Old City is indicated by the fact that the once strongly reserved Prime Minister had "wholeheartedly" endorsed Kahn's Hurvah design on the New Year's Day meeting (correspondence, Yaacov Salomon to Louis Kahn, 3 January 1969). By mid-January, Tamir's ministerial committee gave the project the green light. On 25 February 1969, Kahn received a formal letter from Yehuda Tamir informing him of the resolution to invite him to become the architect of the Hurvah.

With the shifting climate of geopolitical conditions after 1969 and, ultimately, Kahn's death in 1974, the Hurvah's realization would prove untenable as enthusiasm for the project withered. Yet the important features of today's Jewish Quarter owe much to Kahn's vision, namely, his proposal for the enlarged plaza of the Western Wall and its spinal "processional" link to the heart of the Quarter. The integration of archeological grounds, including the preservation of the old Hurvah's ruins as a memorial garden, and the multilevel clustering of residences, yeshivas and institutions around community gardens and public plazas can also be credited, more or less, to Kahn's proposal. Kahn's design for the Hurvah also helped establish Israeli Brutalism as a new paradigm for Israeli national architecture, a minimalist architecture that adopted a primitivistic, "archaeological" sensibility, recalling the muscular forms of ancient Mediterranean structures. Israel, following the exploits of the preeminent archeologist Yigal Yadin, was experiencing in 1968 an unprecedented enthusiasm for excavating, understanding, and culturally referencing its Herodian and Solomonic past. The Quarter's planners were handed Kahn's schematic design for the Quarter and given the charge to musemise where appropriate and to contextualize to local building patterns.

After Kahn was awarded the greatest Jewish commission of the century in 1969, Teddy Kollek lost no time involving him in the greater planning of the city. Not only was Kahn's schematic for the Quarter to be carried out, but on 6 June 1969 Kollek thought it befitting to give him also the chance to direct the planning of one of the important overlooking ridges to the south of the Old City. On a flight to Istanbul en route to Dacca, Kahn would fortunately pen his vision for Jerusalem. Writing to Kollek, he described an environment composed of "a composite order of concrete and stone which would respect each material for its own power and beauty without disguise" (Correspondence, Louis Kahn to Teddy Kollek, 4 July 1969). Kahn's Hurvah boldly demonstrated this very composite order; it was to be an example which, we can securely posit, Kahn intended for the Jewish Quarter as a whole. He then goes on to describe his social vision for the city:

> One of the more important ideas, however, is to give thought to the creation of new institutions which should be offered to Jerusalem and should appear in South Jerusalem. Places of well being, glorifying body beauty as well as the beauty of the mind. I see the places for children, for boys, for young and those older and old as having their own clubs, their own rooms of meeting and places of happening, places of cross invitation, places associated with their gardens, for privacy their courts of entrances, play fields, etc.
>
> I have been proposing for other developments, the establishment of schools of the talents, schools designed to draw out the natural talent of a person in contrast with present ways of examining people on an equal basis. A person does not learn anything that is not already part of him from the start.
>
> A man is born knowing what to do but is not born knowing how to do it or how to express it. This he or she must learn. How timely is now the need for schools which examine only within the talent of the person. The would be good for Arabs and Jews [*sic*]. Israel could be a place of the example.
>
> I know the idea does not apply only to S. Jerusalem but as well, I believe, to Jerusalem S. N. W. or E. as a whole even if only S. J. is being thought of. (Correspondence, Louis Kahn to Teddy Kollek, 4 July 1969)

Clearly, the vision described here is a utopian urbanism that will make Israel "a place of the example"—not through collective heroism (*Mamlakhtiut*), religious or secular, but by its fearless attention to the capacity of the individual, "the would be good" of individuals freed from the constraints of being evaluated

"on an equal basis." This is quintessential Louis Kahn. Kahn's vision is clearly intended for the entire city outside the Old City, but we would be hard-pressed not
to see here some of his intentions for the Jewish Quarter as well.

In the case of the Hurvah, Kahn expressed to Mirkin a desire to respect the
individual by creating a space to serve all levels of comfort with religious obser-
vance. He arranged hierarchically "layered" space: a multilevel great hall (what
Kahn would have referred to as a "served space") completely surrounded by an
ambulatory with alcoves ("servant spaces"). The hall would accommodate up to
1,000 worshippers, with seating for 200 in the lower level, a segregating strategy
to allow the building to look full even with a small number of participants.[6] The
surrounding ambulatory would offer the pilgrim and unattached visitor more intimate areas for personal observation or private prayer. It was to be a space where
no one's faith, perhaps, would be examined on a collective basis.[7] As Mirkin explained:

> Those who are not among the regular worshipers could draw inside. The wor-
> shipers could enjoy the "innerness" of the great hall, while the visitors could en-
> joy the "innerness" inside the alcoves, and no one would be more "inside" than
> the other, and no one would be "outside." (Mirkin 1968)

Kahn's Hurvah demonstrated his desire to preserve Jewish solidarity in Jerusalem *by* serving the centripetal movement of diverse traditions with fluid grada-
tions of loyalty. The new Hurvah Synagogue to Kahn was not to be a mere replacement of its ethnic denominational forebear but a synagogue of the synagogues, a
design modulated to individual particularity. The attempt to present a form of the
Synagogue dedicated to serving a public of different traditions with various individual "levels of commitment" is, it may be noted, essentially nationalistic. Kahn's
Hurvah does subversively escape the mold of a traditional synagogue, much as
the Western Wall does. Still, Kahn would have found it hard to image that the
scale of his Hurvah, while approaching that of other important buildings in the
Old City's skyline, could be taken ominously at all. Monumentally nationalistic
as it was, the building would be nestled in a complex of residences and institutions defining "places of well being" and "cross invitation"—the places of "human
agreement" that naturally enrich the varied, historically layered, and composite
order of the city. From his perspective, he was merely adding another stone to a
jewel-encrusted crown.

While Kahn was invoking a kind of cultural mediation with a religious project, Kahn's social program certainly was not slipping into the kind of semiotic
madness Yasir Sakr claims it was by offering "negations" of religious and nationalistic meanings (e.g. fragmenting the "Form" of the Synagogue into an archeo-

logical relic). Kahn expressed to Mirkin an impatience for subversive architectural programs that strayed into such fanciful social agendas, mentioning his distrust of artists who were "always trying to solve problems" and engineers who did not "have the courage to demonstrate a problem." "Building is not a solution," he exclaimed, "It is nothing but a way to present the problem. The problem remains—and it's art." Mirkin would recount one such encounter with a "problem solver":

> I sat with him for a full evening in the company of young architects, one of whom constantly spoke and explained how the demands of the religious should not be overly respected and cast before him expansive theories of the modern restoration method of ancient cities. Louis answered him, "The basis of all art is respect." Respect and generosity towards the other; respect that is dictated by a specific creation. "Art," he said, "is likened to gold flakes which an artist collects from a certain situation." (Mirkin 1968)

Despite his mildly secular disposition, the anecdote above suggests that the employment of "negational" strategies was foreign to Kahn's sensibilities. Moreover, Kahn consciously evoked the "Origin" of the synagogue as an institution born in religious travail for the hortative task of shoring up the nation in times of crisis. Kahn appreciated the humanizing application of the religiously constituted Quest as a corrective to the dispirited malaise of other nationalistic secular projects.

This fact is best evinced in a single anecdote from Kahn's visit to Israel. When Louis Kahn was shown Solel Boneh's dismal apartment blocks, Dan Mirkin explained to him that the need to absorb immigrants had outpaced any ability to find "clear solutions" to the housing shortage. Unbeknownst to Mirkin, Kahn had participated personally in a modernist housing study during the 1950s to help solve Israel's housing crisis (an occasion that actually led to his first visit to Israel). Remembering his own unrequited, monumental efforts in that unsuccessful endeavor,[8] Kahn would probably have been stung slightly by Mirkin's remark. Mirkin recorded Kahn's reaction:

> The answer left him unsettled in thought. Suddenly he said to me, "Had the people who had built the apartments been religious—of any religion whatsoever, and not necessarily of a ritual faith, but of a faith of the heart—they would not have erected such buildings. It's their tragedy that they had the religion of Solel Boneh." (Mirkin 1968)

By force of necessity, Kahn's clients would attend to his visions while they wisely employed his energy to cross-purposes in navigating the internal disputes of their constituencies or entertaining the subtle expediencies needed to navigate fiscal and political realities. Yet even Kahn's savvier clients could be blindsided by his charisma. Without a doubt, his forceful personality would coax his Israeli hosts into uncharted waters of religious engagement, to the detriment of the Hurvah's ultimate realization. The sheer draw and novelty of his vision among Israelis persuaded the state to temporarily ignore problematic issues surrounding matters of symbol, identity, and sovereignty in Jerusalem. A distance is evinced, as in Kahn's remarks above, between the tempered nationalisms of Israelis (immersed as they were in the cumbersome realities of preemptive statecraft and sovereignty agendas) and the nationalism of Kahn's Diaspora consciousness. As with many among the Diaspora, Kahn's nationalism did not share a strong kinship with either Israeli modernity or Orthodox faith. These diverse motivations for Jewish nationalistic identity were bound to impose new conditions on collective identity that would inevitably raise the importance of Jerusalem's built environment for the recovery of nationalistic expression and global Jewish solidarity. The resurgent importance of Jerusalem to Diaspora identity meant that the state could no longer ignore the Old City or the Diaspora for the aims of Israeli sovereignty. As the political stakes of identity were raised in the process of consolidating new territory or strengthening Israeli control over Jerusalem, the complexities of sibling nationalisms were ignored or, perhaps, all too easily conflated or exploited in the reconstruction of the Jewish Quarter by a leadership managing the complex strains of constituent politics, Jewish settlement, and geopolitical developments.

Kahn was merely an odd forerunner to the long trail of headstrong figures in the Diaspora who would begin to make themselves felt in the internal matters of the Israeli state. Like fellow members of the Diaspora, Kahn had held his breath through the suspenseful days of the Six Day War to encounter in its wake the miraculous rerooting of worldwide Jewry to its ancient past, despite the continuing fragmented state of its traditionalisms and modernisms. Both as an American Jew and as an architect, he was motivated to create a shared space where no one would be more "inside" than the other, and no one would be "outside."

Kahn's Hurvah may be the earliest significant demonstration of the drift of Zionism away from its statist cradle toward a new multiheaded, more postmodern nationalism that expressed without guise the need of the nation to reattach the developing narrative of the state to a more ancient past. The redemptive trajectory of this history did not necessarily entail a religious reawakening, but an affirmation of the significant role of spiritual devotion for the Jewish people. Kahn, no doubt, intended the ruins of the Old Hurvah to remain as a national memorial to warm the embers of this "faith of the heart." The Ruin would signify the constant need of the nation to rekindle its animating faith. Susan Solomon (1997, 431) observed that this poignant symbol proved to be the single most endearing aspect of Kahn's proposal to Israelis. The crumbling artifact set aside is immediately understood by Jews the world over as a symbol remembering the "dual concepts of human frailty and destruction" even in auspicious times. Of course, such a memorial would not just hearken to the razed sanctuaries of the past, like the glass-breaking ceremony in a Jewish wedding. It was one. And today, Kahn's Memorial Hurvah remains in the Jewish Quarter telling us of the marvel that, indeed, a building was made.

Notes

1. I'm indebted to my friend Danny Kopp for his help translating Dan Mirkin's article from the Hebrew. Kahn (who had assistants who spoke Hebrew at the time) preserved a clipping of this article. Clippings of all the newspaper articles referred to below, as well as all letters, carbon copies, and/or telegrams of private correspondence mentioned are held in Box LIK 39 of the Louis I Kahn Collection at the University of Pennsylvania in Philadelphia. The newspaper clippings are in the folder titled "Israel Newspaper Articles Hurva."

2. To many architects Kahn's persona has always resembled something biblical. Alexander Gorlin (1985, 85) recounts how Kahn as a curious toddler had been drawn to inspect the light of glowing coal, which flared up suddenly in his face to permanently scar the features around his mouth. Gorlin thereupon alludes to the commission of the prophet Isaiah (Isaiah 6:5–7), wherein an angel initiates the prophet's lips with a coal from a divine altar. Actually, a startlingly closer precedent occurs in a Jewish agaddic tale (Shemot Rabbah 1.26) that recounts a similar event in the young life of Moses.

3. According to Yasir Sakr, the Rothschilds had provided the funding. Susan Solomon (1997, 398–99; see fn. 16) strangely omits mention of the Rothschilds, either in the procurement of the permit or in the funding. The fact that the construction proceeded on and off for a period of eight years helps confirm that multiple fundraising efforts were involved.

4. As Mirkin recounts somewhat awkwardly in his July 29 *Ma'ariv* article,

and now (Kahn) had completed the plans for a building to be erected on the ruins of Rabbi Yehuda the Righteous, which will incorporate a section of the ancient ruins. . . . (Kahn) explained to me how he planned the lighting to reflect from behind the stone pillars—that taper at their ends and surround the new building—towards the Hurvah. Pointing with his hand towards one of the buildings he added, "The purpose of the concrete and stones is to let the light reach the right spot. The concrete is the silver whereas the light is the gold." As for the ruins, whose design he saw as his life's great work, he explained that the goal was for a prayer or a visit to become a highlight for a pilgrim. Therefore the Hurvah would be built in layered fashion, a type of central hall, and around it a surface area which could serve additional people, a women's court, and around the twenty meter high square building would be very wide stone pillars.

5. Indeed, in at least one instance, it was lampooned as such in the Israeli press. The caricature sketch, drawn by the Israeli architect Mordekhai Ben-Horin, shows a cone-shaped, smoking pyre rising Babel-like to challenge the visual prominence of the Dome of the Rock. The sketch appeared next to Ben-Horin's letter to the editor of *Ha'Aretz* on

9 August 1968, a clipping of which was preserved in Kahn's Hurvah files ("Israeli Newspaper Articles Hurva," LIK 39, Kahn Collection). That Kahn and the project's sponsors began to feel discomfited by reactions to the Hurvah's slightly higher height on the adjacent slope is reflected by the move to reduce the Hurvah's size by twenty percent a year following—at the time, not incidentally, of the first gathering of the Jerusalem Committee in 1969 (Solomon 1997, 451).

6. Solomon (1997, 439) mentions Marvin Verman's recollection that Kahn had posed the same problem to his studio classes: how to design a space that would feel intimate to 200, 700, and 1,000 congregants at different times, "a considerable problem" she notes, "for the post World War II synagogue, which was grappling with how to accommodate a small daily congregation, a somewhat larger crowd each Sabbath, and an entire flock on the High Holy Days."

7. Or: an "egalitarian space, where no one was more privileged than anyone else," as Tsevi Lavi would relate in his article "A Crown-like Appearance for the 'Hurvah' Synagogue," describing Kahn's presentation in the Israel Museum. The article appeared in *Ma'ariv*, 29 July 1968.

8. In January of 1949, Kahn was approached by his associate in the Federal Public Housing Agency, Philip Klutznick, a well-known activist for nationwide, nonprofit Jewish organizations, with the tantalizing project of tackling Israel's housing shortage crisis. Kahn not only immediately accepted the offer to participate, he engaged himself in Klutznick's study team in the Israeli Housing Survey Committee with characteristic self-propelled drive and visionary foresight, albeit to the surprise of some of his colleagues (Kahn, always an individualistic personality, was not noted for exhibiting a stellar attendance record in other such engagements). According to Susan Solomon (2000, 13), "Kahn's willingness to participate in the Israeli Housing Survey Committee was typical of many non-observant Jews who began to play a part in the Zionist world after the creation of Israel. At a time of increased interest in religion, when any religious affiliation was becoming a fundamental way in which to express American identity, Zionism offered a means to identify with Judaism without having to engage in ritual participation." Solomon (2000, 15) shows that Kahn's participation in the housing committee was self-guided almost to the ambition of tackling Israel's housing crisis single-handedly. For him, the crisis offered Israel the chance to introduce in the Middle East the prefab housing and vacuum-formed concrete industries, and thus jumpstart the industrialization of the region, turning a "Building Emergency into a Major Industry." Prophetically, the Israeli government rejected the ideas as too ambitious in favor of temporary housing solutions, a pattern, Solomon later demonstrates, that was to repeat itself constantly in Kahn's work for Jewish clients.

Works Cited

Finkelstein, L. 1928. "The Origins of the Synagogue." *Proceedings of the American Academy for Jewish Research* 1: 49–59.

Gorlin, A. C. 1985. "Biblical Imagery in the Work of Louis I. Kahn: From Noah's Ark to the Temple of Solomon." *A + U* 176: 85–92.

Kahn, L. I. 1973. "The Room, the Street, and Human Agreement." *A + U* 1: 5–222.

———. 1975. "Architecture and Human Agreement." In *The Art of Design Management—Design in American Business,* the Tiffany-Wharton Lectures, XVI, 17–30. New York: Tiffany and Co.

Mirkin, D. 1968. "Louis Kahn versus Architects 'whose Religion is Solel Boneh.'" *Ma'ariv.* 29 July.

Sakr, Y. 1996. *The Subversive Utopia: Louis Kahn and the Question of the National Jewish Style in Jerusalem.* Ann Arbor, Mich.: University of Michigan Press.

Solomon, S. G. 1997. "Secular and Spiritual Humanism: Louis I. Kahn's Work for the Jewish Community in the 1950s and 1960s." Ph.D. diss., University of Pennsylvania.

———. 2000. *Louis I. Kahn's Trenton Jewish Community Center.* New York: Princeton Architectural Press.

Conclusion

Theoretical and Empirical Reflections on Cities, Sovereignty, Identity, and Conflict

Diane E. Davis

This book has examined the interrelationships between ethnic, racial, religious, or other identity conflicts and larger battles over sovereignty and governance, particularly as seen through the lens of cities and the urban built environment. Such analytical concerns may seem particularly appropriate for the study of Jerusalem, a city widely discussed in this volume from a variety of temporal, methodological, and disciplinary vantage points, and whose history displays a complicated layering of multiple identities and sovereignty arrangements. But they are not particular to that iconic city. Equally well known struggles in Belfast and Nicosia exemplify similar tensions between identity politics and sovereignty in the urban realm, and they have made their mark on the physical form of those cities by dividing and/or fragmenting the urban landscape. Less known perhaps, but more current, are similar ethno-national, religious, and sovereignty tensions in Central Asia and Eastern Europe that now threaten to remake both the politics and built environment of a whole new spectrum of cities, ranging from Cizre to Mostar to Kosovo. In these conflicted cities and regions, as well as others discussed in this volume, questions about whose nation-state, legal system, or cultural practices should prevail—and in what parts of the city or for whom—have fueled intense political struggle, often leading to violence.

These examples indicate that, rather than showing themselves to be a thing of the past, collisions of identity politics and sovereignty concerns appear just as often in the current era, especially in those parts of the world where recent post–Cold War boundary drawing has disrupted old patterns of ethnic or religious subordination to a secular nation-state (as in the Balkans) or where efforts to incorporate antagonistic religious or ethnic groups into a single state structure (as in Iraq, Afghanistan and, to a certain extent, Turkey) spark or fan the flames of competing nationalisms. Wide swathes of the African continent may now be among the newest poster children for this politically troublesome state of affairs. Collapsing under the weight of ethnic and tribal violence in an environment complicated by diminished state legitimacy, unstable democratic structures, and endemic poverty, many African nations are caught in a "conflict trap" that fuels the vicious cycle of poverty and violence (Collier 2003; 2008; Collier and Sambanis 2005; Humphreys 2003). Such challenges frequently pull cities directly into the orbit of violence and political struggle, as the recent experiences of Mogadishu, Darfur, and Nairobi so clearly suggest.

In contrast, South Africa stands as perhaps one of the few beacons of hope in the troubled African region. It has transcended the racial and ethnic violence engendered by decades of white-led settler-state sovereignty, in which a majority of the nation's longstanding residents were treated as second-class citizens and where cities served as both physical containers and semiotic representations for coexisting forms of unequal citizenship. Black political struggles against this apartheid system of social and spatial exclusion in South African cities called for white and black inclusion in a common project, structured around a single national state and shared citizenship rather than separate or even parallel systems of urban or national sovereignty based on distinctive racial identities (Beall 2003; Gibson 2004). South Africa's successes suggest that understanding the conditions under which visceral identity conflicts do or do not become embedded in struggles over urban space and/or national sovereignty could be relevant to understanding the prospects for peace and the cessation of identity-based violence.

Clearly, most of the political conflicts noted above have unfolded around more than just sovereignty. They also have involved groups who claim a distinctive social, religious, racial, or ethnic origin or *identity*, often reinforced or formed through political oppression or social marginalization, and whose protagonists seek political autonomy, inclusion, and a form of recognition or viable sovereignty based on those identities. A more elaborated conceptualization drawn from the Stanford Encyclopedia of Philosophy suggests that

> the laden phrase "identity politics" has come to signify a wide range of political activity and theorizing founded in the shared experiences of injustice of members of certain social groups. Rather than organizing solely around belief systems, programmatic manifestoes, or party affiliation, identity political formations typically aim to secure the political freedom of a specific constituency marginalized within its larger context. Members of that constituency assert or reclaim ways of understanding their distinctiveness that challenge dominant oppressive characterizations, with the goal of greater self-determination. (Heyes 2009)

One place where identity struggles have long been embedded in sovereignty questions is Jerusalem. As a location that territorially and symbolically hosts distinct religious and ethnic groupings, and whose residents have battled foreign invaders and occupying enemies over centuries, Jerusalem is known for its overlay of religious and ethnic monuments, symbols, and archeological sites that carry deep meaning for diverse peoples, institutions, and competing nation-states. Historically, it also has experienced a remarkable array of sovereignty arrangements—from imperial to colonial to nation-state rule—that have reinforced or undermined inter- and intra-religious, ethnic, and other identity claims, leading at times to destructive conflict and, even when not, leaving a physical mark on the built environment of the city. Thus Jerusalem has served as an important reference point for reflecting and advancing the major themes addressed in this volume, not just the relationship between identity politics, cities, and sovereignty, but also the conditions under which these relationships might drive further conflict if not violence.

Yet Jerusalem is by no means the only city with a mix of identity and sovereignty conflicts, as the remaining cases in our book make clear, even if it may be among the most recognized. Many cities have suffered through ethnic, nationalist, and/or religious conflicts in which sovereignty questions loom large, or in which local political processes and democratic institutions have been unable to accommodate identity grievances, thereby sustaining a precarious peace. These conflicts have usually been studied through the lens of nationalism or incomplete state formation, or with a focus on the political ideologies that fuel struggle, without taking into account either the urban dimensions of the conflict or the nature of the sovereignty arrangements under contention. Even when they are studied through an urban lens, it is almost always with the presupposition that identity conflicts are fueled by, and most evident in, physical separation—that is, in the form of divided cities (Bollens 2000). The aim of this volume has been to remedy this state of affairs. By focusing on Jerusalem under a range of different sovereignty conditions, by purposefully examining the role that urban conditions have played in fueling identity-based conflicts in that iconic city and elsewhere, by examining urban form and governance in terms of its myriad component parts, and by studying a range of cities in addition to Jerusalem—from Beirut and Bilbao to Hanoi and Pondicherry—we have pursued a wide range of questions about the mix of urban built environmental and sovereignty conditions that fuel, and are fueled by, identity conflicts.

Each of this volume's authors has relied heavily on empirical evidence and/ or case study methods to address these larger concerns. Among the most important questions they pondered has been whether and how the superimposition of certain sovereignty arrangements on identity-diverse urban locales has affected the built environment of the city or its peoples in ways that fan the flames of aggression and violent conflict.[1] Taking this concern one step further, several of our authors have even asked *which* sovereignty arrangements and/or identity claims have been most likely to produce conflict in and over the city, *how* and *why*. They also have queried whether, independent of sovereignty arrangements or the content and intensity of identity politics, certain built environmental conditions or physical aspects of the city have been more likely to mitigate or reduce identity conflict—and conversely, whether certain sovereignty arrangements and identity conflicts are more likely to affect the urban built environment. Through their contributions, this volume has offered a new way of questioning the urban, national, and supranational sovereignty conditions under which cities develop, host, and/or spatially represent or produce difference and diversity without devolving into intractable conflict.

How we understand sovereignty has also set this volume apart. In contrast to much of the literature that invokes *national* sovereignty questions in the context of identity struggles (Gellner 1983; Smith 1995; Weaver 1995; Wright 2004), our concern has neither been nationalism per se, nor the political struggles generated by nationalism, nor even ethno-nationalism as a distinctively violent phenomenon, although some of the urban-based conflicts examined in this book have used nationalism as a discursive reference point for mobilization and could be classified as ethno-nationalist. Rather, we sought to understand the extent to which claims for sovereignty will emerge at a range of territorial scales, both smaller and larger than the nation-state, and to assess the implications for the built form of the city and for the likelihood of conflict among peoples who live in these urban locales.

For all these reasons, we have used the concept of sovereignty not merely to refer to nation-state rule, or nationalism, but rather, as a larger concept defined as "the public authority which directs or orders what is to be done," or more simply as the "supreme, absolute, uncontrollable power, the absolute right to govern."[2] With a focus on sovereignty-related conflicts across a spectrum of conditions— empires, colonial states, national states, and transnational governance regimes— and how these conflicts unfold similarly or differently in a wide variety of ethnically or religiously contested cities and regions, we seek to advance thinking about the relationship between cities, sovereignty, and identity politics as well as the extent to which a focus on these interrelationships can shed new light on studies of urban form.

The nine chapters in this book have addressed these concerns in a variety of ways. For example, the authors in part 1 have asked whether the main triggers for urban conflict or cooperation rest in the *nature* of identity differences (whether religious, ethnic, or otherwise), in the sovereignty arrangements governing these cities, or in the urban spatial environment in which they reside. The chapters in part 2 have carried forward some of these concerns, but also questioned the *causal direction* and/or interrelationship between sovereignty arrangements, urban conditions, and identity-based practices and possibilities. The chapters in part 3 examine whether and how constructs of place, urban function, urban form, or other features of the urban built environment *represent* either sovereignty or identity or both, and whether such representations will reconcile or exacerbate contending identity claims and competing sovereignties.

Although each subsection has focused on a slightly different set of questions and cases, all chapters concerned themselves with sovereignty, whether understood in political or economic terms and whether scaled at the local, national, or international level (or some combination thereof). In addition, they all addressed the physicality of the city—either the urban built environment in which identity groups live and experience the dilemmas of sovereignty, or the ways the built environment manifests sovereignty arrangements. Together, the chapters of this volume have produced collective knowledge of the conditions under which particular sovereignty arrangements and/or built environmental patterns in identity-diverse locales are more likely to lead to the establishment of a genuinely pluralistic, tolerant, and autonomous form of urban citizenship. They also have shown which social and spatial patterns of inclusion will make identity-based differences benign and manageable, rather than erupting into sustained violence or intractable urban conflict.

The Promise of the City

In addressing these general concerns our contributors have drawn inspiration from, and at other times challenged, the literature portraying cities as sites of cosmopolitanism where diversity, tolerance, and democracy thrive. Claims about the political promise and liberatory potential of the city have a grand lineage, dating to Max Weber among others, although similar assumptions also have flowered in many contemporary writings on the city (Takjbakhsh 2001). From Marshall Berman's (1983, 318) notion that "the city offers perhaps the only kind of environment in which modern values [of tolerance, freedom, and so on] can be realized" to Andy Merrifield's (1997, 201) view of the city as host for "togetherness *in difference*" to Ira Katznelson's (1997, 49) claim that "the compound of liberalism and the city promote a liberalism of depth and complexity"[3] to Richard

Sennett's (1977, 295) idea that the city is a place where strangers meet and his attendant proposition that "people grow only by processes of encountering the unknown" (a view prefiguring the political theorist Iris Young's views on the togetherness of strangers in cities), scholars have long celebrated the humanistic potential and endowments of the city. As David Harvey further reminds us, history shows that the notions of city and citizenship are frequently intertwined, such that "[p]rojects concerning what we want our cities to be are, therefore, projects concerning human possibilities, who we want, or perhaps even more pertinently, who we do not want to become" (2000, 157–158).

Many of these same hopes and citizenship ideals also sustain Henri Lefebvre's seminal writings, especially his notion of "the right to the city." This is a proposition that holds great resonance to those living in conflict-ridden cities, where mobility and access to everyday activities and the urban built environment are often hindered or strongly curtailed. It is worth remembering that Lefebvre conceived of the city as "gathering the interests of the whole society" (1996, 158). What may be equally significant about Lefebvre's formulation is his use of society—not the state, nation, or any particular form of sovereignty—as the conceptual reference point for understanding the humanitarian promise embodied in citizenship. For Lefebvre, it is not merely that the political ideals of citizenship are met by the "right to the city" but also that all citizens enjoy social and spatial inclusion. He suggests that such outcomes are often created not through formal citizenship rights, imposed or constitutionally guaranteed by the state, but through everyday urban social practices built on unrestricted flows, "place(s) of encounter," and the "priority of use value" in the natural spaces in and surrounding politically-drawn jurisdictional borders" (1996, 158).

Lefebvre's claims that certain social and physical environments hold the potential to foster inclusion and lay the foundations for citizenship rest not merely on a recognition of the importance of individual access to a wide range of places and spaces, of the exposure to social and class diversity, or of myriad other ways to "rightfully" partake of the city. They also build heavily on an understanding of the relations between cities and nation-states, in a way that is particularly relevant for understanding the impact of certain sovereignty arrangements on cities and the quality of urban life. In a spirit reminiscent of the classical arguments formulated by Max Weber and paralleled in work by Manuel Castells (1983) on autonomous communities in Castilla, Lefebvre and Régulier suggest that where cities and urban activities are dominated by or fused with states, one is likely to see violence and a "vacillat[ion] between democracy and tyranny" (1996, 233).[4] The assumption here is some relationship between cities and sovereignty, although not necessarily a direct one. One of the aims in this volume has been to identify and examine these relationships and their implications for urban conflict.

From City to State

In a general sense, Lefebvre's claims about the tyranny of nation-state domination in the urban realm were recently echoed in writings by Tony Judt. In a highly controversial article (2003) he argued that the persistence of violent conflict and the failure to produce democracy and peace in the Middle East revolved largely around nation-state dominion and its implications for Jerusalem. He suggested that the expansion of Israeli state occupation into further urban territories in and around Jerusalem, particularly those peopled by both Palestinians and Israelis, could be seen as a Gordian knot guaranteeing that "Israel will be either a Jewish state (with an ever larger majority of un-enfranchised non-Jews) or it will be a democracy. But logically it cannot be both" (Lefebvre 2003, 9). For Judt, the state–city nexus holds the key to either democracy or tyranny—whether in Jerusalem or for both Israel and Palestine. The question, of course, is whether problems associated with struggles for nation-state sovereignty among Israelis and Palestinians, which are well reflected in ongoing debate over Jerusalem's status as capital city of one (versus two) states, are relevant only to the contested Israeli/Palestinian history. Or, could principles drawn from a closer study of this contested locale, in combination with analytical lessons drawn from cities as wide-ranging as Hanoi, Beirut, Bilbao, and Pondicherry, hold some larger theoretical or practical questions for other cities with identity conflicts, ethno-national or otherwise? Could such principles predict which paths of urban development are likely to lead to peace, which to conflict (or democracy or tyranny, to use Lefebvre's notions)?

The findings presented in this volume do lend some insight into the issues that concerned both Lefebvre and Judt, but they do not necessarily suggest full acceptance of their claims or concerns. Indeed, several chapters question any blanket claim that state domination of ethnically, racially, or religiously diverse cities will inevitably foster tyranny and limit democracy. This is especially evident in Anne Raffin's comparative study of Vietnam (Hanoi) and India (Pondicherry) (chapter 2), which shows important differences in the nature and degree of urban tensions in these two locales, despite shared French imperial state control. While neither city under study hosted a veritable democracy, given the larger reality of colonial rule, Raffin nonetheless shows that the nature and extent of identity-based political conflict differed significantly in these cities, depending on two general sets of factors: a) the physical character of the colonial built environment, and especially the extent to which French urban planning separated competing identity groups and b) the extent to which the French imperial state imposed urban rule in tandem with existent legal institutions and local governing processes that both fostered local legitimacy and the equitable inclusion of distinctive local populations. Her chapter, as well as Nora Libertun de Duren's discussion of Jerusalem under different sovereignty conditions (chapter 1), makes clear that we must examine both urban specificity (in built environmental and institutional terms) and national or other forms of sovereignty, if understanding identity conflicts and the tendency toward intractable urban violence is the larger objective.

To be sure, if such a research agenda inevitably entails an identification of both urban and nation-state dynamics, and how they combine to make identity-based urban violence more likely, it is wise to recognize the difficulties of analytically distinguishing these dynamics from each other—and not just when de jure arrangements or formal sovereignty mandates fuse the two, as in the case of the city-states that most concerned Lefebvre. The de facto reality in most circumstances is that cities employ states structures, resources, and practices to promote their own local aims, and vice versa, as when states use cities and their resources, populations, and institutions to promote their national aims. The former situation is the subject of Neil Brenner's chapter (6), which shows how and why European cities, enabled if not buttressed by European Union regulations, made demands on their host national states to fund or facilitate urban development projects that increased their own urban global competitiveness. The converse situation, of states using cities for their aims, is implied in Raffin's treatment of colonial urban planning practice and is fully articulated in Lawrence Vale's chapter (8), in which governing officials crafted the urban built form of capital cities through architectural design and land use practice so as to represent and legitimate nation-state sovereignty.

Leslie Sklair's chapter on iconic architecture (chapter 7) takes a similar logic one step further by arguing that it is possible to trace historically shifting forms of hegemonic power and authority through examination of the leading architectural styles in cities. This claim not only leads him to suggest that over time sovereignties will "look" different in built environmental and architectural terms; it also inspires his search for architectural evidence of singular or mixed forms of sovereignty in the physical character of the built environment. Specifically, he argues that in the contemporary era when declining nation-states suffer from reduced capacities in the face of an increasingly powerful global capitalist class, the latter take on the functional properties of nation-states by writing their own global hegemony on the city's built environment in the form of iconic architecture. Granted, the question of who is doing the seeing or interpreting must be seriously considered. To whom will architectural icons represent or embody global economic sovereignty, and why? Will capitalists and public officials offer a different perspective than citizens; and within the latter category, will these buildings manifest a distinctive semiotics to those who work in them as opposed to those who visit them? Clearly, there may be limits to the universality of claims about the semiotic legibility and larger interpretive meaning of iconic architecture.

Notwithstanding this caution, there is plenty of evidence that the interpretive meaning of iconic architecture is not completely randomized. In this volume, the idea that iconic architectural projects are publicly legible as global commodities, not to mention perceived to be capable of enhancing a city's global status, is a thread that runs through Gerardo del Cerro Santamaría's discussion of Bilbao (chapter 4), where the Frank Gehry museum contributed to Basque efforts to assert autonomy by growing their own regional economic prosperity independent of the Spanish national state. As such, iconic projects not only represent or embody the placelessness of global capital and its capacity to represent or recast the sovereignty of a given location as something much larger than the city or the nation. They also represent the transforming nature of sovereignty. And to the extent that the adoption of iconic architecture is intended to move a city's semiotic identity from one set of sovereignties to another, it also should be seen as an active agent in such transformations. Sklair concludes, in fact, that iconic works of architecture can embody multiple sovereignties in both their visual content and scale. This possibility is also echoed in Eric Orozco's chapter on the Hurvah Synagogue (chapter 9), and his discussion of the ways that Louis Kahn's design sought to incorporate multiple historical periods representing multiple religions and/or multiple views of the state's commitment to both peoples and the past in ways that raised questions about the hegemony of religious versus state (e.g. Zionist) sovereignty in defining late-1960s Jerusalem.

While it may seem unusual for a book that concerns itself with identity politics and sovereignties to focus so explicitly on architecture and the built environment, the chapters in this volume have well demonstrated that high-profile architectural projects can give tangible evidence of which actors and institutions hold the power to reshape the built form of cities. In the case of iconic architecture, the role of elites—both investors who fund these projects and state or other public officials who approve them—hold the keys to the representation of power and authority in the city. Still, the urban domain is just as likely to be created through and by citizen engagement, either in support or opposition to urban development plans imposed from outside or above, including plans that promote iconicity in the built form. For precisely this reason, our authors have also found it important to take seriously Judt and Lefebvre's concerns with local capacities for social inclusion and democratic processes, and ask what role citizen-oriented structures and processes play, if any, when urban plans for the city come from elite sources, be it capitalists or the state.

To phrase the issue in terms of this volume's specific concerns about sovereignty and conflict, several authors have pondered what role citizens, as well as the availability of local democratic or legal norms, will play in producing built environmental outcomes. Can socially inclusive structures, urban spatial plans, political processes, and governing practices in cities develop independent of national sovereignty, of formal city-state relations, of global context, or of the local specificities of identity politics? And if so, will local patterns, institutions, and processes have a greater impact than nationally or globally cast sovereignty arrangements or actors on urban space and/or the likelihood of identity conflicts? Such queries are most directly addressed in Raffin's chapter on Hanoi and Pondicherry, as well as in chapter 5, Agnès Deboulet and Mona Fawaz's work on Beirut, in which the focus is everyday urban life and the political institutions, legal norms, or social practices available to residents who struggled over the built environment—using these struggles as a basis to question larger sovereignty arrangements.

The Beirut case is particularly instructive. In contrast to Vale's chapter, where the city is the unit of analysis, and also in contrast to Brenner's chapter, where the units of analysis are urban development projects whose contents are formed in the interaction between city and supranational officials conducted within state agencies without citizen input, Deboulet and Fawaz's study of Beirut introduces both citizens and intra-urban land use conflicts into the mix. In their examination of struggle over an urban restructuring plan built around new highway development, the authors show that negotiations between national states and citizens are conducted in the course of everyday urban governance. This entails communication—if not conflict—between residents and city officials or political party leaders charged with carrying out national visions for the city. Deboulet and Fawaz not only argue that in the course of negotiations the state's larger urban development vision can be recast to accommodate the identities and political expressions of citizens who lack formal power in the national state apparatus. They also argue that citizens and the state will struggle for certain urban policy outcomes in order to sustain or undermine key political and/or territorial bases of control—that is, to sustain or undermine the politico-spatial dimensions of formal or informal forms of sovereignty. In addition, they suggest that religious and ethno-national identities—specific to the community slated for urban policy intervention, to political parties, and to those controlling the national state—are formed and changed in this interaction.

This conclusion could also apply well to Salim Tamari's chapter (3), which details the use of religious confessionalism to divide Jerusalem during the British Mandate period. He shows that strategies of confessionalism employed to secure British sovereignty over the Palestine Territories in the post-Ottoman epoch both emerged out of struggle within and between citizens and the sovereign rulers, and over time reinforced identity differences that fueled nationalist conflicts and struggles over state sovereignty between Israelis and Palestinians in much later periods. In short, both the Jerusalem and the Beirut chapters establish the possibility of upending the Judt and Lefebvrian view that states, by their nature, impose a hegemonic if not tyrannical will on the city and its people. Instead, both Tamari and Deboulet and Fawaz suggest that the nation-state's own "identity" and sovereignty aims are as likely to be formed through ongoing struggles in and over the built form of the city as to exist a priori to such actions. Such conclusions also find expression in Orozco's discussion of the Hurvah Synagogue, mainly by showing how the plans for renovation of this historic site produced intragroup tensions between secular and more religious Jews, who in turn engaged in political dialogue and debate over the site's content. The polemical character of the discussion not only created new fault lines of difference both within and between religious groups and others who claimed a historical right to the city of Jerusalem. It also raised new questions about the representational objectives of the Israeli state, thereby affecting the content and character of both urban and national authorities' claims to sovereignty over the city and its built environmental future.

From Governance to Citizenship

Questions about the relationships between urban political structures and processes at the level of the city, who should control them, and whether or how quotidian decisions about the built form might relate to formal sovereignty arrangements help cast this volume's contributions in light of recent debates in political theory and democratic philosophy, and not merely in the context of claims about urbanism. Remember that philosophical aims concerning citizenship were precisely what motivated Lefebvre's writings about the "right to the city" in the first place. They sustained his normative claim that cities should serve as the starting point for enabling a society's greatest democratic potential, precisely because of the built environment's capacities to make both legible and tangible the workings of power dynamics and social exclusion. This volume's chapters on architecture and representation—as noted above in reference to Orozco's discussion of the

Hurvah Synagogue, Vale's treatment of capital cities, and Sklair's claims about iconic architecture—also make this legibility eminently clear.

Still, if we take seriously the fact that the particular architectural forms discussed in this book have not produced much democratic outcry or political opposition, with perhaps the exception of the moderate and ultimately jettisoned tensions between secular and religious nationalists in Jerusalem noted by Orozco, we must consider whether there is something else besides the architecture and buildings in a city that determines the extent to which citizens focus on them in their struggle for emancipation, inclusion, or alternative structures of power.

We can further specify this by asking under what conditions will active forms of struggle surrounding high profile urban development projects tend to erupt? Why do we see them in Beirut, as underscored by Deboulet and Fawaz, and even in Hanoi, but not in Pondicherry or even Bilbao? One way to answer this general question is to rethink the dynamics of identity politics, and the extent to which local identity conflicts or social allegiances, as opposed to concerns about the urban built form per se, inspire or drive democratic contention in and over the city, either on their own or in the form of partisan political struggle.

Such an approach is in fact suggested by Deboulet and Fawaz's conclusions that in Lebanon, identity issues were deployed in the opposition to the highway by political parties who were ultimately positioning the community against the state with an alternative claim for sovereignty over space. Their claim is consistent with my own writings on citizen struggles to overturn plans to build a Rem Koolhaas–designed skyscraper in Mexico City (Davis 2009). In Mexico neither ethnic nor religious nor other essentialist identities were at stake, but community leaders did use the building as a metaphor for government corruption and state excess, as well as for allying themselves to an oppositional political party. Thus Mexico's outcomes paralleled that which occurred in Lebanon, leading to powerful citizen mobilization and the city's subsequent cancellation of the urban design project.

In theorizing which political structures and processes make citizen mobilization over the city and its built form both likely and possible, we can draw additional insight from the philosopher Jean-Luc Nancy. Nancy shares Lefebvre's desire to normatively celebrate and site the collective experience of urban life as central to democratic struggle and liberating political praxis. As a political theorist concerned with the "excesses of community, national sovereignty, identity politics, and war," Nancy's writings find elective affinity with this volume's originating concerns about identity politics and its relationship to sovereignty struggles. Although he is most concerned with the ways that identity politics, or what he calls "the drive to imagine/create collective frames of experience or connection," can fuel conflict (i.e. the "excesses" of community) and larger sovereignty battles, he is also preoccupied with violence and when it leads to war. In a manner consistent with the premises underlying most work in the field of urbanism, Nancy also identifies the importance of shared experiences, or what he calls the pluralism of being that allows "singular beings . . . [to] variously understand the exigencies of living [together] as beings-in-common" (Welch and Panelli 2007, 349–350). Accordingly, what is key for Nancy is the extent to which recognition of multiple identity groups and full acceptance of pluralism will govern human behavior.

To be sure, Nancy's claims do not invoke the spatiality of the city or its built environmental dynamics in the ways Lefebvre's writings do. Nor do they specify whether certain physical aspects of urban life or urban form would mitigate against the so-called "excesses" of community, national sovereignty, identity politics, and war that preoccupy Nancy. But they do focus attention on the social conditions under which an "imprecise collective of beings" can find ongoing human engagement that will "expose as well as bridge the distances, differences and spaces separating singular (plural) selves." Such claims about the human dynamics of bridging distance, let alone the conceptual notion of a bridge, clearly have a spatial connotation as much as a social one, even as they can be used to refer to political relations (or lack thereof) between citizens and sovereigns. Such concerns echo an argument I made almost a decade ago with respect to social movement theory and the conditions under which citizens will or will not engage the state to express political or identity claims (Davis 1999). But more important for our purposes, concerns about social and physical distance and how to bridge it are replicated in the empirical studies of urban conflict under divergent sovereignty arrangements advanced by this book's contributors.

In her chapter on Hanoi and Pondicherry, Anne Raffin has shown that French imperial efforts to bridge both identity differences and spatial distance (in terms of administering a distant metropole comprised of different ethnic and religious groups) through specially crafted governance regimes and urban development projects produced different outcomes in these two cities, despite the common objectives. Some of this owed to the fact that both urban development patterns and group identity dynamics interacted in different ways to produce greater conflicts between Chinese and Vietnamese in Hanoi than between different castes in Pondicherry. These patterns, in turn, laid different foundations for French–native identity tensions in both locales, driving some unity between (upper-caste) natives and French in India, but more antagonism toward French rule in Vietnam.

Likewise, the Tamari chapter on Jerusalem during the British Mandate period shows that the occupying state's inability to bridge the social and political distance within and between its subjects drove the British to use religious identities to design certain parts of the city, in order to minimize the political tensions between administrators and citizens. Spatializing these identities then had the effect of creating even greater social "distances" between or among citizens themselves, in turn laying the foundation for more intractable religiously based identity conflicts that caused violence in later periods of colonial rule, and saddling the post-1948 state with more complex civilian struggles vis-à-vis both identity and sovereignty. That is, in their efforts to legitimize colonial rule through bifurcated planning practice, the British laid the foundation for greater identity-based conflicts, thus enabling a certain path dependency toward a new (nation-state) sovereignty built on religious identity as well as further challenges to that form of rule.

The path-dependent transformative impact of a sovereign government's urban planning policies is also discussed in the Deboulet and Fawaz chapter on Beirut. They argue that the discursive negotiation between sectarian-religious political parties, unaffiliated citizens, and the Lebanese nation-state ultimately produced a major highway restructuring plan for Beirut that brought certain residents into the political and spatial orbit of the state and its urban development aims, even as it excluded others. When completed, this highway project helped generate greater social and spatial fragmentation of the urban citizenry along religious lines, with these divisions in turn reinforced by competing political parties and later by the physical displacement that combined with local politics to territorially distance the Hezbollah-allied citizens of south Beirut from other actors supporting the Lebanese state and its sovereignty aims. While the negotiation process that led to the implementation of the highway project could be considered only one small manifestation of a much larger area of contestation between Hezbollah and the Lebanese state, it does show how changes in land usage and the built environment both involved and exacerbated struggles over identity and sovereignty.

The Beirut case also underscores the importance of recognizing the transnational dimensions of such conflicts. In their postscript, Deboulet and Fawaz show how the 2006 Israeli war introduced an external, or transnational, manifestation of sovereignty into the complex mix of identity politics in the Beirut metropolitan area and in Lebanon more broadly. The Israeli state's militaristic reach into sovereign Lebanese territory, most evident in the bombings of areas south of Beirut in the 2006 war, did more than physically destroy the urban neighborhoods where Hezbollah had cemented its hold as a consequence of the struggle within and between local groups against the highway project and the factions of the Lebanese state that supported it. The bombings also motivated many others in Lebanon, especially though not exclusively in the southern Beirut areas targeted by Israel, to question current sovereignty arrangements in both Lebanon and in

Israel. Together, these developments revived the complex identity politics align-
ments and realignments underlying questions about the Lebanese state's loyalty
to its citizens, including Hezbollah, as well as its recognition of the sovereign Israeli state straddling its southern border.

When Territorialities of Identity Confront the
Jurisdictional Spaces of Democracy

The ways in which local political structures and identity politics were deployed
in the Beirut highway struggle to bridge the social and political distance between
some citizens and the state, even as they reinforced the greater urban physical isolation of others, underscores again the importance of taking space seriously if one
seeks to understand the interrelationships between cities, sovereignty, and identity politics. An appreciation of the power of urban projects and policies to reinforce or diminish identity conflicts is already part and parcel of Scott Bollens's
path-breaking work on Belfast, Nicosia, and Jerusalem (2000). Bollens has per-
suasively argued that "physical and political qualities [of cities] exert independent effects on ethnic tensions, conflict, and violence" (2000, 19). But one need
not visit the most divided cities of the world to recognize this. In fact, the role of
spatial configurations in enabling democratic participation and/or responding to
identity-based differences is a theme that is relevant worldwide, including in the
U.S., where democracy and sovereignty are not as commonly challenged.

Such concerns are the subject of writings from urban legal theorist Gerald
Frug, who argues that the territorial or spatial context of governance, especially
as reflected in the legal foundations of urban sovereignty, can exacerbate population differences and attendant claims to equitable social inclusion. In particular,
he has highlighted the social and spatial challenges to democracy and social justice that arise when administrative power attributed to communities and cities is
too narrowly circumscribed to generate or guarantee democratic inclusion, arguing that when the legal frameworks for urban governance divide different racial
groups into different politico-territorial jurisdictions, cities are unable to flower
as domains of "plural" decision making (to use Nancy's terms) that "gather" (to
use Lefebvre's) a multiplicity of social collectivities.

In the case of the U.S., Frug further suggests that overbearing "state control
has reduced the importance of cities as instruments of public policy and thereby
diminished the opportunity for widespread participation in public decision making" (1999, 8) in ways that challenge basic philosophical fundamentals of liberal
democracy. Echoing Lefebvre but departing from many other urban democratic
theorists who build on the Tocquevillian tradition of reifying neighborhoods,

communities, and other smaller-scale territorial units as the bedrock of democracy, Frug advocates for empowerment and autonomy on the level of the city—understood as a legal, jurisdictional, and/or spatial entity larger than class- or race-defined neighborhoods but smaller than the nation and subnational states. In fact, he goes so far as to suggest that the legal contours of overly localized power prevent cities from fulfilling their democratic and civil society function by turning them into "vehicles for separating and dividing different kinds of people rather than bringing them together, withdrawal from public life rather than engagement with others, and the multiplication of private spaces instead of walk-able streets and public parks" (Frug 1999, 8–9).[5] Much of this owes to the legal context of localism, which "treats autonomous individuals and the nation-state . . . as interested in pursuing their own self-interest" (ibid., 9) in ways that challenge the independent capacity of cities to guarantee the collective urban interest.

This focus on the legal underpinnings of urban sovereignty and the conditions under which legal frameworks exacerbate identity-based social exclusion and inequality sheds light on claims made by Deboulet and Fawaz in their discussion of Beirut. They argue that the struggle over highways in southern Beirut reinforced identity politics and new sovereignty claims, precisely because residents of lands slated for highway development did not have formal title or legal property rights. The lack of legal title thus helped reinforce further issues of sovereignties and the deployment of these sovereignty issues as strategies in space since it inscribed the contestation of urban projects in a wider framework of contested legitimacies and entitlement to the city.

How the presence or absence, formal or informal nature of urban legal guarantees for citizens can affect the interplay between identity politics, social exclusion, and sovereignty is also a key aspect of Nora Libertun de Duren's chapter on Jerusalem. Like Frug, Libertun de Duren is concerned with identifying the most amenable territorial scales and sovereignty arrangements for ensuring social inclusion of various identity groups that have inhabited or laid claim to Jerusalem. She argues that the gains made in Jerusalem under Ottoman rule owed not to the de jure guarantee of rights associated with allegiance to a particular sovereign, but to the unusual combination of deals and de facto political arrangements that offered certain governance and citizenship rights but not others.

In particular, Libertun de Duren shows that in this early period of empire before the ascendance of national state sovereignty, Ottoman rulers provided customary and legal foundations that mandated widespread social inclusion of all groups in urban governance decisions, albeit through different measures and relationships, despite the lack of formal (Ottoman) citizenship guarantees granted to city residents. Most striking in her argument is recognition of the fact that it was the triangulation of sovereign actors, identified at different scales (imperial and urban) and with different reference points (political versus religious authority), rather than a single sovereignty arrangement, that produced the most stable polity and negotiable urban environment in Jerusalem. Such outcomes, which prevailed primarily under Ottoman rule, were further reinforced by the presence of recognized legal mandates that made possible a set of relatively inclusive urban governance practices, even in the absence of formal citizenship rights. All of this produced less violent identity conflict, more coexistence, and thus a more legitimate sovereignty arrangement than during later periods under British mandate rule, when none of these democratic ideals were met, and even later under national state sovereignty, when citizenship rights were granted to urban citizens, but social inclusion and equal participation in urban governance for different religious and ethno-national groups remained elusive.

Finally, Frug's larger arguments about the legal context of urban governance, inclusion, and citizenship also serves as a key theoretical frame for understanding several of the claims advanced in the Raffin chapter, for yet an entirely different place and time. In this case, legal codes and the ways they included or excluded urban populations from joint decision making with French imperial officials played a key role in accounting for the likelihood of conflict. Raffin found that when French colonial rulers allowed the persistence of customary practice, especially as enshrined in local legal norms, ethnic or race-based identity conflicts between imperial or colonial rulers and the ruled were less likely. But she also notes that informal custom, and not merely formalized legal practice, whether native or imported, framed the extent of collusion between rulers and ruled as well as identity conflicts among the ruled.

From Juridical and Territorial Dynamics to Questions of Scale

Questions about the territorial scale and juridical underpinnings of urban citizenship have become complicated in recent years, as globalization changes the relationships among cities, nation-states, and supraregional entities (like the European Union). In this shifting environment, the question emerges as to which actors and institutions will seek to monopolize the "right" to the city. Such concerns and how they affect or frame identity claims in different territorial dynamics are absolutely central to Neil Brenner and Gerardo del Cerro Santamaría's chapters. In del Cerro Santamaría's discussion of Bilbao, Basque identity-based groups seeking regional political sovereignty from the Spanish nation-state set the content of urban policy in Bilbao, using new urban projects in the city to establish the global economic foundations for claiming their own regional sovereignty rights vis-à-vis the Spanish state. Brenner, too, focuses on the importance of non-national scales of allegiance in the contemporary epoch, and how economic globalization drives new interrelationships between local, national, and transnational territorial scales. But his approach to the "geography of sovereignty" is somewhat different. Rather than focusing on subregional sovereignty claims and how they make urban space, as does del Cerro Santamaría, Brenner examined a supraregional sovereignty that overlies the nation-state system without necessarily replacing it. He further argues that these new territorial allegiances, at least as reflected in membership in the European Union, sustained or generated urban policy priorities that strengthened cities economically, even at the expense of nation-states. These priorities put urban growth and urban development more in sync with global economic objectives than with national political or social integration. Stated differently, for Brenner divergent geographies of sovereignty mediate processes of regional capitalist development and their articulation with urbanization, while for del Cerro Santamaría it is almost the inverse: the interrelationship between regional capitalist development and urbanization mediates competing geographies of sovereignty.

In a way that parallels the Deboulet and Fawaz findings, both del Cerro Santamaría and Brenner suggest that actors and institutions with differently scaled sovereign loyalties—be they political, as in the case of the Basque separatists seeking urban and regional autonomy, or economic, as in the case of efforts to foster global economic integration into a strengthened European Union—will produce different urban policy priorities that feed back on the legitimacy and governing capacities of the nation-state. All three chapters, in short, concern themselves with the interactive dynamics of urban development and shifting scales of sovereignty (understood in terms of authority and governance capacity). As such, this volume's findings support a growing body of work suggesting a "reterritorialization" of governance functions in the contemporary global era and how it emerges at the expense of a "deterritorialization" of the nation-state (Sparke 2005; Appadurai 2003; Devetak and Higgottt 1999; Bhabha 1994). But in contrast to much of the writing on these processes, the emphasis here is the interrelationship and overlap of differently scaled sovereignties—whether cast at levels of action larger or smaller than the nation-state—and how it ensures that the nation-state can still serve as a key mediating force in these dynamics, either as a source of leverage against other competing sovereigns, or as the source of claim-making from cities and their citizens. This argument, while clearly cast in the grounded realities of contemporary Europe, nonetheless echoes insights drawn from Raffin's recognition of the ways that the colonial state in India and Vietnam, despite finding its raison d'être in the logic of French imperialism, leveraged both orbits and local citizen loyalties to maintain a precarious form of rule built around nationalism in which local, colonial, and imperial sovereignty were simultaneously at play.

All these examples suggest the importance of studying *the scaling and rescaling of sovereignties* rather than deterritorializing or reterritorializing, if we seek to represent or understand the contemporary dynamics of cities, sovereignties, and identity politics. This is so because both de- and reterritorialization appear to speak to a single dynamic: either the absence of spatially bounded sovereignty (deterritorialization), or a new, alternative spatial bounding (reterritorialization). As such, both concepts fail to accommodate the possibility that sovereignty arrangements can coexist and overlap across multiple territorial scales at the same time—a situation clearly at play across much of contemporary Europe, in contemporary Lebanon and Spain, and in Jerusalem for centuries. The concept of rescaling, in contrast, not only implies a continuous, if not contested, process rather than an end state: it also allows for a focus on different territorially based scales of sovereignty at the same time, shedding light on how efforts to rescale political authority within and between cities, states, and the globe has implications for the remaking of urban space, and vice versa.

A better understanding of the rescaling of sovereignties also sheds light on processes of urban inclusion and the likelihood that identity claims and conflicts unfolding in cities might connect to national or global agendas. For example, this volume's chapter on Bilbao shows that when identity politics are framed as claims for rights and accommodation in the context of both urban citizenship and global economic aims but not nation-state inclusion, they may be less likely to generate conflict between cities and states or to drive urban citizens to struggle for their own independent nation-state. The reverse effect has also been clear in the cases noted at the outset of this chapter, such as Belfast, Nicosia, Mostar, and Jerusalem, where the imposition of a singular nationalism on these identity-diverse cities has generated opposing nationalisms within that city, in turn fanning the flames of violent conflict.

Rethinking Sovereignty and Conflict through
Spatial and Temporal Lenses

Not that long ago the political scientist Bruce Stanley (2003, 11–12) claimed that "[t]he urban scale, as a site for or actor in the resolution of international social conflicts, ethno-national conflicts or inter-state war," is generally not considered an important subject in international relations literature or practice. The findings in this volume call into question such statements by focusing attention on the role cities play in conflicts over sovereignty. Building on recent work by Saskia Sassen, who argues that the contemporary global era has ushered in new forms of struggle over territory, authority, and rights (Sassen 2007), our findings also underscore the value of recognizing the temporal nature of globalization and how changes in relations between cities, sovereignty, and identity politics are a function of time as much as place (or space).

We are now immersed in an era when the powers and responsibilities of the nation-state are being transformed by globalization. The asserted value of the state as the primordial agent of domestic politics is under question on a variety of fronts, and there is growing evidence that cities themselves are becoming relatively autonomous actors in the global scene.[6] In the words of Manuel Castells, which echo the originating normative concerns of Lefebvre, "the tendency towards state centralism and domination by the state over the city is being opposed all over the world by a massive popular appeal for local autonomy and urban self-management. The revival of democracy depends upon the capacity of connecting the new demands, values, and projects to the institutions that manage society" (2003, 65). Similar normative claims have also been advanced in recent years by scholars who study cities wracked by identity conflicts. Using Belfast as a case in point, for example, Scott Bollens argues that the nation-state has already been questioned "as the territorial answer to the problem of human political, economic, and social organization. The disintegration of many states is compelling international aid organizations, mediators, and political negotiators to increasingly look at sub-state regions and urban areas as more appropriate scales of involvement" (1999, 7). Thus we now face a historic opportunity, grounded in real world changes in the relations between globalization, cities, and states,[7] to raise questions about prevailing theories and analytical frameworks for understanding conflict and peace.

The contributors to this volume who have taken up this challenge by directly examining globalization's impact on the potential for identity-related conflicts have focused upon prior historical periods, primarily imperial and colonial rule, as compared to the more recent epoch of nation-state sovereignty. Yet even within these various sovereignty arrangements, there are differences in the degrees and emergence of conflict, with only some imperial, colonial, and nation-state regimes fueling urban tensions. The question thus emerges: Can we plausibly offer any generalizations about the role that sovereignty, identity politics, or other spatial and temporal factors—including economic globalization—play in producing or mitigating conflict? While clearly we have been somewhat constrained by the evidence at hand, both the small number of case studies comprising this volume and the fact that they do not equally spread across all identity conflicts, historical time periods, and sovereignty arrangements, the combined knowledge emerging from the rich and broadly cast materials presented here does allow for some tentative conclusions about the urban and sovereignty conditions under which identity-based conflicts are most likely to emerge. We can summarize them in the form of several interrelated propositions.

The *first* and most obvious conclusion drawn from the empirical work presented here is that the mere existence of significant identity differences or tensions, whether defined in religious, ethnic, racial, cultural, or other terms, does not automatically lead to conflict. Rather, a combination of sovereignty arrangements and built environmental conditions will interact with identity politics to generate the conditions for conflict. In specifying which sovereignty arrangements will be most conflict-prone, our findings suggest that we move beyond a general classification of sovereignty based on the nature of the state (imperial state, colonial state, or nation-state, democratic or otherwise) to a more nuanced understanding of the governance practices, citizenship possibilities, and degrees of social inclusion guaranteed for different urban citizens under particular sovereignty arrangements.

Understanding sovereignty in a more disaggregated manner means disarticulating the different components of governance and the range of rights and claim-making opportunities offered within each set of sovereignty arrangements. Doing so helps explain why we see identity conflicts turning violent in the cities of certain nation-states or certain imperial states but not others—for example, in post-1948 Jerusalem but not in Bilbao, or in Hanoi but not Ottoman Jerusalem. In looking for correlations between intensity of conflict and sovereignty, the cases of contemporary Beirut and British Mandate Jerusalem also stand apart, because they host low-grade conflict that may simmer below the surface. These two examples suggest that sustained urban violence between competing identity groups does not emerge unless provoked from outside the institutional confines of the given national sovereignty arrangement. Yet external provocation only becomes meaningful if it unsettles the ruler–ruled contract established under a given sovereignty arrangement in a given city. More specifically, if such provocation exposes or reinforces the social or spatial legibility of local identity differences and thus the desire to assert sovereignty over local urban spaces, the outcome will be even more conflictual. This was apparent in Beirut, where the Israeli war of 2006 exacerbated tensions between Hezbollah and Lebanese Christians. Conversely, if external provocation or threat reinforces a shared ruler–ruled contract among city residents, or unites previously divergent or conflicting identity groups, the opposite will occur. This often happens with external invasion or imperial occupation, as we saw in the Hanoi case.

The evidence from Ottoman Jerusalem, Beirut, Hanoi, and Pondicherry further suggests that, independent of state form, urban violence is more likely to be held at bay when a given sovereignty arrangement allows for socially inclusive governance practices, citizenship rights, or some form of symbolic or substantive recognition at the level of the city. Stated conversely, identity-based conflicts are more likely to emerge in cities where divergent populations are denied access to formal or informal institutions for claim-making, for influencing urban policy, or for advocating for citizenship rights or identity aims. These same considerations provide us a basis for understanding whether and when identity-based urban violence might erupt episodically. This is likely to occur when the legitimacy or efficacy of urban governance structures and citizenship rights are called into question by certain actions or decision, or when identity groups are spatially segregated in ways that pit them against each other, as can happen independent of formal sovereignty arrangements.

That particular urban political processes, spatial patterns, or urban policy actions can produce conflict is not a new finding, to be sure. But when estrangement between local citizens and the state emerges in a social and spatial environment where identity differences are already a source of tension, and if such local processes or policy actions disadvantage one group over the other, the interaction effects of this "double-exclusion" can lead to violence. This leads to a *second* proposition: the ways in which the built environment of the city brings citizens together or keeps them apart, either socially, spatially, or politically, will also affect the likelihood that identity differences turn conflictive. That is, the degree to which unity or division among identity groups is facilitated by urban form—whether through symbolic buildings, iconic architecture, or the development of urban projects—will affect the likelihood that inter-group tensions emerge. Political institutions and processes (i.e. sovereignty attributes) can also contribute to these outcomes, as when sovereignty arrangements allow for a continued negotiation or renegotiation of urban forms or urban space within and between identity groups and rulers. In such instances, the hegemony of a single identity group is less likely to be "written on" the city or fixed into its built environment, and thus social, spatial, and political division—or conflict—may be less likely. Stated somewhat differently, it is not merely the physical separation or integration of identity groups in cities that leads to conflict or visceral struggles to dominate or oppress "the other." Rather, identity politics and the attendant social, cultural, and political relationships within and between identity groups are mediated by a variety of factors, ranging from the social inclusiveness of governance institutions to the procedures made available to debate urban policies and urban built forms.

Several chapters here have examined these dynamics, in particular Orozco's, with its discussion of how debate over architectural plans for the Hurvah Synagogue in Jerusalem led to a redesign that, after negotiation, was more accommodating to potentially conflicting identity groups. But even in this case, despite the integration of histories and competing identities in the redesign, the clear exclusion of Palestinians from the dialogue, in process terms at least, left room for continued tensions, despite the accommodating measures offered by the architect Louis Kahn. That both political process and urban form matter is also clear from Raffin's discussion of Hanoi and Pondicherry, where we see that physical separation of groups in the city was not a problem when it was counterbalanced by juridical norms and political institutions that allowed equal access to urban governance or urban policy decisions.

How all these elements can interact to produce more lasting outcomes is perhaps best articulated by Deboulet and Fawaz in their discussion of conflicts over the urban highway project in Beirut. They argued that by contesting technical or professional definitions of how territories should evolve, and through a sequence of multiple and not necessarily coordinated interventions on urban projects, city-dwellers contribute, in a nonlinear way, to redefining legitimacies and sometimes sovereignties. In this project, not only do we see how intractable identity group conflict was avoided by enabling citizens to contest top-down planning solutions for the built environment. We also understand how both sovereignty and legitimacy are constructed and reconstructed through identity-group negotiations over the urban built environment, with the long-term impact of these negotiations and legitimacies laying the groundwork for peace or conflict.

A *third* major proposition generated from a collective review of the chapters in this volume is that among all state forms and sovereignty statuses, identity-based urban conflict appears to have been most likely when the nation-state sought to forcefully impose its rule on a city whose citizens did not share a single identity status. This was especially so when said national rule or nationalist sentiment favored or empowered one group over another, thereby exacerbating identity tensions at the level of the city.[8] Imperial rule seems to have been less viscerally contested from within the city, perhaps because arrangements for urban governance under this form of sovereignty appear to have been more fluid, negotiated, and/ or evenly applied, owing to the physical distance between the city in question and the seat of empire. Colonial state rule, for its part, seems to stand somewhere in the middle, confronted by contestation but showing limited flexibility in response.

Final Remarks on the Interplay of Sovereignty Arrangements, Identity, and the Built Environment in Comparative and Historical Perspective

Some of these conclusions may be an artifact of our "sampling" frame, not in least part because observations of Jerusalem specifically are central to several of these general claims. If one considers that a single case can over-determine sensibilities and that Jerusalem itself faces a unique set of identity and sovereignty conflicts, it is important to consider these conclusions as suggestive at best. The fact that Jerusalem is a capital city also may have mattered, although most of the chapters in this volume likewise focus on capital cities, either as the domain where nation-states need to exert their influence, or as a political and symbolical sites where existent or even competing sovereigns seek to establish authority or legitimacy. Yet, once we recognize that capital cities are important to those seeking sovereignty because they host the main actors and institutions of recognized political authority, we also understand why they tend to be so contested. Likewise, we understand why imperial sovereigns might be more flexible in urban governance: their core legitimacy and authority emanates from a capital city elsewhere, and thus they are more open to negotiation with "subject" actors and institutions, at least if such practices do not undermine their legitimacy at home as well as abroad.

The issue of space also may be important here, because the more expansive the territorial scales of sovereignty (as with the case of empire and colonial versus nation-state rule), the greater the costs and the lesser the benefits of imposing sovereignty on cities, which in turn can account for why imperial states and even colonial ones might be less willing to forcefully impose their will on cities than would nation-states. All this suggests that it is worth considering the following qualification: it is not nation-state sovereignty per se so much as the objectives, expectations, and geographical constraints that come with this particular historical form of sovereign rule that generate the likelihood for conflict.

For one thing, most nation-states are much smaller and more territorially concentrated entities than empires. For another, by their very definition nation-states are granted more legitimate coercive capacity to govern over their own territories. These factors too may help explain why nation-states do not necessarily undertake the negotiated or accommodating political measures necessary to ensure local legitimacy that, say, imperial or colonial states often feel required to adopt in order to maintain rule. This paradoxical state of affairs suggests that nation-states may accept greater social exclusion of identity groups at the level of the city precisely because they work under different legitimacy constraints, pushing them to impose different rules, with different reciprocities and expectations, than do imperial or colonial states. The examination of local practice in Jerusalem under three forms of sovereignty, articulated in Nora Libertun de Duren's chapter at the outset of this book, makes this eminently clear. The findings presented in her chapter, in combination with the materials offered by Tamari and Orozco, show how and why during the transition from imperial to colonial to national state, contemporary Jerusalem became the contested terrain upon which competing sovereigns waged their battles. These struggles reinforced and were reinforced by group identity differences at the scale of the city.

To be sure, identity conflicts in Jerusalem are neither new, nor produced only by the imposition of nation-state sovereignty. Long before the partition of Palestine in 1948, the efforts of religious authorities to imprint their character on Jerusalem brought tension and controversy, leading to efforts to rewrite the history of the city through the lens of particular identity fissures (Wasserstein 2002). Yet despite this fact, deeply grounded in the longstanding history of Jerusalem as a sacred locale for the world's three great religions, it was when nation-states started making sovereignty claims on Jerusalem that pervasive violence and intractable urban conflicts became much more the norm.

An additional explanation for why nation-state sovereignty might invite more identity-based conflict lies in what we might call the "self-selection" bias of national state forms. Historically, the emergence of nation-states as the dominant form of sovereignty has been understood to respond to some "imagined community" in which nation-state boundaries are considered to be relatively coexistent with communal or group identities (Hobsbawm 1992; Anderson 1991). In such instances, there may be fewer group differences, and when they do exist, they tend to be united by shared nationalist aims, including shared experiences of war that sustain these sentiments (Tilly 1992). But such "ideal typical" national states may be less likely in practice than theory, not just in the post–World War II world where global wars led to the redrawing of state boundaries, but also in the recent post-Soviet world where a new set of state boundaries have been cast or are under contention. Accordingly, we might offer a final more qualified conclusion: that nation-states whose boundaries have been in flux historically, where the formal process of nation-state recognition is imposed from outside or above rather than within, or where a transition from one boundary or sovereignty arrangement to another is under way, may be most likely to host urban-based identity group conflict.

A review of the chapters in this volume suggests that many of the problems in Jerusalem as well as Beirut owed not just to the efforts of the Israeli and Lebanese national states to impose their will on the peoples and built environments of their capital cities. They also owed to the fact that populations within those two nations have struggled with and over the legitimacy of the national state: they both have experienced an array of sovereignties, and in many ways, might still be considered in sovereignty "transition"—at least if we accept that these nation-states and how they define themselves vis-à-vis their diverse religious citizenry are still under contestation. This leads us to consider that identity politics may be as likely to devolve into violence in conditions of *uncertain or contested sovereignty,* as under conditions of nation-state sovereignty.

Finally, we also cannot ignore the impact of changing global conditions on the relationships between cities, sovereignty, and identity conflicts. Several of the chapters in this volume examine the shifting or overlapping sovereignty domains produced by the increasing weight of economic globalization on cities and states. Their findings support the claim that economic globalization produces competing tendencies: a freeing of cities and their citizens from struggles over national sovereignty but, at the same time, the production of more diverse and cosmopolitan urban locales where identity conflicts are likely to fester or emerge anew. The first half of this claim is supported by evidence from the Sklair, del Cerro Santamaría, and Brenner chapters, which effectively demonstrate that cities capable of hitching their wagons to global markets or global capitalists can generate economic prosperity that may in turn reduce their political dependence on the nation-state. In such instances, the nation-state may have less legitimacy or capacity to impose its national project on cities, and thus inter-group identity conflicts may remain at bay. Such a possibility is also suggested in the Orozco chapter, in which he notes that Teddy Kollek's efforts to make Jerusalem a global city led to suggested changes in the Hurvah Synagogue design, and helped redirect local attention away from partisan identity conflicts toward a common economic goal.

The second half of this claim, while not our principal subject here, is supported by considerable scholarship showing that economic globalization produces or sustains flows of peoples to cities around the globe, thus increasing urban diversity by bringing new religions, races, ethnicities into the daily life of host cities and nations. In an environment of unstable or transitional sovereignty, such transformations have the potential to generate new bases for identity conflict and urban tensions, which in turn can exacerbate larger sovereignty struggles, or at minimum, more localized struggles over citizenship, social inclusion, and rights to the city. The fact that today we are seeing identity-based conflicts linked to urban citizenship in the major cities of previously stable nations such as France, Spain, the Netherlands, Denmark, and Great Britain, further underscores the urgency of these concerns. To the extent that economic globalization may be increasing the likelihood that identity conflict will emerge in cities, we must be prepared to understand the conditions under which these cities will erupt into violence. Will it depend on the political structures and processes available to accommodate these new identity groups and tensions, including the provision of inclusionary practices and citizenship rights that sustain identity-group capacities to make or remake urban spaces? Or will other transformations linked to globalization counterbalance these tensions? In the era of increased economic globalization we are seeing more transnational exchanges spearheaded by individuals who move back and forth through transnational spaces. Even when the bodies themselves do not move, chains of financial and social remittances continue to circulate, linking individuals to multiple if not competing and overlapping sovereignties or nations, at least in emotional and functional terms. These transnational networks play a large role in sustaining urban development projects and other substantial changes in the built environment of "sending" hometowns, thereby bringing citizens with slightly different sovereign allegiances into conflict over the making of urban space. In such situations, local power structures and citizenship practices will inevitably mediate these conflicts and competing sovereignties, but they will also bring transnational civil society and footloose transnational citizens in collision with local states and local citizens whose lives and futures remained grounded in the city and its built environment.

This suggests that even with economic globalization, *local* sovereignty arrangements made with respect to urban governance, urban inclusion, and everyday citizenship will still matter. If increasingly open borders mean that cities continue to host more diverse populations with different citizenship identities and sovereign allegiances, local officials will still be under greater pressure to make sure that the key components of a legitimate or stable urban sovereignty—whether in the form of governance institutions, socially inclusive practices, or citizenship— are present at the local scale if conflict is to be avoided. However, the nation-state will not necessarily be the only guarantor for rights and for the accommodation of urban-based identity group claims. New forms or institutions on the global level may also emerge to fortify governing practices at the level of the locality, regulate new local–global interactions, or enforce the new territorialities of sovereignty and the promise they offer to cities and their citizens.

Such changes will not only further signal the increasing importance of the city as the key political and spatial location for negotiating rights, political order, citizenship, and other larger principles that in the past were considered to be primarily nation-state projects. They also will uphold the call for bold new imaginaries in the theory and practice of sovereignty, some of which may help to overcome the negative effects of nation-state hegemony on increasingly multicultural cities and perhaps even lead conflict cities on a new journey toward peace.

Notes

1. In the case of Jerusalem, the subject of three chapters in this volume, this is the most pressing queston, since that city and how to physically shape and/or govern it has served

as the Achilles heel of the negotiation process. Without a solution on the nation-state question, peacemaking in Jerusalem has been nearly impossible; yet without solving the Jerusalem problem, and especially the questions of boundaries, settlements, and dividing lines between peoples and governance, peace between Palestinians and Israelis has remained elusive. For a discussion of this dilemma in the debate over the Geneva accords, see Chazan et al. (1991). For an accounting that brings the view up to date from 1991 (where Chazan left off) up through the Oslo Accords and into 2001, see Wasserstein (2001).

2. *Black's Law Dictionary* (Nolan Jr. et al. 1990). Definitions of sovereignty range widely, with some using the concept for describing political arrangements relevant to the modern nation-state (i.e. *Bouvier's Law Dictionary,* 1856 edition) and others finding a more general usage applicable to all forms of governing authority—as with the Hawaiian people's claims for self-determination. For more on this, see http://www.hawaii-nation.org/soveriegnty.html.

3. Katznelson defines liberalism as the divide between public and private, guarantee of individual and group rights, and moral pluralism.

4. They further note that in city-states, or places were there is a fusion of city and state, "the State, whether it be inside or outside the city, always remains brutal and powerless, violent but weak, unified but always undermined, under threat" (1996, 233).

5. Again, it is worth emphasizing that when Frug uses the word city in contradistinction to locality he has in mind the idea of cities as metropolitan bodies which extend in space to include a variety of (fragmented) localities where some form of deliberative power rests.

6. Among the first to make this observation were Jordi Borja and Manuel Castells (1997). For a general overview of the changing dynamics of cities in the context of globalization, see also Short and Kim (1999).

7. Much of the globalization literature also highlights the important role played by transnational actors—ranging from corporations and capitalists to social movements—in molding conditions inside countries in relatively unprecedented ways. For some of the best treatments of this subject, see recent work by Leslie Sklair (2006) and Joseph Stiglitz (2006).

8. Recent studies by Haim Yacobi and Erez Tzfadia on the prospects for peaceful coexistence in multicultural cities such as Jerusalem similarly "[q]uestion the possibility of creating a multicultural urban space in societies that are based on *strong national logic* (emphasis mine), as in the Israeli ethnocentric context" (2009, 289)

Works Cited

Anderson, B. 1991. *Imagined Communities: Reflections on the Origin and Spread of Nationalism,* rev. ed. New York: Verso.

Appadurai, A. 2003. "Sovereignty without Territoriality: Notes for a Postnational Geography." In *The Anthropology of Space and Place: Locating Culture,* ed. S. M. Low and D. Lawrence-Zúñiga, 337–349. Oxford: Blackwell.

Beall, J. 2003. "Uniting a Divided City: Governance and Social Exclusion in Johannesburg." *Urban Forum* 14: 122–125.

Berman, M. 1983. *All That Is Solid Melts into Air: The Experience of Modernity.* New York: Verso.

Bhabha, H. K. 1994. *The Location of Culture.* New York: Routledge.

Bollens, S. A. 1999. *Urban Peace-Building in Divided Societies: Belfast and Johannesburg.* Boulder, Colo.: Westview Press.

———. 2000. *On Narrow Ground: Urban Policy and Ethnic Conflict in Jerusalem and Belfast.* New York: State University of New York Press.

Borja, J., and M. Castells. 1997. *Local and Global: The Management of Cities in the Information Age.* London: Earthscan.

Castells, M. 1983. *The City and the Grassroots.* Berkeley: University of California Press.

———. 2003. "The New Historical Relationship between Space and Society." In *Designing Cities: Critical Readings in Urban Design,* ed. A. Cuthbert, 59–68. Oxford: Blackwell.

Chazan, N., F. Moughrabi, and R. Khalidi. 1991. *Negotiating the Non-negotiable: Jerusalem in the Framework of an Israeli-Palestinian Settlement.* Cambridge, Mass.: American Academy of Arts and Sciences.

Collier, P. 2003. *Breaking the Conflict Trap: Civil War and Development Policy.* Washington, D.C.: World Bank Publications.

———. 2009. *Wars, Guns, and Votes: Democracy in Dangerous Places.* New York: Harper Collins.

Collier, P., and N. Sambanis. 2005. *Understanding Civil War: Evidence and Analysis.* Washington, D.C.: World Bank Publications.

Davis, D. E. 1999. "The Power of Distance: Re-theorizing Social Movements in Latin America." *Theory and Society* 28, no. 4: 585–638.

———. 2009. "From Avenida Reforma to the Torre Bicentenario: The Clash of 'History' and 'Progress' in the Making of Modern Mexico City." In *Mexico City through History and Culture,* ed. L Newson and J. King. Oxford: Oxford University Press.

Devetak, R., and R. Higgott. 1999. "Justice unbound? Globalisation, states and the transformation of the social bond." *CSGR Working Paper* No. 29/99. Warwick, U.K.: University of Warwick.

Frug, G. E. 1999. *City Making: Building Communities without Building Walls.* Princeton, N.J.: Princeton University Press.

Gellner, E. 1983. *Nations and Nationalism.* Oxford: Blackwell.

Gibson, J. L. 2004. "Does Truth Lead to Reconciliation? Testing the Causal Assumptions of the South African Truth and Reconciliation Process." *American Journal of Political Science* 48, no. 2: 201–217.

Harvey, D. 2000. *Spaces of Hope.* Berkeley: University of California Press.

Heyes, Cressida. 2009. "Identity Politics." In *The Stanford Encyclopedia of Philosophy* (Spring 2009 Edition), ed. E. N. Zalta http://plato.stanford.edu/archives/spr2009/entries/identity-politics/ (accessed 15 May 2010).

Hobsbawm, E. J. 1992. *Nations and Nationalism since 1780: Programme, Myth, Reality,* 2nd ed. Cambridge: Cambridge University Press.

Humphreys, M. 2005. *Economics and Violent Conflict.* Cambridge, Mass.: Harvard University. http://www. preventconflict. org/portal/economics/Essay. pdf (accessed 15 May 2010).

Judt, Tony. 2003. "Israel: The Alternative." *New York Review of Books* 50, no. 16: 8–9.

Katznelson, I. 1997. "Social Justice, Liberalism and the City: Considerations on David Harvey, John Rawls and Karl Polanyi." In *The Urbanisation of Injustice,* ed. Andy Merrifield and Eric Swyngedouw, 45–64. New York: New York University Press.

Lefebvre, H. 1996. "The Right to the City." In *Writings on Cities,* ed. H. Lefebvre, 147–159. Oxford: Blackwell.

Lefebvre, H., and C. Régulier. 1996. "Rhythmanalysis of Mediterranean Cities." In *Writings on Cities,* ed. H. Lefebvre, 228–240. Oxford: Blackwell.

Merrifield, A. 1997. "Social Justice and Communities of Difference: A Snapshot from Liverpool." In *The Urbanisation of Injustice,* ed. A. Merrifield and E. Swyngedouw, 200–222. New York: New York University Press.

Nolan, J. R., J. M. Nolan-Haley, M. J. Connolly, S. C. Hicks, and M. N. Alibrandi. 1990. *Black's Law Dictionary,* 6th ed. St Paul, Minn.: West Publishing Co.

Sassen, S. 2000. "Territory and Territoriality in the Global Economy." *International Sociology* 15, no. 2: 372–393.

———. 2001. *The Global City: New York, London, Tokyo.* Princeton, N.J.: Princeton University Press.

———. 2003. "Globalization or Denationalization?" *Review of International Political Economy* 10, no. 1: 1–22.

———. 2007. *Territory, Authority, Rights: From Medieval to Global Assemblages.* Princeton, N.J.: Princeton University Press.

Sennett, R. 1977. *The Fall of Public Man.* New York: Alfred A. Knopf.

Short, J. R., and Y. H. Kim. 1999. *Globalization and the City.* New York: Addison Wesley Longman Inc.

Sklair, L. 2006. Competing Conceptions of Globalization. In *Global Social Change: Historical and Comparative Perspectives,* ed. C. Chase-Dunn and S. Babones, 59–78. Baltimore, Md.: Johns Hopkins University Press.

Smith, A. D. 1995. *Nations and Nationalism in a Global Era.* Cambridge, U.K.: Polity Press.

Sparke, M. 2005. *In the Space of Theory: Post-foundational Geographies of the Nation-State.* Minneapolis: University of Minnesota Press.

Stanley, B. 2003. "City Wars or Cities of Peace: (Re)Integrating the Urban into Conflict Resolution." *Globalization and World Cities Study Group Network (GaWC) Research Bulletin* 123 (October): 11–12.

Stiglitz, J. 2006. *Making Globalization Work.* New York: W.W. Norton.

Tajbakhsh, K. 2001. *The Promise of The City: Space, Identity and Politics in Contemporary Social Thought.* Berkeley: University of California Press.

Tilly, C. 1992. *Coercion, Capital, and European States: AD 990–1992,* 2nd ed. Cambridge: Blackwell Press.

Wasserstein, B. 2002. *Divided Jerusalem: The Struggle for the Holy City.* New Haven, Conn.: Yale University Press.

Weaver, O. 1995. "Identity, Integration and Security: Solving the Sovereignty Puzzle in EU Studies." *Journal of International Affairs* 48, no. 2: 389–431.

Welch, R. V., and R. Panelli. 2007. "Questioning Community as a Collective Antidote to Fear: Jean-Luc Nancy's 'Singularity' and 'Being Singular Plural'." *Area* 39, no. 3: 349–356.

Wright, R. A. 2004. *Virtual Sovereignty: Nationalism, Culture, and the Canadian Question.* Toronto: Canada Scholars Press.

Yacobi, H., and E. Tzfadia. 2009. "Multiculturalism, Nationalism, and the Politics of the Israeli City." *International Journal of Middle East Studies* 41: 298–307.

Contributors

Neil Brenner is Professor of Sociology and Metropolitan Studies at New York University. He is author of *New State Spaces: Urban Governance and the Rescaling of Statehood* and co-editor of *Spaces of Neoliberalism; The Global Cities Reader; State, Space, World;* and *Cities for People, Not for Profit.*

Gerardo del Cerro Santamaría teaches at the Cooper Union for the Advancement of Science and Art in New York City. His books include *Bilbao: Basque Pathways to Globalization.* He is a past Visiting Professor at MIT and a member of the New York Academy of Sciences, the American Academy of Political and Social Science, and the Society for the Advancement of Socio-Economics.

Diane E. Davis is Professor of Political Sociology and Head of the International Development Group in the Department of Urban Studies and Planning at MIT. Formerly Associate Dean of the School of Architecture and Planning, her books include *Discipline and Development: Middle Classes and Prosperity in East Asia and Latin America; Irregular Armed Forces and Their Role in Policies and State Formation* (co-edited); and *Urban Leviathan: Mexico City in the Twentieth Century.* She is editor of the research annual *Political Power and Social Theory.*

Agnès Deboulet is Professor at the Ecole Nationale Supérieure d'Architecture de Paris—la Villette, where she specializes in urban sociology and city planning. She holds advanced degrees in Economics, Sociology, and City Planning. Her books include *La critique architecturale—questions, frontières, desseins; Villes internationales—tensions et réactions des habitants;* and *Dynamiques de la pauvreté en Afrique du nord et au moyen orient.*

Mona Fawaz is Assistant Professor in the Graduate Urban Planning, Policy, and Design Program at the American University of Beirut. Her research explores the possibilities for and capabilities of various groups of low-income urban dwellers to participate in the conception, organization, and production of space.

Nora Libertun de Duren is Director of Planning, New York City Department of Parks and Recreation and Adjunct Assistant Professor of Urban Planning at Columbia University. She holds a Ph.D. in Urban Planning from MIT, a Master in Urban Design from Harvard University, and a Master's degree in Architecture from the University of Buenos Aires.

Eric Orozco resided for three years in the Old City of Jerusalem as a student at the Jerusalem University College (on Mount Zion). He received a Master of Architecture degree from MIT and is now an urban design consultant based in Charlotte, North Carolina.

Anne Raffin is Associate Professor of Sociology at the National University of Singapore. She is author of *Youth Mobilization in Vichy Indochina and Its Legacies, 1940–1970.*

Leslie Sklair is Emeritus Professor of Sociology and Associate Faculty in the Cities Programme at the London School of Economics, Associate Fellow of the Institute for the Study of the Americas at the University of London, and President of the Global Studies Association. His books include *Globalization: Capitalism and Its Alternatives* and *The Transnational Capitalist Class.*

Salim Tamari is Director of the Institute of Jerusalem Studies and Professor of Sociology at Birzeit University. His publications include *Jerusalem 1948; AlQuds Al Uthmaniyya (Ottoman Jerusalem); Mandate Jerusalem in the Memoirs of Wasif Jawahariyyeh; The Mountain Against the Sea;* and *Year of the Locust: Palestine and Syria during WWI.*

Lawrence J. Vale is Ford Professor of Urban Design and Planning at MIT. His many books include *Architecture, Power, and National Identity; From the Puritans to the Projects: Public Housing and Public Neighbors;* and *Reclaiming Public Housing: A Half Century of Struggle in Three Public Neighborhoods.*

Index

Printed and bound by CPI Group (UK) Ltd, Croydon, CR0 4YY

13/04/2025

14656544-0004